BEYOND
PHILOSOPHY

BEYOND PHILOSOPHY

Nietzsche, Foucault, Anzaldúa

NANCY TUANA *and* **CHARLES E. SCOTT**

INDIANA UNIVERSITY PRESS

This book is a publication of

Indiana University Press
Office of Scholarly Publishing
Herman B Wells Library 350
1320 East 10th Street
Bloomington, Indiana 47405 USA

iupress.indiana.edu

© 2020 by Nancy Tuana and
Charles E. Scott

This book is freely available in an open access edition thanks to TOME (Toward an Open Monograph Ecosystem)—a collaboration of the Association of American Universities, the Association of University Presses, and the Association of Research Libraries—and the generous support of the Pennsylvania State University. Learn more at the TOME website, available at: openmonographs.org.

This title is licensed under the Creative Commons Attribution-NonCommercial 4.0 International License (CC BY-NC). Read the license at https://creativecommons.org/licenses/by-nc/4.0/legalcode.

The paper used in this publication meets the minimum requirements of the American National Standard for Information Sciences—Permanence of Paper for Printed Library Materials, ANSI Z39.48-1992.

Library of Congress Cataloging-in-Publication Data

Names: Tuana, Nancy, author. | Scott, Charles E., author.
Title: Beyond philosophy : Nietzsche, Foucault, Anzaldúa / Nancy Tuana and Charles E. Scott.
Description: Bloomington, Indiana, USA : Indiana University Press, 2020. | Includes bibliographical references and index.
Identifiers: LCCN 2020014829 (print) | LCCN 2020014830 (ebook) | ISBN 9780253049827 (hardback) | ISBN 9780253049834 (paperback) | ISBN 9780253049841 (ebook)
Subjects: LCSH: Philosophy.
Classification: LCC B72 .T93 2020 (print) | LCC B72 (ebook) | DDC 190—dc23
LC record available at https://lccn.loc.gov/2020014829 LC ebook record available at https://lccn.loc.gov/2020014830

DOI: https://doi.org/10.2979/beyondphilosophy.0.0.00

1 2 3 4 5 25 24 23 22 21 20

Cover illustration: *Forest View* by Jan Brueghel, c. 1605.
Photo credit: Kunsthaus Zurich.

CONTENTS

Acknowledgments vii

Preface xi

I.

1. Introduction and Beyond   3

2. Nietzsche's Exposure Beyond Philosophy   26

3. Foucault's Unreason   71

4. Anzaldúa's Nepantla   108

II.

5. Border Art Philosophy   145

6. Playing with Fire   163

7. An Infused Dialogue   192

8. livingdying   217

9. Beyond Sensibilities   226

Epilogue   249

Bibliography   253

Index   261

ACKNOWLEDGMENTS

DURING THE years we wrote this book, several groups of people provided opportunities to write and present papers as we developed the ways of thinking that move throughout the chapters. The exchanges between us and those who reflected on our thoughts and concerns infuse our ways of thinking and writing.

Our attunements to beyond philosophy were encouraged and enhanced by influences from many sources. Among the most important have been the dialogues we have had with Alejandro Vallega, Daniela Vallega-Neu, and Omar Rivera. This book would likely not have been written had it not been for Daniela and Alejandro's invitation to direct a course at the *Collegium Phaenomenologicum* in Cittá di Castello, Italy, in 2016 (about which we say more in the introduction). That course allowed us to develop our initial effort to engage Nietzsche, Foucault, and Anzaldúa on issues of temporalities and corporealities, and it became the genesis for dialogues between the five of us. Preparing those lectures and engaging in discussions about them with participants and faculty members of the *Collegium* enriched our thought and provided the wellspring for our emerging thinking in attunement with beyond that was essential to the understanding needed to conceive and write part I of this book. We were inspired not only by those dialogues but also by the border art philosophy exemplified by the work of Alejandro and Omar.

Our chapter on the work of Gloria Anzaldúa and our reflections on intimacy were enhanced by dialogues with members of the American

Philosophies Forum. These annual meetings gave us opportunities to present papers in which we experimented with thoughts and topics that we were in the process of developing and that turned out to be chapters four and seven. Earlier versions of some material appear in publications that resulted from those presentations: "An Infused Dialogue, Part 1: Borders, Fusions and Influence" and "An Infused Dialogue, Part 2: The Power of Love without Objectivity," *Journal of Speculative Philosophy* (2016) 30,1: 1–26; "Nepantla: Writing (from) the In-between," *Journal of Speculative Philosophy* (2017), 31,1: 1–15; and "Border Arte Philosophy: Altogether Beyond Philosophy" *Journal of Speculative Philosophy* (2018) 32, 1: 70–91. We are indebted to John Stuhr and Vincent Colapietro for their leadership and dedication to the importance of those intense philosophical exchanges. We are indebted particularly to those in the Forum who read and engaged our papers.

A series of workshops at Penn State University and at the University of Witwatersrand between 2014 and 2015 on the topic of race and the Anthropocene gave rise to a series of invaluable exchanges with Achille Mbembe, Sarah Nuttall, Robert Bernasconi, and Eduardo Mendieta that influenced our thinking and gave rise to many of the ideas to which we give voice in chapter 6. Earlier versions of some material in that chapter appear in the journal article that resulted from those workshops: "Climate Apartheid: The Forgetting of Race in the Anthropocene," (2019) *Critical Philosophy of Race*, 7, 1: 1–31. The opportunity to bring Anzaldúa to bear on this topic was made possible thanks to an invitation from Alejandro Vallega to participate in the TransAmerican Experience conference at the University of Oregon in 2015. The insights of the participants in these gatherings infuse our reflections.

The Fourth International Conference: *Mosaic* on "A Matter of Life and Death," held in Manitoba in 2014, was the occasion for presenting an early version of chapter 8 that was published in *Mosaic* (2015) 48, 2: 2011–17. We are grateful to Dawne McCance for her support and for making this event possible.

During the last three years, we participated in three Border Thought Workshops. We were stirred and affected by the discussions that developed during those days, and we are grateful to David Ferrell Krell, Omar Rivera, Alejandro Vallega, and Daniela Vallega-Neu for their insights, which opened for us new venues for thought and discernment. We are particularly grateful to Daniela, Omar, and Alejandro for their close and careful reading of the first two chapters of the manuscript during one of our workshops. Their insights and suggestions richly influenced our writing.

The many other people whose influence played important parts in our writing of this book include Del McWhorter, who, during the time we were conceiving many of its leading thoughts, understood what we intended to say even when we did not quite say it; and to David Farrell Krell, who introduced into English-speaking thought the term *twisting free*, with his translation of the German *Herausdrehen*. We use the term and the thought it presents crucially in the book. Alejandro Vallega gave us a wonderful, two-day opportunity to discuss an earlier version of several of the book's chapters in his graduate class at the University of Oregon. The students were exceptionally helpful to us, thanks to their interested reading and persistent questioning of what they read. No one who works closely with graduate students can neglect the impact of their many influences. Although they are too numerous to name, our appreciation of the work of thinkers whom we include within the category of liberatory thought opened up to us in ways that would have been beyond our comprehension had it not been for the insights and interrogations of the many graduate students with whom we've had the opportunity to learn.

Special thanks go to Dee Mortensen, editorial director at Indiana University Press (and to her chickens, who provide respite from the hectic world of publishing), for her support and encouragement, and to Ashante Thomas, assistant acquiring editor at Indiana University Press, who has helped us in so many ways with those countless details of preparing a manuscript for publication.

PREFACE

Well after we began work on this book, we visited the Kunsthaus in Zürich, Switzerland. In its astonishing collection of more than four thousand paintings and sculptures, Jan Brueghel the Elder's circa 1605 composition *Forest View* drew our particular attention.

Surrounded by dozens of exquisite paintings, we found ourselves returning time and time again to this small but commanding painting. Drawn to its complex depths, its movements of light and dark, which created a sense of distance and dimensionality, we found ourselves in the midst of its intensities. The painter's skill in creating dimensions of distance beyond the dell, dimensions with deep darkness and interfusing shades of light, called us.

In it an ancient, deep forest towers over the small figures of two people, one leaning on a long staff and the other, younger one sitting on the ground in shaded light. They are alongside a path in a small clearing in the midst of the dense and serenely dark forest. The everydayness of the moment is accentuated by the relaxed postures of the two people and the presence of two dogs. Behind them, the path with a barely visible, nondescript person walking on it leads into darkness. A distant, small clearing on the path shines beyond the darkness. Farther on, forest darkness. A stream in the foreground makes a leisurely turn and continues down into the forest with three herons on the porous boundary marking the clearing's light and the dark. Far away on the stream's murky course, another clearing appears with barely visible darkness beyond it.

The presented forest drew us in as it opened itself to us. The painting frames the forest and holds a moment . . . it *stills* a moment in the forest as it presents what Brueghel calls a forest view.[1] Those dimensions—the distance beyond people, dogs, and herons; the depth of darkness; the interlacing shades of light—are integral in the people's and animals' presence. Another interweaving is also happening, a fusion of creatures and the non-creaturely forest darklight. That dimension of fusion probably exceeds the people's awareness of it in their site of normalcy. The forest's living depth is at once in and beyond their familiarity; it is present and existent yet beyond and recondite. Unutterable, we thought.

The painting's draw on us and our resonance with it, especially with the unspeakable depth it made available to us, led us to buy the museum catalog so we could see it again. We turned to the page that included the painting—except it wasn't the painting. The painting's re-production flattened the depth portrayed in the original, dimmed the nuance of merging shades of light and dark, and dulled the sense of distancing presented in it. The art of the painting lost much of its compelling intensity and originality on the book's flat page.

One of the challenges we faced in writing this book is speaking of various thinkers, events, and experiences in ways that allow exposure of their dimensions of depth, their dimensions that are beyond the objectification of conceptual grasp and the subjection of grammar, dimensions that are not directly utterable. How are we to disclose in the nuance, attunement, and resonance of our words happenings and processes that exceed intellectual grasp and literal exposition? How do we write so that the art of philosophy does not lose its compelling intensity?

A conviction that guides us in this book is that thinking philosophically can bring people in their everyday lives to the dimensions of indeterminate and unspeakable distance, depth, and interfusing shades of meaning and meaninglessness that give depth and uncertainty in their lives: philosophical thought can bring us to dimensions of events and lives that are beyond schemas, beyond philosophical conception, and beyond normative requirements. How do we and others access and present those

---

1. Not, we note, "A View of the Forest." The original title is *Waldinneres*. Another, better translation would be "Inside the Forest."

dimensions without re-producing them and flattening them, as it were? How might we let them appear in our writing and not dim their distance from our fields of judgment and "normal" perceptivity? Is there an art of thinking that does not flatten and thereby lose dimensions of occurrences beyond philosophy? What kinds of impact can awareness of them have on our everyday comportment, judgments, and authorized knowledge? Neither of us is inclined to what is ordinarily described as mystical, and both of us think and live without what we consider to be metaphysical comforts. How, then, are we to speak of the unspeakable and think of the inconceivable while not mystifying them or domesticating, subjecting, and suppressing them?

BEYOND
PHILOSOPHY

Introduction and Beyond

Things aren't all so tangible and sayable as people would usually have us believe; most experiences are unsayable, they happen in a space that no word has ever entered, and more unsayable than all other things are works of art, those mysterious existences, whose life endures beside our own small, transitory life.

—Rainer Maria Rilke, *Letters to a Young Poet*

How do we think of beyond, a dimension that surpasses our immediate perception or our intellectual comprehension? In some situations when a geographical place is beyond what we can see and we don't know how to get there, maps can help. Imagining helps when something is beyond what we have yet to experience. But beyond, not what is beyond, remains unconsidered. Are we talking about some *thing* when we speak of beyond? We will say more about beyond and our way of thinking of it and with it in a moment.

Two years ago we read an essay on love. It is by an abundantly confident philosopher who wanted to conceive love—to bring it to understandable life in *its* reality, mind you—all by himself. But conceive as he would, he never got beyond the gates of his self-absorbed conceptions. We assumed those gates were locked because in that essay love never made it into his presence. If love had knocked down those gates of his thought and come to him in its bare splendor, would it nonetheless have been beyond him and his leaden formulations? Would a border that marked a remarkable difference have separated them? And if love had come to him, filled him, fused with his reality, destroyed his silly conceptions, transformed him, what then? Would love, that involuntary affective force, still have been beyond him? Him, all by himself? We found the article tedious, but consequent to it we understood better the kind of thinking that will not permit attunement with dimensions of beyond.

Beyond Philosophy began as we worked together on a course for the *Collegium Phaenomenologicum* entitled "Genealogical and Corporeal Temporalities."[1] When we delivered our three-day course, we began with a practice of polyvocality: "There is something different happening in this space today," we said. "A singular difference that is not one but two—two lips, hearts, minds. This is the first time a *Collegium* course has been done together: co-conceived, coauthored, copresented. Neither mine nor yours."[2]

Two voices, two manners of conceptualization, two different individuals speak in this book. They blend into a fusion that does not fully belong to either author. The attunement that infuses our writing emerged from the exchanges between us. We've spent many a pleasant morning or afternoon talking about the themes and authors we here engage. Nancy's philosophical lineages and interests influenced, informed, and infused Charles's thoughts, phrasing, and style; while Charles's lineages and interests influenced, informed, and infused Nancy's thoughts, phrasing, and style. Each one of us has discussed and modified, contributed to, and enriched every idea, chapter, paragraph, movement, and sentence.[3] In the conceiving and writing process, we often found that the ideas and the writing are in-between us, or, perhaps better phrased, the ideas and often the very movements of the written text emerged and at times mutated from our in-between as we thought and talked together.[4] This means in part that this book you are reading is not the product of each of us having drafts of different chapters or sections of chapters and then assembling them into a more or less unified structure. Nor is it simply the result of our sharing our ideas with each other. The process is rather an infused one that issues in a writing that is different from the sum total of our contributions.

---

1. The *Collegium Phaenomenologicum*, founded in 1975, meets in Italy and is an international postdoctoral and graduate seminar designed to explore philosophers and topics in the broad area of continental philosophy.
2. The lectures were written, and copies were handed out to the *Collegium* participants. Although the text is likely still circulating, our lectures were not published.
3. There is one exception, chapter 8, "livingdying." Charles wrote that one.
4. The term *in-between* will play a significant role in the book.

It is a writing that is undergone, not merely undertaken. As we worked in the process of this thinking and writing, attending to the subtle shifts in shade and tone as our ideas, thoughts, and experiences resonated together, something of its own emerged, something that neither of us could write on our own. We find this writing a fusion, an infusion of influences that constitutes an instance of writing that defines itself: something happening in-between in which we, together, find ourselves participant. It's not that the book wrote itself. There were times when we wished that it would!Rather, our interactions and the interplays of our thoughts and feelings formed a process in which something new emerged, a process in which we were intimately involved but did not control.

Beyond Philosophy thus began as we became responsive to polyphony. This responsiveness first happened in our writing as we experienced the multiple simultaneously occurring differences in our meanings, emphases, thoughts, and insights. As we attended to the resonance of these differences, we became attuned to the unsayables and to the silences that emerged with our words. This experience of resonance in the midst of differences happened at times without our intending it and surprised us.

Long before we began to write together, when we were in the early stages of becoming loving partners, we gave papers at a philosophy conference where we and two other philosophers were assigned to the same session. We each authored our respective paper well before our daily philosophical exchanges infused our work. Given our philosophical differences, people, including us, could have reasonably expected papers with vastly different orientations and agendas.[5] We found, however, that although neither of us had the slightest inkling what the other would do in his or her paper, our works were so similar in agenda and guiding thoughts that after the session we shared an anxiety that people would think that one of us had cribbed from the other. That was our first experience when, in spite of our philosophical differences, each of our thinking extended into the other's with a remarkable and constructive overlap. It is an overlap that makes possible what we call an *extended* authorship. Hearing the resonances of

---

5. Charles works with an interdisciplinary emphasis primarily in the broad field of nineteenth- and twentieth-century continental philosophy. Nancy has done major work in feminist philosophy that crosses the academic divides of analytic/continental/pragmatist as well as being richly interdisciplinary.

the one in the other helped us attend together to the unsayables that each of us gestured to in our individual work—what Rilke referred to as "space that no word has ever entered."

Beyond Philosophy thus began as we worked to give philosophical voice to what we experienced between us that happened beyond philosophy. As we became attuned to each other, we experienced each other in-between. Not between. Not between with Nancy's feelings and thoughts there and Charles's thoughts and feelings here and a space of difference between them, but in a happening of feelingthinking *in* the flow of influencing: interfusing thinking and feeling. The experience of in-between occurred initially in the passion of desire. We experienced each other not only as subjects and objects of desire but as fused, interlaced, at once subjects and objects, yet together beyond our subjectivities and objectivities—in-between, an imporing eventuation. These are happenings excessive to being a subject or object, happenings in which there is no distance of one and then the other. Giving voice to these happenings led us to our first experience of extended authorship, "An Infused Dialogue," which in a revised version appears as chapter 7. When we engage in extended authorship, we write out of an encounter that happens in-between. The differences between us in their porosity interweave, and the infusions exceed the differences. The ideas we express in our writing are neither the one's nor the other's; they arise from the exchange. They interplay, and as they play we undergo them. We came to understand that we were experiencing fusions and influences *in* the borders of our identities.

The point of the processes we underwent and that we invite you to experience was not only the production of a written product. It was also to effect a shifting conceptualization and formation of ourselves as we brought ourselves and the book's work together. The aim of giving voice to experiences "that happen in a space that no word has ever entered" is to catalyze a process of affecting, in which affect is neither ours nor yours but a toing and froing in-between. These are movements that attune us to beyond.

BEYOND

Beyond philosophy was not the focal theme of our first experience of extended authorship, "An Infused Dialogue," or of our *Collegium* course. But we became attuned to beyond as we found ourselves in the midst not only of the polyphony of our extended authorship but also of the polyphony of the thinkers we engaged in our course.[6] In the course, we offered a reading attuned to the productive synchronicity and dissonance of the striking differences between—the borders among—all of our voices, differences that often strangely intensified and complemented one another. This attunement to beyond was heightened by each of our years-long concern with borders. These were borders defined by gender, race, class, cultures, differences with and without commonality. We were at times preoccupied with the fusions of borders and with, in Nancy's terms, the viscous porosity of borders that allows both stability for periods of time and the inflow and outflow of influences. Porosity seemed to characterize the borders of differences in the midst of the polyphony of our attunements. Questions of beyond began to emerge from this alertness to dynamic and living borders. These questions concerned intangible, unmeasurable beyond—beyond sense, for example, and beyond identity. In our engagements we became increasingly attuned to the reverberations of dimensions of happening beyond conceptualization.[7] Our attunement was a happening that happened as we found ourselves called to become attentive to the movements, the new prospects, in the thought of Nietzsche, Foucault, and Anzaldúa. Dimensions of happening that we call beyond.

As we became more attuned to these movements, we focused more sharply on such questions as these: How might we speak of the unspeakable? Is there a philosophical art of speaking of the unspeakable? An art of disclosive indirectness? One that our experiences of in-between call for? Would such an art and language have a mandate to stay focused on the ways we live, on what is ordinary in lives, even though the art might be extraordinary in the discipline of philosophy and the language extraordinary in everyday discourse? Perhaps some aspects of ordinary discourse and of the discipline of philosophy obscure ordinary occurrences. Is that possible? Even likely?

---

6. Not only did the course bring us together, two singularly different authors, but it focused on five quite different thinkers—Friedrich Nietzsche, Michel Foucault, Gloria Anzaldúa, Judith Butler, and Lee Edelman.

7. We note the distinction between happening and what is happening or a happening.

Perhaps not surprisingly, Nietzsche's "beyond" sounded the clarion call. In his conception and appropriation of "beyond good and evil," we began to sense unsayable experiences, attunements to happenings in the borders of reason and reflective thought that are often silent or, if glimpsed, rendered nonsense. But we would not have heard so clearly Nietzsche's refrain had we not been in the midst of attending to Anzaldúa's "nepantla." This Nahuatl word names the indeterminate happening of differences coming together, an indefinite in-between out of which new happenings emerge.[8] Anzaldúa crafts an attentiveness to nepantla that opens her to movements beyond habituated ways of thinking and living. In our movements with the question of beyond, we also found Foucault's account of truth and his experience of the legacy of "unreason" to embody a sense of beyond that is kin, in spite of important differences, to Nietzsche's beyond in the phrase "beyond good and evil." Here, the timbre of Foucault's homophony was as resonant as his polyphony.

As we intensified our emphasis on the importance of the word *beyond*, we realized that we needed to distinguish among its various meanings in specific contexts. We and our thinkers often use the term in its multiple meanings. We sometimes talk about things that are beyond in the sense of measurement—farther away spatially or temporally. Anzaldúa grew up, for example, in the Rio Grande Valley of Texas, a region just beyond the Mexican border. Sometimes we, or our authors, talk of things that are outside the limits of a subject or activity. Anzaldúa, for another example, often uses Spanish to say things that go beyond what can be said in English. As we noted at the beginning of this introduction, the word *beyond*, in our particular focus, refers to dimensions of happenings that are beyond the limits of conceptualization and organized patterns of association and meaning. It names dimensions of happenings that are beyond schemas of value and judgment. This book is about those dimensions.[9]

In the interplay of Nietzsche, Foucault, and Anzaldúa—in their various ways of destabilizing unquestioned stabilities, in their unending critique of dualisms, in the unsayables nuanced in their texts, in their

---

8. For a discussion of the Nahuatl meanings of *nepantla*, see Maffie 2013.

9. We will develop the thought that beyond is in no sense a thing and that it lacks sense. Our intention throughout this book is to use language that does not subject dimensions of beyond to the illusion of being subjects or objects.

commitments to transformations, in their indirect disclosures of what cannot be said directly and their styles of presentation—we encountered dimensions of beyond that lack identity and happen as incalculable, non-literal, conflicting, in-fluencing, fusing, imporing processes, such as the dynamic processes of lineages. This beyond that we speak of in this book is not something we can capture in words. We cannot sufficiently define it for you here or even in the conclusion to this book. Our intention in this writing is to occasion a practice of attunement to unspeakable dimensions of experience. Such attunements emerge in part from the desire of those of us who, in the words of Foucault, "write in order to change [ourselves] and in order not to think the same thing as before" (2000, 240). Beyond, we will suggest, is a hitherto seldom noticed dimension of liberatory thought, a dimension that in part explains our choice of interlocutors.

Our aspiration in part I is to offer a reading of these three thinkers that reflects our engagement with the dimensions of beyond that resounds in their texts and also to attend to the processes that are beyond philosophy in their thought. We will neither strive for a comprehensive reading of our chosen authors nor engage secondary literature or debates over interpretations. We choose to stay within our selected texts to offer a reading that gestures in a direction that others might find productive and that might animate attunements beyond.

We begin with three different thinkers, three very different voices. We do not see our work as offering a comparative reading. Indeed, it is a nonjudgmental reading. Each of our authors has their own singular experiences of beyond. Each of them has cultivated their own inimitable habits of attunement that, while likely changing each of them in profound and perhaps at times unsayable ways, transformed both of us in our experiencing of their unsayables. The subtle differences in tone and intonation and not so subtle differences in focus between them carried us beyond our normalized ways of thinking. As the differences between them, and between us, and between us and them resonated in our thinking, we experienced moments of liminality, unspeakable in-betweens. The new experiences engendered by such a reading opened up futures that did not exist before our study began—new thoughts, new values, new perspectives. We hope to be as successful as they in writing in such a way that not only changes us but serves as an occasion for creative transformations of our readers.

In addition to the term *beyond* and its various meanings, there are several additional terms central to our conception of beyond philosophy that will play significant roles in both parts of the book. Our goal in the remainder of this chapter is to provide an introduction to these terms.

IN-BETWEEN

The word *between* suggests a relationship of two or more individual entities in which there is a connection of differences. You might get between two friends who are beginning to push each other in their anger, or as a mediator you might find yourself between people attempting to hear and be heard. An open space might be between two buildings. We often find ourselves between a rock and a hard place, between the devil and the deep blue sea. *In-between*, in our usage, however, means an immediacy of contact when there is a blending of differences as well as the continuing presence of the differences. In-between is a continual happening, a reminder of the deep interconnectivity of things in the making (James 1958). We will consider in this context, for example, occurrences of human intimacy, the ways in which lineages blend and mutate, human life in-between the immediacy of environments. The term *in-between* will be particularly important when we speak of transitions, transformations, and the viscous porosity of borders.

As we speak of in-between, consider the word *chiasmic*, with an emphasis on its suggestion of a crisscross structure, like the Greek χ (*chi*). In that structure two irreducibly different lines cross each other to form a crossing, a chiasm. Such a formation requires the immediate, connected, and simultaneous happening of the differences. The differences, in the language we are using, are in-between and do not constitute a bifurcation or dualism. A chiasmic eventuation happens when, for example, a conceptual structure allows the manifestation of processes and events beyond the limits of conceptual and grammatical structures that happen with the structures.

Our emphasis in this book falls on the experience of in-between. Not on an occurrence, for example, of Martin Buber's I-Thou (1970) but experiences of connection in which differences remain differences and at the same time interfuse. Interfusion: the experienced in-between, a mutual opening with the other. Some people call it "a moment," as in, "You and she had a moment! I saw it happen." In chapter 7 we will describe what some therapists call a therapeutic moment. As we think of it, the moment is neither active nor passive.[10] We find occurrences of in-between as ordinary parts of everyday lives. People might be closed to such happenings, frightened by them, or incredulous regarding them. Our experience is that they do happen often in many circumstances to many people. Including us.

One kind of in-between can happen in relation to works of art and in relation to texts. Our preface says, in effect, that we experienced Brueghel the Elder's painting as an occurrence of in-between. "The presented forest drew us in as it opened itself to us," we said. We were Nancy and Charles as we know ourselves, *and* we were also *in a border* where the painting opened to us and we to it. In that meeting we were beyond ourselves. We were ourselvesbeyondourselves. In-between. When we approach texts with the primary intent of listening to them, making ourselves available to them, feeling what it's like to think and know in the work's terms and in its sensibilities, we often experience them in-between. We do not always like what we experience. Each of us at times might want to back off, move away from the experience, and resist what we engaged and came to understand in fusion with it. Whether we resist or want to return to it, however, we can know the work on the basis of our intimate experience with it and respond to it in many different ways. We can be infused experientially with the work and able to some degree to speak of it from it, speak of it from the in-between happening.

We hope that readers of this book will find themselves in-between with it.

LINEAGES

Genealogical literature speaks of various lineages, such as: lineages of authoritative hierarchies, formations of institutions, identities, religious

---

10. As we will discuss explicitly in chapter 7, the middle voice, which is neither active nor passive, is a resource for thinking about in-between in which the focus is on the activity of the action, not on the doers or receivers of an action. We will often use this voice in our writing.

emotions, punishments, subjections, rejections of physical desire. The image of a line embedded in the word is unmistakable: *lineage* derives from the Latin *linea* and means linen string or thread. The Old English word *line* and the Old French *ligne* derive from the Latin word. Each of those words referred originally to a guideline, cord, or string and suggested a tool used by builders to make things level. The terms could also mean track, course, direction, or a procession of followers. *Lineage* can connote bloodlines, with the lines of begats, descent in a line from a common ancestor, tribe, species, or the ascending line of parentage. *Lineage* can have an attractive sense of straightness, neatness, purity, exactness. In the midst of the chaotic mess of the world's fusing, interconnecting, interbreeding things, one might hope to find uncomplicated clarity about certain origins by establishing a distinct line of descent from a common ancestor or an uncorrupted (we hesitate to say virginal) originary site. We do not, however, deploy that particular sense of *lineage* but instead agree with Foucault that "at the historical beginning of things is not the inviolable identity of their origin; it is the dissension of other things. It is disparity" (1977, 142).

Linea, linen string or thread. People have long used linen thread, not only to set a straight line or as a means of measuring, but to weave cloth and to connect the various parts of shoes, sails, and saddles.[11] It can be twisted, knotted, entwined with other threads. It can be fused with wax or polyester threads, for example, to make connections more durable, or it can be infused with dyes for various colors. Linen thread can be crisscrossed to form designs, shirts, clothes of many shapes and turns. It is a connector that invites many different influences, shapes, and interpenetrations. It can connect complex, diverse things together, as lineages do. But even when it measures, a line need not be straight to be a line. You need a "lesbian rule" should you wish to measure irregular curvings.[12] For when the thing is indefinite, the rule also is indefinite. It is not the straightness of the line that matters here but the twists, turns, and intertwining of many threads, as it were, their tensions, tears, and interlaced mesh.

---

11. Our thinking in this section was animated in part by the writings of Tim Ingold in his marvelous *The Life of Lines* (2015).

12. As Naomi Scheman reminds us, "the rule determines the measurement of the world" and will be "dictated by interests and values" (1993, 207).

A complex lineage might include such opposing differences that happen simultaneously as cruelty and love (as we will find in Nietzsche's work), oppressive power and drives toward liberation (Anzaldúa), and orders of disorder (Foucault).

When we use the word *lineage*, we will thus have in mind, not a straight line of descent, but interconnected, interpenetrating, and interfused groups of processes that include developments of normative practices, changes in hierarchies of authority, mutating values, and much else. Lineages also include all manner of powerful environmental influences and infusions such as climates, precipitation patterns, shifting ocean currents, and species migrations. They include the effects of wars, mediums of exchange, human migrations, new knowledge, linguistic mutations, institutional developments, governmental transformations, alliances, and whatever else flows or fights its way into the inheritances of a culture or society and thus into the physical, enfleshed lives of environments and individual beings. Far from being like a chain, lineages are more like a dynamic weave of processes—like a dynamic area of simultaneously happening factors—that a genealogical investigation might well consider in their specificity and power of continuing influence.

GENEALOGY

Genealogies have to do with such a variety of things! With developments of values, distinctions, identities, hierarchies, dualisms, polarities, descents, the emergence and growth of practices, habits, authorities, and sensibilities. Genealogies such as those found in Hebrew Scriptures trace not only ancient family trees, the lineages of priests, prophets, and kings, but also the divine guidance that formed a chosen people to reveal and carry out God's will. Greek mythology is filled with genealogies of Goddesses, Gods, and Demigods. Genealogies in the contexts of Nietzsche's, Foucault's, and Anzaldúa's work have to do with formations and transformations of ways of life and the images and powers that guide them.[13]

---

13. As we will show in chapter 4, although Anzaldúa does not identify herself as a genealogist, she does give accounts of formations and transformations and the powers that move them in lineages that are active in various ways of life. In our terminology, her work constitutes one kind of genealogy and is informed by her genealogical sensibilities.

In some instances genealogies give accounts of the formations of such capacities as reason and conscience. Genealogies, as Foucault thought of them, find, "not the inviolable identity of... origins... [they find instead] the dissensions of other things" (1977, 142). They find conflict, friction, strife, discord, contention, and, in Foucault's words, the "disparity" of multiply interrelated things that give rise to many beginnings. Attunement to conflict and the emergence of new beginnings is also a key component of Nietzsche's and Anzaldúa's thought.

In this book the genealogies we focus on will be especially alert to the ways that fusions (which we at times call imporings) and mutations characterize the lives of lineages as they bring to bear in people's lives experiences and practices vastly different from their own. Vastly different, and yet constituent in our cultural genes—in our languages, social practices, religions, moralities, and even in our dreams. These genealogies can be interlaced with describable relations of power that accompany the dissensions and persist with the mutated lineages that infuse, stabilize, or destabilize institutions, identities, values, habits, senses of commonality, and social boundaries. We attend also to genealogies that make possible alternative knowledge, such as the knowledge generated by Nietzsche, Foucault, and Anzaldúa. They are alternative to established knowledges and structures of authority, and they often interrupt them, put them in question, and shake their foundations of certainty. These genealogies aim to create new values, new ways of using languages, new formations of authority, and new ways of thinking. Our chosen genealogies are not intended to be abstract; they are meant to affect lives and sensibilities. They are often motivated by and arise from experiences of domination and oppression. These genealogies emerge out of such things as clashes among different standards for normalcy, departures from regimens of prayer and meditation, or from dedicated forms of insubordination and disciplines of refusal. Such genealogies thus arise from dispute and defiance, passions and anxieties, fear and strong wills, cultivated inclinations toward critique and disagreement, and anger in the presence of perceived entrenched injustices or what is identified as corruption—corruption not only of individuals but of institutions, societies, or cultures. The genealogies we consider also arise from experiences of suppression, ostracism, and harmful prejudgments concerning such things as gender, sexual practices, physical appearance, unquestioned axioms of meanings and values, or other economies of inequality. Such passions, encounters, and experiences, when they create new ways of seeing and knowing and behaving, impact the sensibilities and systems of practices in which they arise.

The genealogies we consider not only impact the formations of authorities and sensibilities; they also arise *from* and bring to expression sensibilities, often sensibilities that are in processes of transformation or aspects of sensibilities that various structures of power and meaning have occluded or suppressed. The genealogies we emphasize aim to disclose hidden inclinations, assumptions, and evaluations in lineages of practice and ways of living, as well as to interrupt and recast the ways people recognize the world around them. Such genealogies can enact suppressed lineages and reveal and perform the undulations of broad-ranging sensibilities as axiomatic values begin to change perceptively in them and normal practices begin to erode. In these processes what has been unacceptable can move into the birthing of still-vague practices of acceptance or legitimacy, or what has been acceptable can begin to feel unsettled and vaguely disturbing. Genealogies, as we will see, can be attuned to the interconnections among lives and things, to their deep and shifting rhythms.

In both their performative expressions and their discursive content, genealogies can contribute to the slowly developing awareness of, for example, subjecting values of domination, habitual forms of recognition and identification, and institutional practices that attach to genders, sexual preferences, skin colors, and cultural practices. In their transformative contributions, these genealogies often help to create shifting attunements that increase social power for marginalized people. At their best, genealogies can incite change in the ways people think and feel and predispose them to expect that their most cherished beliefs and values are in processes of transformation. The genealogies we consider show that much of human experience occurs well beyond the sense people make of those experiences.

In addition to contributing to slow transformative processes in sensibilities, genealogies might come in times when an interconnection of those transformative, imporing processes culminates in sudden and striking change. Indeed, the inception of genealogy as we will engage it came at such a time. Such genealogies might be attuned to the movements, vibrations, tensions, rifts, and instabilities that, if not erupt, reach a turning point, like that reached when the earth quakes and a new terrain emerges as an older terrain disappears. In such turning points, a genealogy might bring to expression the mostly pre-reflective, shifting passions, desires, and tacit knowledge in ways that join the diverging, heaving, and stressed forces breaking through cultural borders. Then accounts of the death of the traditionally conceived knowing subject, the death of god, or the questionability of axiomatic values strike a deep and involuntary chord of anxious, perhaps still resistant interest and affirmation. Or a genealogy of mental institutions works a revolution in the treatment and understanding of "the insane." Or Latin American people begin to consciously feel discordant rhythms in their lineages as they find possibilities for different senses of identity. Or a genealogy of sexuality serves as a catalyst for those who have been persecuted and closeted for their queerness to find pride, solidarity, and a new opening for their social lives. As we will show, a puzzling element in the power of some genealogies has less to do with their correctness than with transformations of sensibilities.

SENSIBILITY

Dictionaries define the word *sensibility* as the *ability* to perceive, the *capacity* for emotion or feeling as distinguished from intellect and will; it happens as mental receptivity, ready discernment, awareness, and especially responsive feeling. Our particular use of the word gives priority to its emphasis on feelings and affect and on pre-reflective perceptivity as well as on sensibilities' power to generate meanings and values. Sensibilities in this sense allow people—predispose them—to make sense of and be especially alert to some values, practices, and things while ignoring, rejecting, or finding senseless other values, practices, and things. While we distinguish sensibility from intellect and will, intellection and willing are not separated from it as people function in their lifeworlds. Sensibilities happen in-between affect and cognition, feeling and knowing, sensing and thinking. Sensibilities incorporate and generate many borders as they infuse ways of knowing, affective responses, habitual dispositions, bodily comportments, forms of desire. We note with emphasis that while the word *sensibility* names aspects of awareness and alertness, it also can name cultural and social capacities and abilities that exceed those of individuals in their particular will and intellect. Sensibilities allow sense to be made. We use the term to name dynamic, cultural factors that are historical in their origins and that inform specific institutions, rituals, symbols, and what we will call for the moment *cultural atmospheres*. People can live in-between sensibilities and experience meanings, values, institutional inclinations, and social movements, and hence their own predispositions, happening simultaneously and in strikingly different ways.

We want to make clear that sensibilities can constitute highly complex, dynamic, and mutational types of pre-reflective agency in the beliefs, symbols, interrelations, organizations, and environments of groups of people. These types of agency are shared and are not the province, as it were, of autonomous individuals. For human awareness and identity, sensibilities function effectively like our ability to breathe, in the sense that they are already complexly and dynamically formed and actively in place when we find ourselves in them and begin to think, recognize, or evaluate. Their capacities and contents are dynamic aspects of the world we inhabit. They are effective in language, works of art, interconnections of institutions, and the multiplex of lineages and practices to which we belong. Sensibilities in this sense are largely pre-reflective and inherently relational. Our awareness arises *from* them. We might become reflectively aware of them to some extent *within* their affects. Sensibilities do not reduce to any particular awareness of them.

How such reflective awareness might emerge and develop will be one of our defining issues as we engage Nietzsche's, Foucault's, and Anzaldúa's works. By way of anticipation, we also note that sensibilities have aspects of different, often conflicting lineages. The predispositions they occasion might be simultaneously conflicting ones, such as feeling a strong dislike of a person because of their moral standards and yet feeling an inclination to affirm them at the same time. Or a person might deeply affirm the importance of freedom from discrimination for all people and nonetheless feel that some types of people are inferior. Sensibilities might be characterized as borderlands.[14] They are not unified but are more like spaces of dynamic predispositions, shifting borders of differences. With that differential dynamism also comes the possibility for affirmation of sensibilities

---

14. *Borderland* is a term that Anzaldúa frequently uses in several different contexts.

quite different from our own and a greater likelihood for living, in Gloria Anzaldúa's words, in borderlands without the felt requirement for unifying agreement in our language, conduct, and thought. The porous borders of these differentiations constitute the openings, fissures, and excesses that can provide sites for transformations and give rise to differences other than those to which we are habituated.

ANONYMOUS AGENCY

We, Nancy and Charles, think of human agency as an event with multiple influences and determinations that are enacted as the individual acts intentionally; a self is an event that includes all manner of determining influences. The image of human subjectivity as an autonomous reality that is, at its core, free from all determinations is a powerful fiction in the modern Western philosophical tradition. The term *anonymous agency* in our usage does not refer to something like efficient causation or intentionally directed action. It names indifferent influences that enact themselves without intention and that can directly affect people, institutions, and things.

Consider the enactments of lineages, for example. Lineages are neither mental nor intentional, and yet they are enacted in the languages we speak, the foods we eat and the ways we eat them, the ways we connect with one another, and so forth. Nietzsche, Foucault, and Anzaldúa each work explicitly with lineages, the ways they function as anonymous agents, and the force of their many influences. Art will constitute other examples of anonymous agency. In this book's preface we noted a painting's anonymous agency as we were absorbed by it. We will see in chapter 7 the way Wassily Kandinsky describes the anonymous agency of paintings.

People are vulnerable to so many anonymous agencies, including those that arise from our natural and cultural environments. Indeed, sensibilities, as we understand them, function as an assembly of dynamic anonymous agencies in individuals' lifeworlds. We people are in our choices and intentional actions extended agents, as distinct from nucleus-like centers of free, intentional power. We live *in* our interrelations. We *are* interrelational, and significant parts of our interconnections are anonymous agencies.

As we wrote this book our intention was to inscribe in it our affirmation of the importance of anonymous agencies and hence of affectional vulnerabilities in our lives, and to affirm as well the implications they have for the ways we think and the ways we experience our environments. These are important steps for us in thinking and writing in the force of genealogical sensibilities.

GENEALOGICAL SENSIBILITY

In the context of this book, we use the term *genealogical sensibility* to name sensibilities that are alert to lineages of oppressive practices, to silenced or suppressed lineages, and to the tensions and fissures in them. Such lineages, for example, as those in particular types of authoritative knowledge, in some moralities and religions, in racial and gender classifications, or in class structures. *Genealogical sensibility* in this context has a distinct nuance of liberation and transformation, as in the affirmation of the freeing and transforming power that Anzaldúa found in the fissures in and among the multiple lineages active in her life. Individuals do not need to carry out genealogical studies to have genealogical sensibilities. They might or might not be familiar with Nietzsche's or Foucault's genealogies when they are inclined to reanimate suppressed lineages or to put in question practices and policies that carry out oppressive mind-sets. When people are familiar with those genealogies, whether or not they agree with what Nietzsche or Foucault specifically says, they, in their genealogical sensibility, will be inclined to affirm the genealogists' spirit and directions of thought. They will be attuned to power vectors, to the often ignored or obscured ways that relations of power function in social structures, systems of justice, and standards of normalcy. They will be alert to quests for purity. They will question unquestioned stabilities. "Who is served by these values?" is always an appropriate question for people who make sense of the world in genealogical sensibilities.

At the end of the last section we spoke of the force of genealogical sensibilities. Consider the experience of entering into the writing of Nietzsche, Foucault, or Anzaldúa, "entering" in the sense that you are guided by a desire to experience the writer's desire, undergo the living dimension of the writing, feel the feelings in what the writer writes. You want to attune yourself to the writing in the writing as you read, and you want to hear what the writing says and means to communicate. That degree of subjection is similar to what a well-trained actor experiences when becoming—acting—a part, becoming so much the character in the play or film that the character can take over the actor's gestures, change the scripted words, and feel its own feelings. When people read Nietzsche, Foucault, or Anzaldúa that way and, to the extent possible, leave aside for the moment desires to argue or to remain in their own state of mind, they will experience a genealogical sensibility. It might be very different from the readers' own basis for making sense of the world. Some readers might want to have nothing further to do with *that* experience and its implications. Others might be affirmatively drawn to it and want to carry out the sensibility's strong intention to disrupt what appears as delusions of permanence in a world of becoming, to unsettle illusions of unfractured unities without lineages filled with dissension and mutation, or to interrupt fantasies of unchanging truths and values in always-changing cultures. The forces of genealogical sensibilities impact those who engage them. They—the sensibilities—collide with unquestioned assumptions and axioms. They push toward personal and social transformation. In our experience the push is toward taking decisive, liberatory action to loosen the soil of fixed beliefs and practices in ourselves and in what we will call normalizations, to expose relations of power that silence and marginalize certain kinds of people, and to open new prospects of exposure to what we cannot now perceive or think.

Some of the people we engage do genealogies, and each has distinct sensibilities expressed and accessible in their work. We engage with others whose work emerges from and expresses what we are naming genealogical sensibilities. Some of them keep the genealogies of others alive by stirring the ground those genealogies have rendered instable. We too are not writing a genealogy in this book. But we identify ourselves as writing in a genealogical sensibility.

PHILOSOPHY AS BORDER ART

Our intention is to connect with the works we engage in a way that brings to expression an attunement—a resonance—with dimensions of occurrence that happen outside the grasp of philosophical thought and the boundaries of normative values. This intention means that while we want what we say about the texts to accord with those texts and want to interpret them responsibly, our primary goal is not a thorough account of the authors' works. Our expositions are means to express attunements to what the authors cannot convey directly or literally yet make evident indirectly. Attunements, for example, with lineages that are dynamic and forceful in people's lives and beyond people's grasp and control, like those that Nietzsche, Foucault, and Anzaldúa encounter. Attunements with silences, for another example, at thresholds of transformative processes, silences that are unspeakable.[15] We want to be aware of happenings beyond exposition in our expositions so that we can stay focused on the regions that are beyond philosophy, normative values, and literal expression.

When people's awareness is attuned to dimensions in their experiences that happen beyond what responsible description or exposition can say, they are *in* borders of expression and experience that happen as an occurrence of in-between. We are referring to being *in* borders and not between them as between two houses or between two ideas. Being in borders is rich with possibilities for attunements and resonances with happenings, none of which survives objectification or literal expression. We, Charles and Nancy, are thinking in our experiences of being in borders as we, in our specific differences, experience attunements to happenings beyond the borders of comprehension or schematization in the writing of others or in our own compositions. To write of such happenings, to elicit attunements with what cannot be directly expressed, calls for an art of indirect disclosure—a border art, we call it. We intend our writing to constitute such a border art, to carry overtones, resonances, nuances, and shades of meaning that allow more to appear in the ways people live their everyday lives than they can say or ordinarily expect to say. We will see, for example, that lineages in their mutational dynamism require border art philosophy if philosophers are to invoke the dynamic happenings of lineages in their accounts of them.

---

15. Silences that are not anything in particular and that yet occur are indeed strange. Uncanny, we might say, as they slip our grasp.

We found the *ascesis*, the discipline, of being alert in the borders of our lives difficult at times and always enlivening. We experienced this kind of awareness as one of the privileges that came with the efforts of composition, something like a gifting that joined our personal experiences with our professional experiences and made the jointure of our thought interpersonal in, for us, a new kind of intimacy—a *poiesis* happening again and again as we worked together philosophically. The word *intimacy* gained enriched meaning for us. Intimacy with a painting? With philosophical cogitation? Intimacy with, of all things, Nietzsche? Yes, and with much more, as you will see in the course of this book. When we speak of philosophy as border art and of being in-between, this intimacy and the kind of vulnerability it brings with it are like the tain of a mirror that invisibly allows the reflection of something that is not a reflection at all.

A NOTE ON READING THIS BOOK

We have said that we intend to develop ways of speaking of the unspeakable, to find how to speak in attunement with dimensions of experience that happen beyond formations of representation and objectification, dimensions that happen beyond meaning and sense. As we think, we cultivate forms of expression in attunement with happening beyond forms. In the poet Mary Oliver's words, our concern is with "the edge and making forms out of the formlessness that is beyond the edge" (2016, 28). As we think of edges where meaning and reason cease, our emphasis falls on nuance, feeling, resonance, and release from expectations of transcendent meaning and reason. We are thinking of such edges as we write, and we are on them as we think.

Our attention to dimensions that happen beyond meaning is cultivated through our reading of the three thinkers—Nietzsche, Foucault, and Anzaldúa—whose work we find to be particularly salient to our efforts to cultivate habits of attunement to beyond, three thinkers whose attention to unsayables and silences deeply resonates in our own thought and in our own efforts to speak about attunements to silent happening outside the borders of reason. There are other thinkers, both past and present, whose work connects with questions of happening beyond philosophy. Our aim is not to provide an exhaustive list or to offer comparative or historical studies of such thinkers. We hope, however, that our efforts in this book will catalyze others to attend to thinkers and artists who write and create in attunements with indeterminate beyond and in so doing to thicken the dialogue we begin here and further animate indirect disclosure of unsayable dimensions of experience.

In the chapters that follow we offer practices of attunement—both our own practices of attunement and those of our three thinkers—with unsayable dimensions of beyond. We will not compare our three thinkers or interconnect them directly, as we find that doing so mutes our attentiveness to beyond. Each writer has their own engagements with happening beyond philosophy. So readers do not need to read the chapters focused by Anzaldúa, Nietzsche, and Foucault in a particular order. One chapter does not presuppose the others. If readers have more familiarity with one of the authors, they could begin with that chapter before reading the others. The point is to get into each author's performative thought, its variations of tone and shades of meaningnonmeaning. The goal is to experience the ways the author's language and thought engender further, elaborating language and thought. The aim is not agreement or disagreement, critique or consent. We want to create opportunities for readers to find or intensify their own experiences and thought with the issues and questions engaged by us and the thinkers we address.

Each chapter in this book is oriented, not by notions of supernatural entities or processes or by transcendental a priori formations, but in the context of everyday living by experiences of happenings beyond conception and by experiences of liberation in circumstances generated by sensibilities. That is, circumstances formed by the influences of lineages, porous borders, oppressive or enlivening practices, life-enhancing or life-denying mores, insistent stabilities, the power of authoritative knowledge, experiences of certainty and uncertainty within systems of belief and commitment, processes of self-formation, experiences of loving, of dying.

We hope this book, attentive as it is to dimensions of experience that are beyond formations—beyond identities, values, and meanings—and to the liberatory power that attunements with beyond can occasion will engage readers who have a wide variety of convictions and leading interests that resonate with these happenings. We hope that readers will experience their own edges where differences begin to meld and something else that is nothing else becomes wordlessly, formlessly apparent.

We note in conclusion that the book is divided into two parts. In part I we find that resonance and attunement with beyond are shaded in the thought of Anzaldúa, Foucault, and Nietzsche. In the complex depths of their resonance and attunement with beyond, literal clarity in their thought fades out. Nuance, metaphor, and performative indirection become indispensable as borders blur, become shadowy, disappear. Meaningful intentions lose their directive power in this aspect of their work. Reading them deeply is like living with them. This experience can be tantamount to moving into a penumbral area where shadows intensify in a crosshatch of receding light and growing dark until there is no thing. Formless nothing. It is like coming, not simply to an edge, but into an edge, being in an edge. Form and formlessness seem to blend, to fuse, like lightdark at a periphery when the verge of light is dimming out and darkness fuses with formlessness. *Beyond* names a silent formlessness that is apparent in formless darkness, in dimensions of occurrences with which Anzaldúa, Nietzsche, and Foucault, in their strikingly different ways, are exceptionally attuned.

We hope that the chapters in part I will provide openings for readers to attunements with beyond that are not within the authority or power of any formation but that can have transformative power for people who form their lives in affirmation of that attunement. Isn't it true that we can be incited to think when we experience not knowing, incited, not to fill in the blanks of ignorance, but to grapple with and learn from not knowing?

In part II we intend to write and think in attunement with beyond in the impact of our engagement with Foucault, Nietzsche, and Anzaldúa as we develop what we call border art philosophy. In these five chapters and the epilogue, we will put to work the words and concepts that we discuss in the introduction as we engage such socioenvironmental issues as anthropogenic climate change, infusions of racial exploitation and environmental exploitation in the lineages of slavery, and the impacts of the use of nitrates to increase food production. We will also speak of the normativity/antinormativity debate, extended agency, anonymous agencies, erotic desire without objectification, Wassily Kandinsky's experience of his paintings, and the immediacy and feeling of livingdying. Throughout part II we engage questions of how to advance transformative, liberatory lifeways, of how to live viably and creatively in common with others, how to live with uncertainty and decisiveness *in* the liminality of thresholds. These questions give us occasions to trouble the ground—"to rattle the cages of our certainties," we say—of normative assuredness in the context of our affirming the importance of normative values. Can people be committed in affirming the importance of their values and at the same time know that values and their meanings are formed in sensibilities that are infused with shifting, often incompatible lineages? Can they carry out their commitments, carry them out hyper-actively (we use Foucault's term), without the illusion of fixed certainty or of the finality of justice? Can people stand the instability of where they stand? Stand the instability of intangible beyond in the midst of their ever-so-tangible lives?

Nietzsche's Exposure Beyond Philosophy

PREFACE

We begin this chapter by noting that one of our goals in this book is what Johann Wolfgang von Goethe called augmenting people's activity. Nietzsche particularly liked this statement: "In any case, I hate everything that merely instructs me without augmenting or directly invigorating my activity."[1] For Goethe, invigorating his activity meant intensifying his sense of being alive and creative. We want to carry out our engagement with beyond in Nietzsche's phrase "beyond good and evil," with the purpose of augmenting and invigorating people's activity. Instruction is not our goal. Nor is finding the truth about any particular thing. We listen carefully when Nietzsche says, "It is no more than a moral prejudice that truth is worth more than appearance. . . . Is it not sufficient to assume degrees of apparentness and, as it were, lighter and darker shadows and shades of apparentness—different 'values,' to use the language of painters?" (1996a, section 2, subsection 34, 45; translation altered). We have

---

1. This statement by Goethe begins Nietzsche's forward to "The Uses and Disadvantages of History for Life" in his *Untimely Meditations*. Nietzsche elaborates the statement: "We need history, certainly, but we need it for reasons different from those for which the idler in the garden of knowledge needs it, even though he may look nobly down on our rough and charmless needs and requirements. We need it, that is to say, for the sake of life and action. . . . We want to serve history only to the extent that it serves life" (1997, 59).

degrees of apparentness and shades of lighter and darker in mind as we turn to Nietzsche's exposure beyond philosophy.

Nietzsche uses the word *beyond* in several different contexts. It can refer, for example, to what runs counter to our natural instincts and animality, to a fantasized God and an "eternity of torment without end, as hell" (1997, Second Essay, section 22, 92). In the course of this chapter, we will also find that human bestiality—human corporeality with its natural instincts—is, in Nietzsche's view, beyond the reach of the type of rationality and philosophy that functions to make sense of the world, even though natural instincts function *in* the corporeality of rationalities and moralities. Our primary focus now will be on *beyond* as Nietzsche uses the word in the phrase "beyond good and evil." We will find that his resonance with that sense of beyond is crucial for his development of genealogical knowledge that uncovers lineages and puts in question our most cherished values, institutional practices, and meanings. His usage of the word points us in one of the directions we follow as we consider the philosophical importance of attunements to regions of occurrence that the defining boundaries of reflective thought make obscure and often conceal. Attunements in our lives to occurrences beyond values and good sense, we will show, constitute thresholds—simultaneous endingsbeginnings—to life transformations, whether for good or ill. Our intention as we engage Nietzsche's work is to think and speak in these attunements, to think on the borders where syntactical language comes to its limit and an art excessive to skillful, clear thought becomes important if we are to speak in resonance with the unspeakable. We will draw on Michel Foucault's and Gloria Anzaldúa's work as well as Nietzsche's when we call this philosophical art *border art*.[2]

In 1886 Nietzsche addressed directly the importance of art in connection with the formations of careful thinking and morality.[3] He says that in *The Birth of Tragedy*, his first published book, he wanted "to look at

---

2. See chap. 5, where we engage Anzaldúa's use of the term *border arte* to elaborate her attunement to occurrences beyond the reach of conceptual formulations and her ways of communicating that attunement.

3. In that year he published *Beyond Good and Evil* as well as an introduction to the reissue of *The Birth of Tragedy*, "Attempt at Self-Criticism." In this prefatory paragraph and the one that follows, we will refer only to that introduction.

disciplined knowledge [inclusive of philosophy] in the perspective of the artist, but at art in that of life" (1966b, 19).[4] This fecund intention in writing *The Birth of Tragedy* and giving primary attention in classical Greek culture to art—the art of tragedy as well as to mythmaking—that might impact people's experience of knowledge, thought, and values. This intention meant that he experienced an "instinct that aligned itself with life and that discovered for itself a fundamentally opposite doctrine and valuation of life—purely artistic and *anti-Christian*" (1966b, 24).[5] He is also creating and articulating a perspective that gives priority to the imaginative artistry and mortality of all formulations, including philosophical conceptual formations and sacred beliefs and, of course, his own conceptions and beliefs; he gives priority to their being always in processes of transformative becoming. They are formations that are deforming—as they provide experiences of beauty, knowledge, truth, sense, and bordered stability as well as oversimplification, superficiality, inscripted fear, lust for power, and much foolishness.

In this book, as he focuses on the emergence of the art of tragedy, he thinks in the context of the two primary forces of nature that were figured in Apollo and Dionysus. Both figures have long lineages from many prehistoric cultures. Apollo: for Nietzsche, primarily the God of stabilizing formations and appearances. Dionysus: the God of deformation and destructuring. They represent for Nietzsche the two basic forces of life: on the one hand, the power to stabilize the chaos of uncontrolled life energy by such formations as identities and works of art, and, on the other, the power of sheer unformulated urge to be that cannot be harnessed for long by any formation. The classical Greek tragic dramas by Aeschylus and Sophocles, as Nietzsche interprets them, were able to bring together artistically these two life-powers without compromising their incompatibility. The borders between them are found in the continuous tension between

---

4. We have changed the translation of *Wissenschaft* from "science" to "disciplined knowledge" in order to make clear its meaning in English usage.

5. His goal is "to learn the art of *this worldly* comfort first." To accomplish this goal, he says, "you ought to learn to laugh, my young friends, if you are hell-bent on remaining pessimists [i.e., continuing to see clearly the suffering and meaninglessness of life]. Then, perhaps, as laughers, you may some day dispatch all metaphysical comforts to the devil—metaphysics in front" (1966b, 26).

the formed stories, actions, and characters in the play, on the one hand, and, on the other, the chorus that perceives forces far beyond the reach of human control, meaning, and reason, fateful forces entwined in human lives that will destroy what is heroic and good. The chorus also provides the wild and senseless dithyrambic, discordant, wailing rhythms that arise from lineages of ancient Dionysian festivals. We recognize Nietzsche's presentation of those tragedies as one kind of border art, an art that happens on the borders of communicability, not in between two or more incommensurable forces and regions but in-between—*in the chiasmic eventuation* of the incommensurable forces and regions. Border art makes manifest far more than what people can articulate directly. Can thinking occur as another kind of border art that in its artistry exceeds the reach of thinking and the norms by which we live? Is disciplined thought—philosophy—able to instill an attunement with nonrational and nondiscursive processes, an attunement that in an art of thought allows thought to resonate with dimensions of occurrence beyond itself and the borders of meaning and judgment? Are we philosophers able, as philosophers, to communicate in such attunement and resonance?

We feel a draw to philosophers who think in this attunement. Part of this chapter concerns the way Nietzsche developed philosophical alertness that is beyond philosophy's conceptual grasp. That is, alertness to occurrences that are beyond good and evil and good sense. Nietzsche's art is found in his ability to make such alertness manifest by nuance, indirection, contextualized silences, styles of presentation, and experimental types of knowledge (such as genealogy).[6] We hope that our readers will experience an intensified predisposition toward border art philosophy and toward greater uncertainty in connection with their certainties, experiences, and values. Perhaps they will even develop a predisposition to laughter and an affirmation of being alive in the midst of the mindless brutality, lack of justice, and indifference that characterize the world—and possibly experience also an inclination to make a livable difference

---

6. We will discuss such occurrences in the context of mutations and fusions of lineages, the formations and deformations of, in Nietzsche's words in *Beyond Good and Evil*, "the human soul," and the moments of creation and emergence of new realities.

in our environments with full acceptance of the reality that indifferent transformations and mortality trump everything we value, do, and are.[7]

TRUTH?

Are we creatures who seek truth? Nietzsche thinks yes and no. We will consider first the voice of a "free spirit" in sections 24 and 296 in *Beyond Good and Evil* (1966a). That is, we will begin this discussion of Nietzsche in the context of beyond philosophy with his understanding of truth in connection with the truth of his own work, especially the truth of what he says about truth.

Section 24 begins part 2 of the book *The Free Spirit* with these words: "*O sancta simplicitas*! In what strange simplification and falsification man lives! One can never cease wondering once one has acquired eyes for this marvel! How we made everything around us clear and free and easy and simple! how we have been able to give our senses a passport to everything superficial, our thoughts a divine desire for wanton leaps and wrong inferences! How from the beginning we have contrived to retain our ignorance in order to enjoy an almost inconceivable freedom, lack of scruple and caution, heartiness, and gaiety of life—in order to enjoy life! And only on this now solid, granite foundation of ignorance could knowledge rise so far—the will to knowledge on the foundation of a far more powerful will: the will to ignorance, to the uncertain, to the untrue! Not as its opposite but—as its refinement!" (1966a, 35).

We are creatures who seek the simplicity of falsifications about the world and its lives in order to enjoy being alive, in order to enjoy *creating*

---

7. In *The Birth of Tragedy* Nietzsche develops the observation that in classical Greek culture many people fully accepted the Dionysian "wisdom" that human life, when considered only in its natural state, is miserably tragic, that not living is preferable to living. But this culture, without rejecting tragic pessimism, found life worth living by creating beautiful works of art ranging from their myths, mores, and architecture to their great dramatic tragedies. They developed a pessimism of *strength*, "An intellectual predilection for the hard, gruesome, evil, problematic aspect of existence, prompted by well-being, by overflowing health, by the *fullness* of existence." In their inclination to make their existence a matter of life-affirming art, they "seduce us to life" in spite of its dimension of massive indifference (1966b, 17). See also the encounter of King Midas and centaur Silenus (1966b, 42).

values and scruples and the conscience they require, and to do so with a shocking lack of scruple and caution. We are creatures who instinctively seek the gaiety that learned ignorance of the chaos, destruction, cruelty, and utter indifference of life makes possible. We are wily creatures who in our instinctive will to knowledge create the value of truth and certainty because of our also instinctive will to the uncertain and untrue. We build our culture on the remarkable, even beautiful, foundation of ignorance—*educated* ignorance—remarkable and beautiful because it shows a will uncorrupted by the corruptions it engenders, a malicious will that is intrinsic in our lives and that finds its pleasure in creating, creating even formations that constrict the world around us, formulate it, enframe it, and subject it (bring it forcefully under our control)—in order that we may enjoy being alive.

Would you like to see primordial cruelty? Nietzsche directs us to look to what we creatures do to the dense, dynamic uncertainty and brutality in life with our truths, our truths about life that in life's obscure liminality cannot be circumscribed by something universal called *truth*. Far from the beauty of the Greek Gods and the classical Greek tragedies, as Nietzsche reads some of them, that are conceived in the dark shadow of the horrors in being alive, people now with their normative truths create ugly, warped structures of obligation, belief, and fear that compose nothing more than hideouts from life itself.

Is any of Nietzsche's formulation about truth true? We turn now to the last paragraph in *Beyond Good and Evil*, that is also written by a free spirit, not in the cheerful mood of section 24 but rather with a sense of mourning, in the context of "What Is Noble": "Alas, what are you after all, my written and painted thoughts! It was not long ago that you were still so colorful, young, and malicious, full of thorns and secret spices—you made me sneeze and laugh—and now? You have already taken off your novelty, and some of you are ready, I fear, to become truths: They already look so immortal, so pathetically decent, so dull! And has it ever been different? What things do we copy, writing and painting, we mandarins with Chinese brushes, we immortalizers of things that can be written—what are the only things we are able to paint? Alas always only what is on the verge of withering and losing its fragrance! Alas, always only storms that are passing, exhausted, and feelings that are autumnal and yellow! Alas, always only birds that grew weary of flying and flew astray and now can be caught by hand—by *our* hand! We immortalize what cannot live and fly much longer—only weary and mellow things! And it is only your *afternoon*, you, my written and painted thoughts, for which alone I have colors, many colors perhaps, many motley caresses and fifty yellows and browns and greens and reds: but nobody will guess from that how you looked in your morning, you sudden sparks and wonders of my solitude, you my old beloved—*wicked* thoughts!" (1966a, 236–37).

"You sudden sparks and wonders of my solitude." The moments and exhilaration of conception, creation, coming to form as something new emerges into life. Sparkling . . . exciting . . . birthing . . . unwritable and beyond direct articulation. What happens when nascent thoughts are set into stabilized words? When they become nouned, verbed, subjected, objected—when they become grammatical and fitted into nets of decent prose? Are such moments like weary birds not far from their deaths? We can *experience* conception and creation and unfolding into life, but we cannot write *about* them without losing *their* events. Can such experiences be *experienced in* the writing? Prosaically written, they—these sparks and wonders—are past and exhausted as we attempt—hysteresis-like—to hold them and contain them. But perhaps they—both the sparks and the wonders and experiences of them—are alive in nothing literal but in styles, performative enactments, nuance, interactive attunements . . . in what we will call the sensibilities of some texts and some kinds of awareness, and in the art of presenting what cannot live as an object. The *wonders and exhilaration* of births and, for Nietzsche, the solitude that accompanies them, when they are held long enough to write about in a conventional, straightforward manner, lose much of their lives in translation. They—the creations and silences that pervade *Beyond Good and Evil*—wither. They become like something that doesn't seem to die, like truths . . . but "so dull." Can those wonders live in the still, releasing solitude that can permeate a piece of writing? Could we experience such a sensibility in sections 24 and 296? In what they do not say, in the gaiety and lack of truthful seriousness in 24? In the grief expressed in 296, the grief of losses buried in truths and literality, grieving sadness that seems to allow undisturbed the stillness and solitude and wonder reflected in the grief? Can those wonders live in grief, grief not simply as a disposition tied blindly to death but as inclination to live in the glow of the creation's twilight with anticipation of births yet to come? Birth and death at once? Birth and death forming a liminal threshold?

Can the sparks, playfulness, and wonder come to live in a type of innocence, a dimension of conscious life that is far below or above (Nietzsche would say they are the same) knowledgeable sophistication? A dimension of conscious life that can be like a child's joy over something new and sparkling, the innocence of a child's indifference to the big problems of serious living? A geist or spirit that has mutated out of a soul that carries the heavy baggage of lineages of life-denial like an overloaded camel in a desert? Nietzsche's account in "The Three Metamorphoses" in *Thus Spoke Zarathustra* has the camel mutating into the lion, a beast of prey. The lion who—in its aggressive anger, resentment, and rage toward the burdens, toward the imposed, God-given "thou-shalts" that have as their progeny guilt, self-denial, resentment, and hostilities toward corporeal life—fights to destroy the burdening load and moralizing sublimity carried by... let's now call it the Western human soul.

Another spiritual mutation occurs in what we might call the region that once harbored the moral/religious soul, a mutation from the deconstructing lion to the child that embodies the soul's full self-overcoming, an image of the apex of the will to power in which the will to power wills itself without hindrance and composes the child's being: "The child is innocence and forgetting, a new beginning, a game, a self-propelled wheel, a first movement, a sacred 'Yes.' For the game of creation, my brothers, a sacred 'Yes' is needed: the spirit now wills his own will and he who had been lost to the world now conquers his own world" (1966c, 27). That sounds like the sparkling moments of creation and wonder, doesn't it? The sparks and wonder that break out of constricting formations of normative values and meanings. The child's conquest happens by virtue of its *willed*, its *lived*... its *physical* affirmation of the urge to be alive. Its metaphorical dimension happens beyond the reach of the free-spirited, deconstructing beast of prey, although, ironically, the dimension of the child is forecast by a free spirit. Nietzsche forecasts the self-overcoming of his own free spirit in a living affirmation of creation—a living affirmation of spiritual birthing, self-overcoming, and emergence. An affirmation, perhaps, in which the "alas" of the last paragraph of *Beyond Good and Evil* is overcome by the wonder "of a new beginning," "a first movement." With this new beginning we are now far beyond philosophy, but we are also thinking philosophically. This is an observation that we will develop more fully in the following pages.

Are sections 24 and 296 written in what we might call the nuance of the metaphor of the child? We will speak for a moment of *physicality* to underscore its importance in our engagement with truth and occurrences beyond truth. Consider the root word for physicality, *phusis*. It has the sense of the springing up of earthy, living things, at once enfleshed and growing, entwining, entangling, imporing outside the range of good and evil, the living and arising of things in their interconnections without norms or values, ongoing processes of physical-spiritual birth, growth, and death in a tangle of processing lives. The child is attuned to the world's physical (*phusic*) eventuations, finds wonder and delight in them, and in this wonder and delight has no desire to injure or subject.[8] It—the child—is a metaphor for the *ecstasis* of creative moments. Its power, as we understand it, permeates its environment and is itself earthy, enfleshed, entwining and entangling with the lives of things, imporing and infusing with their lives as it shines out to grow and die without resentment or immobilizing anxiety. The child is the *Yes* when creation happens, an affirmation that continues to reverberate in relation to worldly life when a changed sensibility emerges from experiences of this *Yes*. Such reverberation should make Goethe happy: it invigorates activity. And that activity should be read as inclusive of thinking in attunement with events and processes that are quite beyond thinking's jurisdiction.

The metaphor of the child as Nietzsche projects it thus embodies one of the culminations of the human geist's self-overcoming transformations (living in affirmation of eternal return is another). People who enter into the sensibilities of his literal and nonliteral worlds are turned to the marvel of creative energy and events—turned even to the creation of truth and the cheerfulness with which he speaks of the holy simplicity of that falsification (i.e., of created truth and truths), cheerfulness, indeed, vis-à-vis the perverse and perverting ignorance of truth's creation. It—the

---

8. From Latin *subjectus*, "brought under," past participle of *subicere*, from *sub-*, "under," + *jacere*, "throw."

creation—is beyond the dichotomy of truth/lie, and when free spirits are able to find joy in a creative happening they can laugh with the human foolishness that they also find. They—the free spirits—lose their deep-seated desires to contain, control, and dominate the drives to live, desires that Nietzsche finds inherent not only in people but also in the environments they have created and in which they usually live. We can think of these environments as herd cultures, about which we will say more. We might even say, with a smile, that they are cultures of truth-made-normal.

Were what Nietzsche says in *Beyond Good and Evil* only literally true, the book would have missed the point of its writing, its freedom, its creativity. When we hold these two paragraphs from *Beyond Good and Evil* together, supplemented by "The Three Metamorphoses," we could well think that free-spiritedness, exhilaration in creative moments that are felt as ends in themselves, and *geistige* birthing combined with joy in discovering that a will to simple superficiality supports knowledges and truths—we could think that these factors all arise from a *sensibility* unique to his created and written world of thinking and writing. We might discover that these elements are simultaneously enfleshed in the desires, wills, and feelings of those people who have come to live in the motivational power of that sensibility. We could think that Nietzsche's primary purpose in writing was not only to discover, express, or pursue truths (although he also often wished that what he wrote and said were true). Is the book not only about thinking and living in attunement with life—physical life—as beyond good and evil but also about *being* oneself beyond truth? Does the book perform what it also talks about as it talks about it? What would that beyond *be* like? A sustained encounter with these questions could provide us with an entrée to the way this book, a book that Nietzsche wants to elaborate in his *Genealogy of Morals*, enacts far more than he can say directly. We shall see if the book's enactment constitutes *its* corporeality and its attunement with a sensibility far different from the dominant strands of sensibility we find in most of our Western cultures.

THE HUMAN SOUL

In order to emphasize the dynamic corporeality of spirit (*Geist*), soul (*Seele*), and beyond (*Jenseits*), we turn for a moment to part 3, section 45 of *Beyond Good and Evil*.⁹ The section is called "Das religiöse Wesen." Although that title could well be translated "What Is Religious" or "The Religious Being," our preference is "The Religious Creature." It directly concerns the lineages and constitutions of the Western *Homo sapiens*' soul . . . the human soul, the *geistige* self . . . the soul grown in a vortex of lineages, like a womb webbed with historical vortices. It concerns the ensouled creature: given its maelstrom of constitutive lineages, perhaps the most dangerous to itself and to others of all living beings—a creature that can create as it destructively turns against its own power of life. It also concerns how the soul might be transformed.

For his genealogical purposes, Nietzsche accepts the widespread claim that we humans have souls. Or, better said, humans are besouled. Hear his opening sentences: "The human soul, and its limits, the range inner human experiences has reached so far, the heights, depths, and distances of these experiences, the whole history of the soul *so far* and its as yet unexhausted possibilities—that is the predestined hunting ground for the born psychologist [i.e., the specialist in the logos of the soul] and lover of the 'great hunt'" (1966a, 59).

He metaphorizes the soul and the reach of its embodied complex legacies as "this huge forest, this primeval forest." The hunter needs "a few hundred helpers with good, well-trained hounds" to "drive into the history of the human soul to round up *his* game" (59). His game? The hunter's game? The progenitors of fearful, religious creatures who prey upon bodies—their own and those of others—with their morals, rituals, and fear of flesh, those who fear the consumptive power of pleased, caressed skin, of corporeal passions and intense, absorbing pleasures, those who fear the very energy of life without divine sanction, those who fear the loveless indifference of the world that impores the permeable borders of their most cherished loves and God-given moralities. His game are the anonymous begetters of creatures haunted by the grim liminal sense of darkness that shadows forest light, haunted by cold, loathing forest wraiths that seep through crevasses of emptiness and bedevil the very

---

9. The word *geist* has been adopted in the English language and does not require capitalization as it does in German. We use it at times to name the human soul. Nietzsche also uses *Seele* when he speaks of soul.

heart of the soul. In this primeval forest he has already discovered living, embodied lineages of self-sacrifice that would crucify even God incarnate and would abuse their own spirits until it "hurts indescribably" (section 46, 60). He has found clearings surrounded by thickets where continual suicides of reason take place—often for the sake of believing absurdly that their souls will live eternally as a gift for despising the only life they have.

But Nietzsche has found few volunteers who are able to carry out the hunt "where the great danger begins" (59). Why? Because at issue is not an abstract soul. The issue is one's own physical, living soul, the soul that reaches back so far, that lives with and contains previously unimagined depths, heights, and distances of uncountable, multiply fused lineages, the soul that is one's entanglement with strange passions, cruelties, hatreds, and fears, the soul that is the continuous wellspring, corrupted as it is, of the person's meanings in life, the person's source of desire (and this is Nietzsche's desire too) to find the soul's "nature." As the psychic history begins to come to light, one's desires, wills, and senses of purpose are shaken as storms of discovery and the spiritual undulations that go with them break open the forest darkness, and the history-enmeshed individual is exposed as the light of one's own soul shines on itself. Webs of lineages wrap around this awareness, and the volunteer hunters face the specter of meaningless insanity as they find the full meaning of "*beyond good and evil.*" That meaning is not insanity. It is the experience of being beyond the compelling power of the meanings, values, and desires that have provided a normative ground of consciousness-in-the-world for the hunter. It is coming to know that there is no purity in the soul, that our best values often carry with them active, pre-reflective lineages of their opposites, that identities arise from a muddle of differences and chance happenings. Finding the meaning of "beyond good and evil" means discovering that in the absence of one nature or a divinely given scaffolding of norms people must find (preferably, create) and embody their own primary values and meanings. It means being a free spirit, the friend of the camel, the lion, and the child—all at the same time—as one sheds light on, interrupts, and destructures the power of one's own soul.

The great danger is one that Nietzsche knew well. Most of what he so maliciously, so immorally, so very irreligiously exposed and criticized also inhabited his own soul. He writes out of a struggle of self-transformation, of "self-overcoming" and transvaluation of all values in his language, of radical transformation, that, in his experience, allows one group of powerful prejudgments and beliefs to weaken until another group can take their place with the growing lightness of a free spirit and the myth of eternal return at their center.

BEYOND

So, how does beyond happen in Nietzsche's genealogical sensibility? We could sensibly and correctly say that *beyond* names both a dimension and a goal. Beyond is "where" the theo-moral dualism, good/evil, loses its power. There are certainly many valuations of goods and bads in his work, but they are without an infusion of transcendental validation. And since *evil* has so much theo-metaphysical baggage, we can say with Nietzsche that it's better to drop the word and let it be one of the more fortunate casualties of God's loss of the power necessary to create a civilization-wide moral universe of dualisms and opposites as distinct to degrees and gradations of mortal, regional differences.

We could also say unproblematically that Nietzsche's use of the word *beyond* suggests a goal by which aspiring free spirits might measure their movement toward freedom from the oppression and ascetic, life-denying subjugation found in Western morality and religion. That's not an easy movement according to Nietzsche, as we have seen. It requires physical transformation, and he is not only talking about the transformation of slavish types of spirits who still have *geistige* strength adequate to the effort. He is also talking about the possible transformation of people with passionate and strong spirituality, if they can be found, people who have turned their backs on milksoppy morality and religion with their happy religious comforters, bland relativisms, pity for weakness, fear-based civility, and insistence on being children of a Lord of Life. He is not talking only about people who in their spiritually fearful lives bear living testament to the death of God as Nietzsche understands that death. He also has in mind people with robust moral and religious values—*passionately willed* values, enfleshed values that engender structures of living. He has in mind people able to make, in awe-filled wonder, their bodies a sacrifice to an Almighty Power—more in the direction of early Christian communities or of Savonarola or Pascal. There, *in those bodies*, is where God lived, in their wills, souls, enchained spirits. But such strong-spirited people are scarce. The people Nietzsche found, who were mostly in Europe, lived as herd creatures who together felt protected from the jungle depths of their souls and their webs of lineages, their dangerous passions, and who unconsciously made weakness of spirit their cause. *Beyond* for him is beyond the herd and its guards of conformity, beyond those satisfied with their goodness, and beyond the evil created by their God. But not beyond the night sounds of the forest, the deep howls from the darkness that lead them to huddle, lead them to punish deviations from goodness and to isolate those who might want to know more about life without herds, life beyond herd morality, truth, and religion, and life beyond the moral and theoretical conceptual formations that arise out of herd cultures.

We are, of course, talking about ways of living. We are talking in all of these instances about physical—corporeal—ways to be. Free spirits transform into different ways of willing and different kinds of perceiving in comparison with herd creatures. Herd creatures: those who have sacrificed their wills to God, to normal truths and morals, or to systems of already-packaged truths and beliefs, as well as those who have never had or lost the capacity for deep soul-passion.

The word *beyond*, as Nietzsche thinks of it, thus suggests a kind of physical goal as well as a dimension, living in attunement with which requires enormous physical change—that is, attunement with beyond requires transformation of souls and daily comportment. We will also consider the meaning of the word as we move toward an engagement with Nietzsche's genealogy in the context of beyond philosophy. We understand *beyond* in this context as an unschematized dimension of human occurrences, genealogical temporalities. Beyond is "where" incalculable, uncountable processes happen. Beyond is beyond chronological time. We christen *temporality* in this context of beyond with the meaning of ongoing physical processes of transformation, willing to be, and simultaneous and unsynchronized infusions in porous webbings of lineages (we will say more about the porous webbings of lineages). These eventuations are not measurable by schemas that give order to the flow of moments, eventuations not defined by any particular confluence of influences. Temporality in this context is the happening of liminal in-betweens, mere transfiguring processes without order, identity, teleology, or origin—a Dionysian temporality for Nietzsche, or, to say the same thing, the becoming of occurrences beyond schemas of sense. Temporality in this dimension of Nietzsche's work comprises composed lives that eventuate in the flux of their multiple lineages where the liminality of in-between dissolves the clarity of boundaries, where tried-and-true differences meld, where there is neither truth nor lie nor logos. Like a Dionysian mask behind which there is nothing. We speak of Dionysian temporality, of processes beyond good and evil, in this context to emphasize the physical, processional dynamism of fusing lineages and hence the dynamism of bodies beyond the sense (schema) of time and meaning. Perhaps you can see that this use of *temporality* forecasts the meaninglessness of time both in the myth of eternal return and in Nietzsche's understanding of genealogy. Time without meaning is nothing. Yet the circle of lives circles, bodies *are*, beginnings begin to end, endings happen without end, always in-between, always multiple thresholds, all-ways . . . always. Dionysus smiles absently from behind a mask where he isn't.

We are aware of how difficult and counterintuitive language and conceptuality are when one enters the sensibility of beyond in Nietzsche's discourse. But upon entering it, we are also aware of the original depth of his affirmation of life as he finds living to take place; we are aware of how demanding it is to free ourselves, even to a small degree, from transcendentally authorized schemas, good sense, truths, and boundaries of meaning that circumscribe our worlds and hold us at a safe distance from the great forest where meaning, value, and truth lapse. When we speak in upcoming sections of the meaning of *temporality* in Nietzsche's genealogies we will speak of the events of complex, mutating, and uncountable lineages in the lives of *Homo sapiens*. We will describe these events of lineages that are purposeless, dynamic processes of imporing, mutating, infusing—processes that are outside the jurisdiction of ordered time and succession. The historian's time is composed of systems of counting and ordering, but physical/*geistige* processes beyond such counting and ordering happen. Some of these processes can be traced, but not, for Nietzsche, as a historian's history (although he was an extraordinary scholar, philologist, and classical historian). Such processes can be traced in what we call a genealogical sensibility, a sensibility that in establishing its claims and giving priority to corporeality (physicality, flesh) releases its own interest in truth in order to allow a new kind of knowledge. That knowledge is attuned to truthless physicality and the liminal world of *geistige* formation where something happens like an "obscure moon lighting an obscure world of things that would never be quite expressed" (Stevens 1954, 288). In this sensibility, fables, stories, and combinations of "facts" and suggestions open into a kind of spirit fundamentally different from that of mainstream Western scholarship and cultures. As we turn now to *On the Genealogy of Morals* our interest is in its sensibility in connection with particular lineages, their mutations, and the power they embody. The occurrences of the lineages, mutations, and embodied power are beyond philosophy, and yet *On the Genealogy of Morals* is a philosophical work. How can this genealogical knowledge be both philosophical and nuanced in a way that is beyond philosophy? Beyond all disciplined knowledge? Before we can be clear about that "how," we will need to encounter the threshold of beyond, the kind of border that it composes, and the art of speaking of it without losing it.

GENEALOGY: A PHILOSOPHICAL STUDY BEYOND PHILOSOPHY

In its subtitle, Nietzsche describes *On the Genealogy of Morals* as a polemic. *Polemic* is Kaufmann's and Hollingdale's translation of *Streitschrift*. That is an unproblematic translation, although indirect reference to Pólemos is not found in the German. *Streit* may be translated reasonably as "battle" but not as "war" (*Krieg*). *Polemic* also does not mean war, although it carries the sense of "attack" as well as "argument" and "contestation." Nietzsche does not have argumentation in mind in *On the Genealogy of Morals*. Rather, he is waging a battle, and we find the imagery of war helpful in interpreting aspects of genealogy as he carries it out. The irony we will highlight is that, although he does have head-on battles with the ascetic ideal and its figurations, he carries out his *Streit* primarily by turning away from direct confrontation—confrontation that would hold in presence the very thing he wants to eliminate—and developing a different kind of knowledge that originates in attunement with beyond as he accounts it in *Beyond Good and Evil*. His genealogy is an interlacing of philosophy and attunement to processes that are beyond philosophy.

We hold Pólemos in mind, however, when we read "polemic"—polemic → Pólemos, the God of war. We read *On the Genealogy of Morals* as waging a war by means of a shifting sensibility and a production of a new kind of knowledge as Nietzsche uncovers and follows the genealogies of various human capacities and values. Since this book is intended as an elaboration of *Beyond Good and Evil*, and since *Beyond Good and Evil* is a prose presentation of some of the leading, poetically conceived thoughts and processes of Zarathustra's self-overcoming in *Thus Spoke Zarathustra*, when we read *polemic*, we may also think of an affirmation of an ongoing battle that is found in *Thus Spoke Zarathustra* and *Beyond Good and Evil*, as well as in such books as *Twilight of the Idols* and *Joyful Wisdom*.

Nietzsche's war is a strange one. He wages it with no interest in refutations—"What have I to do with refutations!"—and in a "positive spirit" (1967, 18). He is neither a spectator nor a field commander of battles. This positive spirit issues in such "arts" as those of refiguring exegeses, an example of which is the Third Essay in *On the Genealogy of Morals*, "What Is the Meaning of Ascetic Ideals," and ways of reading that he calls the art of rumination (1967, 23). Among his pronounced goals in the polemic is the discovery of the ways morals and values live in people's interconnected lives, discovering their multiplex beginnings, as well as the ways the value of morality itself happens. *How* do morals and values produce consciences and subjections to life-denying affirmations? *How* do they create certain kinds of living and censure of other lifeways? He is developing an art that creates in attunement with "beyond good and evil," "a rendezvous ... of questions and question marks," a new knowledge of the lives of goods and bads and of goods and evils at the same time that he is thinking philosophically about morality and its lineages (1966a, part 1, section 1, 9). He is at once deconstructing the human soul as he engages it in *Beyond Good and Evil* and, as we have noted, intensifying a different sensibility that in a self-overcoming movement turns out of those sensibilities that have informed, during most of his life, his senses, recognitions, feelings, and inclinations. He is carrying out—performing—this changing sensibility as he generates his genealogical knowledge, and as he lives and creates in this changing sensibility, he is carrying out his struggle, his war. It is a *Streit* that twists out of and away from the "enemies" on whom he has declared war. All of that in the context of an art that is attuned to living processes that are beyond the strictures of conceptual grasp and sense and thus beyond philosophy. This art of thinking, nuance, and style turn creatively out of the war zone—away from it and into a new prospect and sensibility. This turn away from direct confrontation constitutes the main thrust of his attack.

In this conflict the enemy that he must creatively outflank is "the [imagined, posited, and powerful] *origin* of our moral prejudices" and the forceful authority that accrues to them. The issue is "the *great* danger to mankind," that is, the *value* of morality (1966a, 5). The *great* danger of European moralities is that by their guidance the will, the very energy of lives, turns against life—turns against itself and creates a suicidal spiritual sickness. For Nietzsche, *On the Genealogy of Morals* is a continuation of a struggle for the emergence and survival of a creature capable of a *Geistigkeit* that is in fundamental, affirmative attunement with its own life-energy. His agenda is not so much to attack and weaken the valence of particular values such as pity or self-abnegation, although he encounters them in many head-on skirmishes. His underlying agenda focuses on the systemic problem with European moralities in their functions as organizing, power-giving, hierarchizing, bifurcating, and identity-forming cultural realities. He finds the systemic issue in the enormous power this life-denying energy—the energy of moralities—silently exercises in most aspects of daily living. Even if he were to make some moral values weaker, that would be only a slight wound, a small reformation, in the life of moral normalizations if morality as such retained its powerful, positive, and normative value. He intends rather to undercut the *system* of moral values through the creation of another kind of knowledge and sensibility that will put in question the value of morality as such. To do that he must put the spotlight on... we will call it for now... the posited ascetic (unblemished) purity of moralities' beginnings. (Earlier in our discussion, we found him making a similar systemic move in questioning the value of truth.)

Hear what he says about the big shift he experienced in his own sensibility when he learned how to ask certain kinds of questions: "Whoever sticks with it and *learns* to ask questions here will experience what I experienced—a tremendous new prospect [*Aussicht*] opens up for him, a new possibility comes over him like a vertigo, every kind of mistrust, suspicion, fear leaps up, his belief in morality, in all morality, falters—finally a new demand becomes audible. Let us articulate this *new demand*: We need a *critique* of moral values, *the value of these values themselves must first be called into question*—and for that there is needed a knowledge of the conditions and circumstances in which they grew, under which they evolved and changed (morality as consequence, as symptom, as mask, as tartufferie, as illness, as misunderstanding; but also morality as cause, as remedy, as stimulant, as restraint, as poison), a knowledge of a kind that has never yet existed or even been desired. What if a symptom of regression were inherent in the 'good,' likewise a danger, a seduction, a poison, a narcotic, through which the present was possibly living *at the expense of the future*? Perhaps more comfortably, less dangerously, but at the same time in meaner style, more basely?—So that precisely morality would be to blame if the *highest power and splendor* actually possible to the type man was never in fact attained? So that precisely morality was the danger of dangers" (1967, 6). This would be a knowledge that does not cling to its enemy through desire, confrontation, or lineage.[10] Rather, *in* the geist's self-overcoming transformations the aborning sensibility and knowledge spawn new directions, new values, new meanings in the fading twilight of morality's reign.

Two different genealogical temporalities are invoked in the quoted passage. At first Nietzsche reports his experience of the emergence of beyond philosophy and beyond morality in his sensibility due to the questions he learned to ask—beyond good and evil, beyond truth and untruth, beyond mutually excluding opposites, beyond bifurcations. That experience brought with it a radical shift in the way he perceived and experienced the world. This dimension of beyond refers to the interfusing mutating play of multiple lineages in unschematized and non-processional processes, the temporality of beyond without the measurements of time.

The second temporality that plays a significant role in Nietzsche's polemic invokes a schema of possible growth and decline of intensities that compose human geist—of the human soul with its depths and possibilities as well as with its brutalities, anxieties, fears of life's actualities, and inclinations to oppress and cause pain. This second sense of temporality

---

10. See *Beyond Good and Evil*, section 41.

also invokes the human spirit's *as yet* unexhausted possibilities as it looks toward the possibility of a different future for humankind in comparison with its present, active lineages. In this second temporality of *geistige* possibility for growth and decline there are multiple lineages. They compose ongoing past and mutating formations of all manner of values and such *geistige* capacities as the ability to be responsible and the courage to authorize one's own values. The effects of dynamic lineages emerge in many different, present situations of disparity, such as situations of power imbalance in institutions and practices, long-standing structures of habitual discrimination, and deeply ingrained religious bifurcations: forceful values and evaluations that emerged in the midst of wars of doctrine, in violent disputes over territory, in ancient practices of sacrifice and rituals of worship, in justifications of torture and punishment—implemented lineages that inspired pleasure in acts of torture, punishment, abuse, and subjection. There are so many processes (as distinct to subjective agencies) in which values formed in recountable random ways. People often posited transcendental origins for these values to give them originary power that validated the important worth of those values and thereby stunted or corrupted people's transforming, self-overcoming lives. Spirits can grow, flourish, decline, and die in this troubled, contested, and often confusing temporality. The future of *geistige*—spiritual—life is at stake. It is a vulnerable future foreseen by Nietzsche in a prospect attuned to the flow of eventuations beyond good and evil, beyond truth and untruth, a prospect attuned to an in-between of differences that has no nature, no natural boundaries, no guiding transcendental law, and no intended origin, an in-between—a dimension, if you will—that is beyond philosophy and morality.

A final introductory note about Nietzsche's engagement with genealogy, his new project that he sees with the new eyes that emerged with the new prospect opened by his attunement with being beyond: "To me," he says, "there seems to be nothing *more* worth taking seriously [than undertaking a genealogy of morals], among the rewards for it being that some day one will perhaps be allowed to take them [the problems of morality] *cheerfully*. For cheerfulness—or in my own language *joyful science*—is a reward: the reward of a long, brave, industrious and subterranean seriousness, of which, to be sure, not everyone is capable.[11] But on the day we can say with all our hearts, 'Onwards! our old morality is too a part of *the comedy!*' we shall have discovered a new complication and possibility for the Dionysian drama of 'The Destiny of the soul'—and one can wager that the grand old eternal comic poet of our existence will be quick to make use of it" (1967, 21–22).[12] For Nietzsche the last word is never *tragedy.* The last word is in fact not a word. It is laughter and cheerfulness. Perhaps we could appropriately call it the gift of Dionysus.

THE TEMPORALITY OF ETERNAL RECURRENCE

Before we engage Nietzsche's genealogical knowledge, let's take a summarizing glance at our major thoughts up to this point and then consider his myth of eternal return in order to orient ourselves in the turn he makes away from the senses of time that often guide traditional histories and philosophies. We have said that Nietzsche's *On the Genealogy of Morals* is conceived and written in a sensibility that is attuned to the sense of beyond in the phrase "beyond good and evil." He conceived of genealogy as constituting knowledge that embodies a "new prospect" that opened for him when he learned how to question values and practices that traditionally have not been subject to question, such as the value of morality and truth (as distinct to morals and truths). A precondition for this new genealogical project and transforming sensibility is the passing away—the death—of "God's" power to determine the limits, values, and truths in major sectors of Western culture. Other images and powers now define people's, governments', and cultures' values and identities. Religious passions have weakened and become signs of normal niceness. Where are the Savonarolas, Pascals, Beatrices, and Hildegards? he asks in effect. He conceived of his genealogical approach in the wake of "God's" deteriorating soul-power and social power. His thoughts and perceptions

---

11. As we noted earlier, the word *Wissenschaft* is often better translated in English with the word *discipline,* as distinct to *science.* The German word can refer to such humanities disciplines as philosophy, French literature, nineteenth-century English novels, etc. On the other hand, *joyful discipline* for *fröliche Wissenschaft* would sound absurd in English. *Joyful wisdom* or *joyful knowledge* would be preferable translations.

12. *Fröliche* has been changed from *gay* to *joyful.*

developed in the possibilities for creation and sea change that the abyss of God's absence engendered.

In our focus on beyond philosophy, we have emphasized that Nietzsche's thought is philosophical as an interconnected, interacting group of concepts that function in the formation of an open system of hypotheses, exploratory claims, and styles of presentation. These concepts, hypotheses, etc. are conceived in interaction with major figures in the Western philosophical canon. The concepts of his thought are formulated so as to require their own self-overcoming, and at their best they carry out (or perform) attunements to processes that are beyond philosophy. They—Nietzsche's concepts in their interactions—affirm their own porous, dynamic limits. The processes that draw our particular attention are lively lineages that in their fertile, mutational occurrences constitute the "inner experience," "the souls" of *Homo sapiens* (1966a, section 45, 57). The combination of philosophical thought and the art of presentation that communicates attunement to dimensions of occurrence beyond philosophy holds our attention in this engagement with *On the Genealogy of Morals*.

The nuance of eternal recurrence runs through Nietzsche's account of the genealogy of morals like a moon shadow that appears as a reflection of a reflection. It—the nuance—has a shade of sense in the context of Nietzsche's thought that is a reflection of beyond indicated in the phrase "beyond good and evil." It is a reflection of no sense at all. His understanding of temporality in the myth of eternal recurrence literally says that all moments in every detail recur eternally, that time is a circular movement, a mandala-like becoming that has no teleology, no intrinsic meaning. Time is mere repetition in which the present past is now at once the future present. All that has been and is will be.[13]

---

13. "'Behold,' I [Zarathustra] continued, 'this moment! From this gateway, Moment, a long, eternal lane leads *backward*: behind us lies an eternity. Must not whatever *can* walk have walked on this lane before? Must not whatever *can* happen have happened, have been done, have passed by before? And if everything has been there before—what do you think... of this moment? Must not this gateway too have been there before? And are not all things knotted together so firmly that this moment draws after it *all* that is to come? Therefore—itself too? For whatever *can* walk—in this long lane out *there* too, it *must* walk once more.

What happens if we live as though the myth in the context of Nietzsche's thought were nonliterally true, if we *fancy* it to be true, if we find it worthy of being appropriated into the texture of our awareness, if we are able to embody its nuance in our ways of life? Nietzsche found that when the myth of eternal recurrence is appropriated the past appears as upcoming and not simply as a region of fixed and unchangeable bygone events. Past events are yet to be, and people are able to affirm the *life* of whatever has happened—the life with all that is tragic and horrific as well as everything valued, loved, and enjoyed.[14] The sense of the recurrence of the same finds its finite, present enactments in life-affirmation. The time of the repeating circle of events is meaningless even though what happens and recurs eternally is filled with meanings and values. To accept and appropriate the myth of eternal recurrence means the loss of any sense of temporal or cosmic teleology. It means that people are free to affirm life, to say with the Ugliest Man in *Thus Spoke Zarathustra*, "My friends, what do you think? Do you not want to say to death as I do: Was *that* life? For Zarathustra's sake! Well then! Once More" (1966c, 318).

How could people make this turn and find this new prospect? This way of living presupposes a transformation similar to the one that Zarathustra experienced and the one we discussed in the section on the human soul. The process of a conversion like this one for people who

---

"And this slow spider, which crawls in the moonlight, and this moonlight itself, and I and you in the gateway, whispering together, whispering of eternal things—must not all of us have been there before? And return and walk in that other lane, out there, before us, in this long dreadful lane—must we not eternally return?

"Thus I spoke, more and more softly; for I was afraid of my own thoughts and the thoughts behind my thoughts'" (1966c, part 3, section 2, 158).

When Nietzsche, after a period of deep anxiety and depression as the image and thought of eternal recurrence emerged in his awareness, fully accepted its literal meaning in addition to embodying its nuance in his sense of life and time, he believed it should be accepted as a scientific doctrine. This belief defines one of several unresolved contradictions in his work. He, at least at times, also believed, for example, that will to power is literally real. Such beliefs are incompatible with his emphasis on creativity, the moment of birthing of new realities, and the untruth of "truth." One of the arresting dimensions of Nietzsche's work, however, is the way it bridges, on the one hand, the Western sensibilities in which he is participant and that he so roundly condemns and, on the other, the emerging sensibility of beyond that is our focus in the context of beyond philosophy.

14. We distinguish between life and what happens in life. The point is to affirm life regardless what happens.

live in a sensibility defined by linear time includes a painful, dangerous deconstruction of the soul's lineage-infused consciousness. It is a turning—a transfiguration—of the very basis of the meanings and values with which a person has lived—a metamorphosis of consciousness and the way the world appears. One enters a new spiritual environment, feels alien, alone. Zarathustra's life-instincts, his inherent inclinations to affirm life regardless of its content, tell him to heal himself after the soul-trauma of transfiguration that happened as he came to appropriate the implications and nuances of eternal recurrence. They tell him to be active in his convalescence, to become future-oriented, to learn to replace the spirit of seriousness with laughter in the midst of transformation, to compose new songs, to dance, to create new concepts—to become, in our terms, a border artist—and, in Nietzsche's story, to become the first teacher of eternal recurrence.[15]

The temporality embedded in *On the Genealogy of Morals* is not simply a repetition of the myth of eternal recurrence. Its conception emerges after the conversion and convalescence occasioned by Nietzsche's full acceptance of the myth of eternal recurrence. The temporality of his genealogy, in addition to the kind of historical evidence and formulations of descriptive clusters of concepts he uses in the book, presupposes the self-overcoming journey of Zarathustra and the nuanced, attuned sensibility expressed in the conceptuality of *Beyond Good and Evil*. In the course of our discussion, we will show that *On the Genealogy of Morals*, as it engages past beginnings, ongoing mutations, and descents of lineages, is conceived in alertness to the nonpurposive temporality of eternal return and beyond in the phrase "beyond good and evil." His genealogical project is philosophically oriented by fusions and occurrences of lineages and temporal schemas that are beyond philosophy. He finds their sense in their enactments and dynamic formations as they infuse peoples' ways

---

15. In this affirmation, Nietzsche is affirming and adapting the classical Greek affirmation of tragic life by means of the mythologically infused beauty of art. Eternal return is a myth that poetically expresses the meaninglessness of time. For Nietzsche's account of the classical Greek affirmation of tragic life, see his *The Birth of Tragedy*, sections 3–10, and his "Attempt at Self-Criticism," section 1, which is included the 1967 edition of the Walter Kaufmann translation. To follow the process of Zarathustra's convalescence and the advice of his life-inclined instincts (metaphorized as birds and animals), see *Thus Spoke Zarathustra*, part 3, section 13.

of living. He does not present the formations of the lineages he describes from a stance of moral judgment. He is presenting a "new" knowledge, a new way of creating knowledge without a perspective of transcendentally authorized origins, moralizing sublimity, or ethical concern. But he does indeed have the goal of developing a kind of knowledge that will stimulate refigurations of sensibilities and souls. He wants to begin the development of a kind of knowledge that metamorphizes its readers' affect, and he wants to trace some of the mutations and infusions that compose lineages and constitute anonymous agencies in the formations of practices, values, and meanings that are forceful in human lives. Appropriation of the imagery of the silent, meaningless, unceasing coming to pass of eternal recurrence, beyond philosophy and beyond the confines of literality, pervades the richly meaningful work of *On the Genealogy of Morals* with its purpose of human transformation.[16] The book presents the new prospect that Nietzsche found consequent to his learning to ask questions—malicious questions—and to follow the questions that do not resolve into static definitive answers.

THE ASCETIC PRIEST

In "What Is the Meaning of Ascetic Ideals," we meet the figure of Nietzsche's archenemy, the ascetic priest.[17] In this confrontation, the second sense of temporality that we discussed, the temporality of the ebb and flow—the decline and growth—of human geists and souls, plays an important role. The struggle is over the will to live, the meaning of suffering, and the priority of physicality. For both Nietzsche and his figure of the ascetic priest, the stakes are focused by what each finds best for the

---

16. Isn't his interest in human transformation an ethical one? Human transformation is better than existing comfortably in a herd, isn't it? Yes. Turning away from the ascetic ideals of Western religions and moralities is better than living ascetically, isn't it? Yes. But we note that he has no prescriptive morality in mind and is thinking outside the bifurcation, normativity/nonnormativity. He advocates nothing that will attempt to stabilize life with fantasies of either enduring goodness and truth or sociocultural normativity.

17. See *On the Genealogy of Morals*, sections 15–22. We begin with the figure of the ascetic priest in order to elaborate the specific meaning of the "polemic" that constitutes part of the book's motivating force, that is philosophically conceived, and that takes us beyond philosophy.

suffering, physical human creature. This is the way Nietzsche sets the issue with the ascetic priest: Is the best alternative for people affirmation of a suicidal energy of earthly life enclosed in a titanic religio/moral system, with the consequence that their life-energy turns against itself? Is it best to live now in the force of a spiritual cannibalism that is stabled in formations of slavish fear of one's own mortality and the prospect of *nothing* when one dies? Is it best to recognize that the human being is fundamentally a weak, depressed creature that needs Meaning for its suffering, Meaning that it cannot create, capital-M Meaning for life and not merely mortal meanings alongside profound soul/spiritual pain and the loss of everything beautiful and good? *Or* is it best to attend to life as it happens in all of its suffering, terror, and ecstasies, to learn how to live in life's indifference to human creatures and to live with affirmation of fleshly, sensuous desires and pleasures as well as with tragedy without resentment, cruelty, or revenge? The latter would be, in Nietzsche's words, to live with nobility. In the war (far more than a struggle) between Nietzsche and the ascetic priest, Nietzsche has as his primary weapon a genealogy of ascetic values and of the high priest of Meaning, while the ascetic priest has as his primary weapon the extraordinarily creative perversion of psychic life by means of the promise of eternal reward for lives lived self-sacrificially, lived with moral goodness and in obedience to a judgmental God.

The figure of the ascetic priest—the *figure* of ascetic denial of the goodness of physical desires and bodies of pleasure and meanings that are bound by the mortality of the physical world in favor of suffering abnegation now for the sake of a life to come, eternal life—can you imagine such transvaluing power as the ascetic priest exercises? People can live in God's presence and with capital-M, divinely inspired Meanings and the ways of living that such Meanings generate. These souls can be happy in their fanaticized hope and in the sacrifice of the desires and mortal life-instincts invested in their physicality. Nietzsche recognized that the power of the ascetic ideal and its promises transformed the deep despair that pervaded suffering human creatures, transformed that despair into hope for eternal lives free of suffering. This power transformed despair into a will to feel alive by virtue of life-denying values. A transformed sensibility emerged that is empowered by soul-sickness, a sickness that is engendered by the promise of a sweet by-and-by and that has no sense of the wonder and delight of creative births without Meaning or transcendental hope. This is a sensibility that changed the Western world, a sensibility with no sense of Dionysus's gift. It had no sense of the beauty of ever-ongoing life that is without Meaning, filled with creation, values, meanings, suffering, death, and laughter. Soul-weakness and fear became the basis for a civilization.

Trust in such invented Meanings can indeed bring comfort and often a striking degree of deep happiness in addition to solace in times of death and loss, as is manifest in the lives of many people who practice a multitude of different types of religion. Nietzsche was fully aware of the effective force he was up against as he turned toward the formation of a new kind of knowledge and a new sensibility. In this project he was not looking for solace but rather for creative spirits who are struggling to be free of life-denial and who feel joyful affirmation of life with its suffering and tragedies; he was looking for people who are attuned with the dimension of beyond and who live affirmatively in the shade and power of its nuance.

This war brings together the schematized processes of soul-growth and soul-decline with the processes outside the range of measurements and beyond philosophy. The Third Essay of *On the Genealogy of Morals* is defined by a war for ensouled bodies, for the very sensibility of humankind. The war and its processes can be put into meaningful words, told, even measured by various standards of success and failure. But the manifest darkness in the soul in Nietzsche's genealogy of the meaning of the ascetic ideal? The forest darkness that we discussed as the hunting ground for a genealogy of morals in connection with the religious creature? Concerning the genealogical light that exposes the scam of Meaning, Nietzsche, the struggling free spirit, says of himself and all who join him, "Probably, we, too, are still 'too good' for our job; probably, we, too, are still victims of and prey to this moralized contemporary taste and ill with it, however much we think we despise it—probably it infects even *us*" (1967, 139). In his corruption—in his goodness and moralized taste—he nonetheless fights his war. He does far more than irritate or enrage. He wants to create a new alternative to goodness and moralized taste and to make impotent the system of morality that is based on the fabrications of Gods, universal moral laws, moralized reason, and above all the disparagement of sensuous corporeal life. He wants to eliminate the adhesive that holds the system together and that is indicated by the figure of the ascetic priest.

He wants to expose the invented value of morality and to turn his readers toward new prospects, new desires, transforming desires to join the war in the spirit of beyond all dualisms and monisms—indeed, beyond all *-isms*.

But the exposure initiated by his genealogy—is this exposure a new kind of interruption and disparity? Is it authored solely by a confessed corrupted soul? We think not. "His" genealogy is not an exposure that Nietzsche completely discovers and authors. It is one that goes beyond his authorship, deep into the agential power of his transforming sensibility. His genealogy invokes temporality, the one that we discussed in the context of beyond morality and conceptualization. This sensibility thus stretches to a dimension that is beyond the difference between corrupted and uncorrupted, beyond Meaning and meanings, beyond the mask it appears to present in language about it (such as the language we are now using). This temporality that is beyond Nietzsche's conceptual reach, plays a major role in *On the Genealogy of Morals*, as Nietzsche, who probably *is* "too good" for his task, finds enough attunement with it to bespeak it, to let this unschematized temporality, as it were (it's always as it were in this arena, isn't it, when we put transitive verbs with the dimension of beyond!?), cast its dark, illuminating shadow in his project, in his nuanced words and concepts, lets it, as it were, have *its* say in its silence, in its undistinguished stillness, in its objectless happening, and have its say in his transvaluing war.

We turn now to the first two essays to intensify and to broaden our engagement with the temporality of the dimension of beyond as Nietzsche engages it. Our goal is not to provide a thorough commentary but rather to provide a vocabulary and prospect that is alert to the pervasive Dionysian dimension in his work, the beyond dimension of this thought, at the same time that it is alert to what we may call the applied dimension that is within time's schema. Accompanying this intention is our conviction that without a wide-ranging and comprehensive change in our sensibilities, critiques of various values or clusters of mores will be extremely limited in their worldly impact as the implanted system of transcendentally founded morality holds its sway and quietly infuses the language and conceptuality of opposition to it. Our hope accompanying our intention in this study is that as people come to feel the impact of Nietzsche's shifting sensibility—and of our sensibility as we present his sensibility—they will experience how the world feels and appears in it. Only when we experience the strange force of beyond can a personal and philosophical departure from Nietzsche be of much value. Standing on the outside of genealogical sensibilities and lobbing arguments against his perceived "arguments" or interpreting his statements without a thorough engagement with their context constitutes an unprofessional interpretation.

Developing genealogical knowledge, for Nietzsche, we have said, includes paying maximal attention to the powers, mutating formations, imporings, and dissensions of lineages. Developing genealogical knowledge also includes interrupting the serene authority of broadly accepted, often transcendentally founded moralities and religions by exposing the frequently shocking practices and opposing values that are incorporated in their lineages and thus pre-reflectively shadowed in their rituals and mores. This kind of work presupposes what we will call genealogical responsibility. Genealogists are answerable for their authorial intentions that play out in the creative processes of developing a body of knowledge, *and* they are responsible for their attuned affirmation of a dimension of processes that are beyond the region of responsibility and authorial intention. This latter dimension, christened Dionysian by Nietzsche and described as beyond good and evil, is "where" senseless infusions of influences, inheritances, environments, and emerging values and meanings interbreed and mutate without the intrusion of human intention. It is a dimension without responsibility, without opposite values and antitheses; it is a dimension of our corporeal/spiritual lives. It is the dimension of lineages in their dynamic, interfusing lives. When people live with genealogical sensibilities they are answerable for the genealogical work they do and for their attentiveness to dimensions of beyond in the context of which their responsibility has no resonance.

RANKING VALUES: NIETZSCHE'S GENEALOGY OF THE *AND* IN "GOOD AND EVIL," "GOOD AND BAD"

"The future task of the philosophers: this task understood as the solution of the *problem of value*, the determination of the *order of rank among values*" (1967, First Essay, section 17, 56). In this ranking, this determination, the value of morality as such is the foremost problem; it is "what is at stake" (1967, preface, section 5, 17). In order to begin this task, Nietzsche says, we must begin with the descent [*Herkunft*] of the judgment, "good" (1967, First Essay, section 2, 25; translation altered). "The judgment 'good' did *not* have its situated emergence [*Entstehungsheerd*] with those to whom 'goodness' was shown! Rather it was 'the good' themselves, that is to say, the noble, powerful, high-stationed and high-minded, who felt and established themselves and their actions as good.... They first seized the right to create values and to coin names for values" (1967, First Essay, section 2, 25–26; translation altered).[18] *Good* names the exceptional people who bestow the status of value to all manner of things. They create and rank values. They are the ones who *feel* the power—the *geistige* power—to put normative sounds (such as words) together with actions and states of affairs, to give definitive force (or positive valence) to some things and not to others.[19] Nietzsche is speaking in part of warriors, people who

---

18. See Michel Foucault, 1977, "Nietzsche, Genealogy, History." We accept the distinction Foucault makes in his interpretation of Nietzsche between *Entstehung* and *Herkunft* on the one hand and *Ursprung* on the other, as well as his view of the implications of the distinction: "*Entstehung* and *Herkunft* are more exact than *Ursprung* in recording the true objective of genealogy; and, while they are ordinarily translated as 'origin,' we must attempt to reestablish their proper use. *Herkunft* is the equivalent of stock or *descent*; ... the traits [an analysis of *Herkunft*] attempts to identify are not the exclusive generic characteristics of an individual, a sentiment, or an idea, which permit us to qualify them as 'Greek' or 'English'; rather, it seeks the subtle, singular, and subindividual marks that might possibly intersect in them to form a network that is difficult to unravel. Far from being a category of resemblance, this origin allows the sorting out of different traits.... Where the soul pretends unification or the self fabricates a coherent identity, the genealogist sets out to study the beginning—numberless beginnings whose faint traces and hints of color are readily seen by an historical eye. The analysis of descent permits the dissociation of the self, its recognition and displacement as an empty synthesis, in liberating a profusion of lost events ... to follow the complex course of descent is to maintain passing events in their proper dispersion; it is to identify the accidents, the mute deviations—or conversely, the complete reversals—the errors, the false appraisals, the faulty calculations that gave birth to those things that continue to exist and have value for us; it is to discover that truth or being do not lie at the root of what we know and what we are, but the exteriority of accidents. This is undoubtedly why every origin of morality from the moment it stops being pious—and *Herkunft* can never be—has value as a critique" (1977, 145–6).

19. Nietzsche uses etymological evidence found in a variety of languages to identify the beginning of the value of *good*: "The basic concept from which 'good' in the sense of 'with aristocratic soul,' 'noble,' 'with soul of a high order,' 'with a privileged soul,' necessarily developed: a development which always runs parallel with that other in which 'common,' 'plebeian,' 'low,' are finally transformed into the concept 'bad'"

commanded by means of their physical power and forceful presence. But we can expand his designation and refer to the type of people we now designate as natural leaders or forces of nature: people who have an exceptional energy to take charge; meet challenges head-on; create new things, whether in art, cooking, philosophy, war, politics, or other areas of relation and endeavor—unusual people (Shakespeare, for example, who introduced 1,700 new words in the English language, or those unknown individuals who discovered that sticks could be used as weapons), extraordinarily gifted and effective people, whether they are dangerous, cruel without malice, charismatic and constructive, or reclusive. The emphasis that develops in the lineages of warriors and unreflective, almost beastly tyrants now falls on people who were and are dominant, proactive, and naturally predisposed to put their stamp on the world around them. Nietzsche calls them the noble.[20] What they esteem is good, and *esteem* names a feeling from which concepts and values arise, a feeling in affirmative touch with the force of life. These people are distinguished from "all the low, low-minded, common and plebian" reactive people who are "the bad": "The pathos [the intense feeling] of nobility and distance ... the protracted and domineering fundamental total feeling on the part of a higher ruling order in relation to a lower order, to a below—*that is the origin of the antithesis 'good' and 'bad'*" (1967, First Essay, section 2, 26). *Good* comes to be conjoined (usually with the conjunction *and*) with *bad* as opposites based on people with creative dominating energy and superior, creative power as distinct to people who are ignoble, coarse,

---

(1967, First Essay, section 4–5, 27–31). See also section 10 for Nietzsche's use of philology to support his account of noble and ignoble people in ancient times.

20. "The noble mode of valuation: it acts and grows spontaneously, it seeks its opposite only so as to affirm itself more gratefully and triumphantly.... [The noble ones are] filled with life and passion through and through—'we noble ones, we good, beautiful, happy ones!'" (1967, First Essay, section 10, 37). They create and act out of their own spiritual strength and life-energy. Slavish spirituality, on the other hand, emerges out of *ressentiment*, out of natures "that are denied the true reaction, that of deeds, and compensate themselves with imaginary revenge. While every noble morality develops from a triumphant affirmation of itself, slave morality from the outset says No to what is 'outside,' what is 'different,' what is 'not itself'; and *this* No is its creative deed. This inversion of the value-positing eye—this *need* to direct one's view outward instead of back to oneself—is of the essence of *ressentiment*: in order to exist, slave morality always first needs a hostile external world: it needs physiologically speaking, external stimuli in order to act at all— its action is fundamentally reaction" (1967, First Essay, section 10, 36–37).

low minded, cowardly, and socially impotent, people who are comfortable in herds.

Further, Nietzsche finds in his genealogy certain traits that are effective but usually overlooked and that constitute what he calls a *"quiet problem*: . . . it is of no small interest to ascertain that through those words and roots which designate 'good' there frequently still shines the most important nuance by virtue of which the noble *felt themselves* to be men of a higher rank."[21] The word *good* carries the nuance of a "*typical character trait*. . . . They call themselves, for instance, 'the truthful.' . . . The root of the word coined for this, *esthlos*, signifies one who *is*, who possesses reality, who is actual, who is true" (1967, First Essay, section 5, 29; emphasis added). The "quiet" move here is *from* externally incited controlling, creative power *to* affectively based, creative power of spirit that is not externally motivated. It is a move from emphasis on people in action, the doers, to a nuance sometimes found in people in action with genuine, *geistige* nobility whose truth is found in the ways they really are. It is a move to a richly affective state of mind that is manifest in such actions as establishing values in ranked orders; these are people who are actually *truthful* in *being* as they are.[22] We could say they are the genuine item. In this nuance we can see that the high-ranking noble people are conjoined, not by opposition, but by *geistige*, felt difference in connection with "the *lying* common man," the disingenuous ones who lack *geistige* nobility, who in many quiet ways feel inferior. The noble ones do not need or establish moral oppositions. Rather, they recognize differences of power and creativity.

This unintended, happenstance conjunction engenders a space of meaning that connects power, good, and truth on the one hand with powerlessness, bad, and lying on the other (1967, First Essay, section 5, 29). This formed and conjunctive space—this conceptual/*geistige* space—is separable from the specificity of "those" genuinely noble people and "these"

---

21. He continues: "Granted that, in the majority of cases, they designate themselves simply by their superiority in power (as 'the powerful,' 'the masters,' 'the commanders') or by the most clearly visible signs of this superiority, for example, as 'the rich,' 'the possessors' (this is the meaning of *arya*; and of corresponding words in Iranian and Slavic)" (1967, section 5, 28–29).

22. In this distinction, *truth* connotes "being noble through and through." *Lying*, in Nietzsche's sense of the word, however, suggests acting out of fear, weakness, and resentment. We might say that lying is actually inferiority through and through.

really ignoble people. A multiply applicable pair, good and bad, is born without the benefit of intentional human agency in various, random situations of living.[23] Whoever has the power to take control of the pairing has the power to rank values that guide people's comportment and their degree of importance in their societies. At stake is "true" value and "true" knowledge. The question is, who fills the space and decides the content of good/bad, true/not true? To repeat for emphasis, the power to fill this space of conjunction, good *and* bad, bestows the social power to rank what is good and what is bad and to use or not to use the axle of opposition (as distinct to difference) in this ranking. Whose spirit will assume the mantle of good and triumph? Could the impotent and ignoble become dominant—could they begin to control the *geistige* space operative in a culture and authorize themselves and their values as good? Might they impose formations of spiritual ignobility by creating a structure of obligatory morality that brings to expression a transvaluation of values that makes the resentful ignoble spirit good and the noble spirit bad?

During this part of his analysis, Nietzsche has his eye on a conjunction in which each member of the pairing brings the other into view. He describes the complex beginning of this conjunction with no suggestion of a founding subject or transcendental validation, and one of the implications in this account is that the lives of people are filled with goods and bads.[24] In other words, there are values and rankings of values aplenty that guide people's (including Nietzsche's) actions and give lives meaning in the absence of transcendental Meaning and teleological temporality. Nietzsche gives no direct critique of the progressing and multiply

---

23. The observation here is that the region of mores and normativity has its beginning without human or transcendental grounding. It emerges by virtue of the conjunction of noble and ignoble types of people.

24. On the issue of an autonomous subject that founds actions and judgments, he says: "A quantum of force is equivalent to a quantum of drive, will effect—more, it is nothing other than precisely this very driving, willing, effecting, and only owing to the seduction of language (and of the fundamental errors of reason that are petrified in it) which conceives and misconceives all effects as conditioned by something that causes effects, by a 'subject,' can it appear otherwise. For just as the popular mind separates the lightning from its flash and takes the latter for an *action*, for the operation of a subject called lightning, so popular morality also separates strength from expressions of strength, as if there were a substratum behind the strong man, which was *free* to express strength or not to do so. But there is no such substratum, there is no 'being' behind doing, effecting, becoming; the 'doer' is merely a fiction added to the deed—the deed is everything" (1967, First Essay, section 13, 45).

influenced ways "good and bad" began, although there is a decisive departure from any suggestion of transcendental foundations and meanings in an origin of "good." Instead of direct critique, he gives a genealogical exposure of very different types of spirituality. The conjunction of good and evil, however, is another matter.

In order to understand genealogically the good/evil conjunction, Nietzsche shifted from noble power to priestly power. When the priestly caste is in political ascendency, "pure and impure confront one another" (1967, First Essay, section 6, 31). Although in their early history the purity of priests consisted simply in physical cleanliness and dietary fastidiousness (and thereby composed the budding of the ascetic ideal), unhealthiness nonetheless characterized these clean and cautious people. A brooding, morbid neurasthenia, Nietzsche says, seems to have run through the caste because of an insufficient ability to dominate by proactive physical actions. They lacked adequate options for "joyful," physical release of their life-energy (1967, First Essay, section 1, 33). Their turn of energy was toward an inward, *geistige* self-inspection that set them apart from the world around them. In their intensifying, reflective awareness, their emphasis on purity created a growing sense of corruption and purification in their bodies, an alertness to the dangers of pleasure, a finely honed perception of their own predisposition to degeneration. This kind of sensibility, combined with a passion for power, engendered a type of menacing spirituality that was suspicious of the world, sick of itself, and yet self-important: "For with the priests *everything* becomes more dangerous, not only cures and remedies, but also arrogance, revenge, acuteness, profligacy, love, lust to rule, virtue, disease—but it is only fair to add that in the soil of this *essentially dangerous* form of human existence, the priestly form, that man first became an *interesting animal*, that only here did the human soul in a higher sense acquire *depth* and became *evil*—and these are the two basic respects in which man has hitherto been superior to other beasts!" (1967, First Essay, section 6, 32–33). Evil begins in a spirituality that not only makes self-reflection, judgment, and conscience possible but also raises "badness" to a transcendental dimension of Meaning and Value, a dimension that casts a religious and theological pall over morality and goodness.

The internalized, priestly awareness—the very capacity for self-reflection and judgment operative in *On the Genealogy of Morals*—has its ancient genealogical beginnings in the development of the priestly caste, with all the feelings and mentation that came with its lack of physical release, its pent-up, restrained, repressed energy that turned on itself in the absence of a warrior-like release. This spirituality that described itself as incorporeal, was born, as Nietzsche accounts it, not in wonder, from an inherent soul, or by a divine act, but in self-inflicted cruelty (denial of free-spirited pleasures, for example, or denial of spiritual release of violence that spends itself in its action in the world). Hatred is a companion with such self-infliction, with the often subtle, smiling, innocent-seeming, blind and intense ill will that shuns and does injury to life-enhancing feelings. This cauldron of self-domination, self-sacrifice, lust for power, and disingenuous love inspired the coupling of transcendental badness—Evil—with transcendentally grounded Good. Here in the forming priestly soul we find the birth of good conjoined with evil.[25]

---

25. Nietzsche found the Jews to be the archetypal priestly people in Western civilization. Although his genealogical claims about the Hebrew/Jewish traditions are severely critical, he also admired (with significant qualifications) the power inherent in their signature accomplishment, which he called "this unequaled creativity" (1967, First Essay, section 6, 34). He said that the Jews effected the most radical "revaluation of their enemies' values, that is to say, an act of the *most spiritual revenge*.... It was the Jews who, by awe-inspiring consistency, dared to invert the aristocratic value-equation (good = noble = powerful = beautiful = happy = beloved of God) and to hang on to this inversion with their teeth, the teeth of the most abysmal hatred (the hatred [bred] of impotence), saying 'the wretched alone are the good; the poor, impotent, lowly are the good; the suffering, deprived, sick, ugly alone are pious, alone are blessed by God, blessedness is for them alone—and you, the powerful and noble, are on the contrary the evil, the cruel, the lustful, the insatiable, the godless to all eternity.... With the Jews there begins *the slave revolt in morality*: that revolt which has a history of two thousand years behind it and which we no longer see because it—it has been victorious" (1967, First Essay, section 6, 34). This revolt includes Christianity, which for Nietzsche is basically a branch of the Hebrew/Jewish tradition that is considerably hellenized via the influence of Platonism. In effect, Nietzsche is saying that he—his very spirit—is within the powers of the lineage of slave revolt and that his genealogy is intended as a turn out of it and away from it. We also note his venomous tone when he turns his attention to other religions and to the quality of spirituality in European civilization, especially in Germany and, of course, including most particularly Christianity. He distinguishes between his critique of the Hebraic lineages and antisemitism. See, for example, his unconditioned distancing of himself from the antisemite, Eugen Dühring, in *On the Genealogy of Morals*, Second Essay, section 11. In this context, the German National Socialist Party and its genocidal program appear as an especially horrifying expression of spiritual sickness and abysmal lack of what Nietzsche calls nobility.

We should understand Christianity as bringing with it this conjunction. From the slave revolt of the Jews, "there grew something equally incomparable, a *new love*, the profoundest and sublimest kind of love" (1967, First Essay, section 6, 34). This love "grew out of the crown [of Jewish hatred]" and pursued the inherent goals of the revaluation of all values: "victory, spoil, and seduction [conversion]." "This Jesus of Nazareth, the incarnate gospel of love, this 'Redeemer' who brought blessedness and victory to the poor, the sick, and the sinners—was he not this seduction in its most uncanny and irresistible form, a seduction and bypath to precisely those *Jewish* values and new ideals? Did Israel not attain the ultimate goal of its sublime vengefulness precisely through the bypath of the 'Redeemer,' this ostensible opponent and disintegrator of Israel? . . . [the] undermining power of that symbol of the 'holy cross,' that ghastly paradox of a 'God on the cross,' that mystery of an unimaginable ultimate cruelty and self-crucifixion of God *for the salvation of man*?" (1967, First Essay, section 6, 35).

Nietzsche shows that beyond family lives, secure in their rituals and tribe-like loyalties, beyond the warm hearth and home, beyond the values that define social normalcy and goodness, beyond the values that tell us who we are, beyond our causes and loyalties—*beyond* the conjunctions of good and bad—lineages are infesting our most intense loves and senses of identity. In addition to institutions and symbolic systems, such lineages as that of the conjunction of good and evil arise from primal instincts and erupt in beastly violence in the texture of people's securities and normal behavior—in the very texture of their ranked values and the mores and comportments to which those values and their hierarchies give rise. Subterranean resentments, fears, and anxieties produce the kind of deceptions and inclinations that fabricate redemptive crucifixions, societies of self-sacrifice, and, most importantly for our purposes in this section, the need for an ignobly conceived transcendental Reality that gives Meaning to the misery and horror people visit on each other: a need for Evil, a cosmic opponent, conjoined in mortal combat with the Goodness of God—just the kind of war that Nietzsche will not engage. Disclose appalling beginnings and meandering descents of such Divine war? Yes. Show the effects of its lineages in his own work? Again, yes. But describe the conjunction of Good and Evil as evil? Never. Rather, Nietzsche moves outside and away from the dichotomy of Good and Evil as he carries out his genealogy and shifts to *"the problem of value, the* determination of the *order of rank among values*" (1967, section 17, 56). As he accepts the important differences between good and bad, he has no interest in becoming an ethicist. He wants options that allow the blur among ordered values, and he wants uncertainty to impregnate the values with which we live and for which we would die. He "knows" that the differences from the top of the order to the bottom of the order are not fixed and are available for transvaluations that can happen at times gradually, at times quickly due to subtle shifts in sensibilities, authoritative knowledge, or political climates: values and their orders are porous. In their permeability they are protean and mutable.

Nietzsche knew that his spirit was a battleground for the two pairs of conjunction—good and bad, Good and Evil. He also knew that Good and Evil had not totally prevailed in spite of the many victories accorded it (1967, section 16, 52). He knew that he must keep a distance from the battleground at the same time that it engaged his deepest awareness, his spirit. He must become a prospector in the new regions that his questions and problems opened up. Instead of conjoining opposites, he must fully accept—even love—being multiply split and beyond conjunctions, just as the lineages that both plagued and enabled him were multiply split without concomitant connectors. He must write and think in the liminal thresholds of the many boundaries that lived in his spirit and let himself find attunement with nuances and hues without promise of clear and defining lines of difference and identity.

Nietzsche's developing genealogical knowledge thus calls for a discipline that problematizes posited value-bestowing origins of values and cultivates the art of asking questions. In the midst of such displacements and uncertainties, however, people cannot overestimate the importance for Nietzsche of passionate affirmation, the kind of affirmation we discussed at the end of the section "Genealogy: A Philosophical Study Beyond Philosophy" and in the section "The Temporality of Eternal Recurrence." His is passionate affirmation of life, its occurrence, its immediate, aesthetic quality that generates wonder and all of the arts. Passionate affirmation without ethics? Without a supporting, normative morality? How now (as Nietzsche might say)? Passionate affirmations without certainty? Love of the fate of life, far beyond good and bad, good and evil, or compassion for suffering? Affirmations that enhance life and thus lives? Affirmations that create values? Affirmations that, being alive, love creation? A creature whose event is immediately life-enhancing? These are Nietzsche's hopeful, motivating, questionable dreams.

Keeping in mind that the nonreligious meaning of the word *redemption* is recovery, restitution, retrieval, hear what Nietzsche has to say: "But some day, in a stronger age than this decaying, self-doubting present, he must yet come to us, the *redeeming* man of great love and contempt, the creative spirit whose compelling strength will not let him rest in any aloofness or any beyond, whose isolation is misunderstood by the people as if it were flight *from* reality—while it is only his absorption, immersion, penetration *into* reality, so that, when he one day emerges again into the light, he may bring home the *redemption* of this reality, its redemption from the curse that the hitherto reigning ideal has laid upon it. The man of the future, who will redeem us not only from the hitherto reigning ideal but also from that which was bound to grow out of it, the great nausea, the will to nothingness, nihilism; this bell stroke of noon and of the great decision that liberates the will again and restores its goal to the earth and his hope to man; this Antichrist and antinihilist, this victor over God and nothingness—*he must come one day*" (1967, section 2, 96).

This dream, with its vulnerability and fragility, its quasi-messianic anticipation of a bell stroke of redemption, this "man of the future," composes a powerful, affirming force in Nietzsche's formulations and passions as he undergoes a self-overcoming turn out of a quasi-Christian sensibility and comes into thought and passion in the complete absence of a sense of living divinity or God. It makes his understanding of genealogical responsibility especially important as dimensions of beyond (of beyond good and evil, beyond good and bad) and earthly reality find concurrence in both a "knowledge"—a conceptual scheme—and ways of existing that in their happening constitute their own values and truths. Nietzsche is speaking of reality beyond the power of morality and disgust with life as it happens, beyond guilt and ascetic ideals. It is his dream of sensibilities and ways of life that restore (redeem) a sense of living with no sense of debt, no need for metaphysical comfort, and no desire for future rewards for life-sacrifices.[26]

---

26. Note that on Nietzsche's own terms, the content of his dream is a mortal figuration. Distinguishing between the content of specific fantasies that arise from attunement with the dimension of beyond and the attunement itself is especially important. No fantasy or dream that arises from the attunement authorizes the attunement.

GENEALOGICAL RESPONSIBILITY

At the end of the section "The Ascetic Priest," we noted that in the context of Nietzsche's thought genealogists are answerable for their affirmation of a dimension of processes that are beyond good and evil, unsusceptible to conceptual order, and totally insubordinate and irresponsible as far as schemes of meaning, obligation, and order are concerned. Nietzsche's affirmation of life as well as his affirmation of such processes as the mutating development of lineages do not constitute or lead to a normative ethics. We have also said that such genealogical knowledge as Nietzsche develops presupposes considerable and ongoing changes in people's sensibilities; these changes are processes of transformation that are often spiritually dangerous as the grounds of many values and meanings tremble and shake, and they usually happen outside of the range of reflective consciousness. They initiate changes of inherited and ingrained consciousness—in Nietzsche's language, definitive changes of one's spirit/soul: the soul—the dynamic lineage-filled stretch of inner experience—is the site of its own transformations. Those changes inaugurate radical shifts in one's ethos—in one's way of living, one's comportment—and these transforming processes are not burdened by prescriptive norms. How are we to understand a person's being responsible for affirmative attunement to such a dimension beyond good and evil as well as beyond good and bad? How might we understand an ethos-changing process that is outside the realm, draw, authority, or value of morality? How might we think philosophically about events that are beyond the circumference of meanings and conceptual formulations?

First, we will consider Nietzsche's account of "the right to make promises" (1967, Second Essay, section 1, 57).[27] That account is "the long story of how *responsibility* originated" (2, 58). In order to make promises, the creature must be predictable, calculable: "With the aid of the morality of mores and the social straitjacket, man was actually *made* calculable" (2, 59).[28]

---

27. Unless otherwise noted, all quotations in this section will be from *On the Genealogy of Morals*, Second Essay. The subsection will be parenthetically noted in the text.

28. In 1.3 he calls the process of creating a capacity to keep promises "mnemotechnics": "If something is to stay in the memory it must be burned in: only that which never ceases

This was a long "breeding" process in which "the animal," *Homo sapiens*, "bred in itself" the faculty that overcame the natural forgetfulness that characterized it: enough memory to be able to make promises. That process involved "severity, tyranny, stupidity, and idiocy," as it made painful, often severely painful, forgetting or blindly adjusting to changing circumstances that diminished the felt importance of an earlier promise (2, 59).[29] In this slow and punishing process, human desire slowly changed. As a new reflexive capacity emerged, a capacity to relate oneself to oneself, people began to want to be reliable and to expect reliability from others. But also mixed into this transformative process was a desire for freedom from such limiting socialization, a desire for irresponsibility—a longing that is intrinsic to the very energy of life to be one's own event without the cultural imposition of a social straitjacket of mores and without the oppression of those dominating people in the direct lineage of ancient warriors who created their own values and imposed them on weaker people.[30] These seemingly incompatible desires to be reliable and

---

to *hurt* stays in the 'memory'—this is the main cause of the oldest (unhappily the most enduring) psychology on earth.... pain is the most powerful aid to mnemonics" (61).

29. "These Germans [for example] have employed fearful means to acquire a memory, so as to master their basic mob-instinct and its brutal coarseness. Consider the old German punishments; for example, stoning (the sagas already have millstones drop on the head of the guilty). Breaking on the wheel (the most characteristic invention and speciality of the German genius in the realm of punishment!), piercing with stakes, tearing apart or trampling by horses ('quartering'), boiling of the criminal in oil or wine (still employed in the fourteenth and fifteenth centuries), the popular flaying alive ('cutting straps'), cutting flesh from the chest, and also the practice of smearing the wrongdoer with honey and leaving him in the blazing sun for the flies. With the aid of such images and procedures one finally remembers five or six 'I will not's,' in regard to which one had given one's *promise* so as to participate in the advantages of society—and it was indeed with the aid of this kind of memory that one at last came 'to reason'! Ah, reason, seriousness, mastery over the affects, the whole somber thing called reflection, all the prerogatives and show pieces of man: how dearly they have been bought! how much blood and cruelty lie at the bottom of all 'good things'" (Second Essay, section 3, 62).

30. See sections 17 and 18. As we have seen, Nietzsche posits, on the one hand, a warrior-type, pre–*Homo sapiens* creatures who ruled according to their own wills and, on the other, enslaved creatures. Over time these two fundamental types of individuals metamorphosed into people who formed values and meanings that were affirmatively attuned to their ways of living. The warrior type becomes the aggressive masters, conquerors, and enslavers who established their own senses of what is good and bad by means of their

to be nonresponsible in their many incarnations over a long period of time fused, mated repeatedly, if you will, in such ways as to produce a different kind of creature whose strength of self-direction and self-control became the deed, the very event of its living: "*the sovereign individual*, like only to himself, liberated again from morality of custom, autonomous and supramoral (for 'autonomous' and 'moral' are mutually exclusive), in short, the man who has his own independent, protracted will and the *right to make promises*" (2, 59). This creature, emerging in the complex lineage that created a type of being who policed itself, who wanted to be reliable, and yet who desired its own freedom from externally and internally imposed values and obligations . . . this creature internalized what had been the imposing external powers, began to create its own values in the circumstances in which it found itself, and thus found its freedom in self-creation.

Processes that are without any hint of responsibility thus produced a form of conscious life that finds its freedom in being a living affirmation of its own event and in ranking values that are congruent with its life. Its life is an event composed of lineages, an event linked with the prolonged formations of conscious, human life, and one moved by the dynamic, originating forces of formation and deformation. The sovereign individual who has the right to make promises and who is answerable to itself is thus intersected and determined by a vast array of lineages and traditions and by the inherent powers of life. The happening—the event—of the sovereign individual, in its sovereignty, is formed in histories of development and is culturally interdependent in its life. It has the strength of reflexive self-affirmation and does not fear moral censure and misunderstanding by others. It alone is its complex, interdependent eventuation. It is able to be true to its words and acts without obedient dependence on a body of mores and rules for living. It lives on its own terms—"like only to [itself]"—and gives value to what it finds to be estimable (2, 59). We can say that the sovereign individual is free as it calculates itself with its determinations.

---

assertions and preferences. The enslaved or colonialized people find their meanings for life, not by immediate means and externalized expressions of their feelings and inclinations, but in internalized forms of obedience and self-sacrifice that bring spiritual rewards in life after death. Inner experience and the formation of soul and conscience arise in the genealogy of what Nietzsche calls slave morality.

And yet it is not similar to a Cartesian or Kantian subject. It is an event, not a substance or an a priori capacity with its own nature. Its *event* is composed of multiple interdependencies, shared lineages, traditions, the value rankings that it leaves behind, and those beings in relation to whom it feels a spiritual kinship or superiority.

The sovereign individual, as Nietzsche finds it, with its instinctual, dominating freedom, thus arises from a present and temporary culmination of a complex historical, developmental process. It constitutes the formation of individuals' ability to be responsible to their own freedom as they make their promises and forge their values in their cultural environments. They become responsible to a dimension of living events beyond good and evil and beyond responsibility. Their inclination to live in responsible resonance with nonresponsible freedom, in Nietzsche's account, is both instinctual and self-aware.[31] It is the eventuation of a self-conscious, dynamic intersection of lineages and environmental factors that knows itself to be answerable to itself. It becomes its own conscience.

Nietzsche's genealogical account of the development of the capacity to be answerable to oneself exemplifies his own responsibility to the genealogy that lives through him and to the unschematized dimensions of life that are beyond his conceptual grasp: he is answerable to the nonresponsible, interfusing lineages that constitute his deepest sensibility, and he is answerable to the nonresponsible and nonschematized dimensions beyond value and meaning. He, Nietzsche, is attuned to anonymous processes in the formation of cultural values, beliefs, and meanings that include, as we have seen, terror, torture, cruelty, sacrifices, and mutilation. They are processes that happen without intentional subjects forming them or directing them, and those processes give rise to conscious subjects who are freely self-directing and who find themselves answerable only to themselves. "We modern [people]" are inclined to avoid knowledge about these processes and their progeny. We are inclined to make that

---

31. "The proud awareness of the extraordinary privilege of *responsibility*, the consciousness of this rare freedom, this power over oneself and over fate, has in his case penetrated to the profoundest depths and become instinct, the dominating instinct. What will he call this dominating instinct, supposing he feels the need to give it a name? The answer is beyond doubt: this sovereign man calls it his *conscience*" (2, 60).

avoidance a basic part of our epistemic and ethical blindness.[32] He, however, made descriptions of these processes a central part of the genealogical knowledge he constructed as he, for example, traced the formation of the capacity for "the human creatures" to become sovereign individuals with a robust conscience. Of course, on Nietzsche's terms, sovereign individuals are not necessarily just, even when they intend fairness, and will often do harm even if they intend kindness. They too will generate knowledge that makes the world simpler than it could ever be as they—Nietzsche included—are driven by a will to truth as they create their own truths. They will enjoy their injustice and cruelty as they celebrate their justice and hospitality. So life will have it (as he understands life). Purity does not happen in *Homo sapiens'* lives, not even pure impurity or pure ambiguity. Differences happen by degrees and shades in an interrelated complex of fusions, similarities, deviances, disparities. In this intricate and complicated assemblage, the bottom line for the responsible Nietzsche is found in his strong predisposition to put in question traditionally unquestionable values, truths, and meanings, as well as his own values, truths, and meanings, in the midst of heartening and unqualified affirmation of being alive. He lives with passionately affirmed values and meanings that he expects to transform in continuous processes of self-overcoming. His genealogies compose experiments in epistemology that celebrate life's eventuation with its cultural formations, values, and meanings as well as with its—life's—lack of a civilized nature and its utter indifference to particular events and specific lives.

SILENT ELISIONS

And what are we doing in this chapter that you are reading? In it we have inscribed a sensibility that welcomes Nietzsche's experimentations,

---

32. "It seems to me that the delicacy and even more the tartuffery of tame domestic animals (which is to say modern men, which is to say us) resists a really vivid comprehension of the degree to which *cruelty* constituted a great festival pleasure of more primitive men and was indeed an ingredient of almost every one of their pleasures; and how naively, how innocently their thirst for cruelty manifested itself.... To see others suffer does one good, to make others suffer even more: this is a hard saying but an ancient, mighty, human, all-too-human principle to which even the apes might subscribe.... Without cruelty there is no festival: thus the longest and most ancient part of human history teaches—and in punishment there is so much that is *festive!*" (2, 67).

his discovery of the creative power available to thinking without transcendental comforts, his initiation of a new kind of genealogy for his time that communicates his responsibility to dimensions of human lives that are beyond good and evil, good and bad, and schemas of time and meaning—dimensions that are beyond responsibility as well as beyond philosophy. We are not inclined to speak of our particular agreements and disagreements with his claims. Agreement and disagreement are not the primary issues in this chapter. Rather, we are disposed to encounter his sensibility, to engage the ways in which his thought and language, in their coincidental connections, mutations, and transformations—in their mergers and omissions, in their elisions—expose us to dimensions beyond good and evil, beyond good and bad, beyond bifurcations and meanings.[33]

As we speak of our purposes and goals in this chapter, what we cannot say directly is elided in what we directly say. But we do join together our exposure to what we cannot say with what we can and do say. That is also the case with sensibilities: they happen in whatever makes sense, inclusive, of course, of words and feelings—feelings such as those of inclination toward many things and situations, and aversion in relation to many other things and situations. Sensibilities happen in manners of perception, recognition, evaluation, and conception. And they happen in alertness to what cannot be articulated, to borders of sense and nonsense; they happen in the elisions intrinsic to being *in* borders, intrinsic to in-between. The lives of sensibilities escape direct and objective articulation even as they manifest themselves in language that speaks of them. Because so much is beyond the careful grasp of disciplined, conceptual thought and because we find disciplined thought so valuable, we find philosophically crucial our resonance with happenings and dimensions of awareness that are beyond the range of conceptual order. That is, we find crucial developing a discourse of elision in the sense that what we bring together in our writing omits dimensions of beyond that constitute a primary issue in both this chapter and this book. We are considering and experimenting with an art of thinking in the borders of conceptual understanding and ungraspable events. We are cultivating an art that creates a border alertness, an expressed attunement and resonance with events and processes in the

---

33. We have in mind one meaning for the word *elisions*: processes of joining together, merging things, and omitting things.

elision of which intuition and feeling become especially important types of awareness. In this process, traditionally stable meanings, values, beliefs, and truths often become volatile and limited in their power to secure people's sense of certainty. Instead of a sense of certainty, a sense born of alertness to the finite mortality and inconstancy of careful constructions gives motivation for our thinking. When thinking is attuned with events that are non-reasonably beyond rational grasp and moral authority, a philosopher's opportunity is to develop a skill—an art—that brings together questions and answers, problems and solutions, clarifications and unsettling possibilities, brings them together in a sensibility that joins them with a sense of responsibility to processes that have no resonance with responsibility: the philosophers' opportunity is to make evident the silent, elided unspeakable in the way the philosophers speak of and nuance the material they address. The silence of what we have called beyond is conserved in the elision constitutive of the border art we cultivate.

3

Foucault's Unreason

PREFACE

Flattening Michel Foucault's work is easy to do. We can read it as though its purpose were primarily historical, as though his intention were to establish truths about past events and social configurations by means of his archival research. We can read his thought as though he gives accounts of institutional and epistemological configurations with primary attention to the improvement of contemporary organizations, practices, disciplines, and ways of recognizing people and the world around them. Or we can read his work through the lens of such beliefs as those concerning sexuality, colonialism, gender, or race. With the exception of a fundamental misreading of Foucault that separates forms from relations of powers, all of these other ways of reading him appropriate aspects of his oeuvre. And all of them flatten his thought, the art of his thought, if they lose touch with the often chaotic-seeming play of "unreason" in the way he conceives the genealogical stories that he tells. As he says, "Yet the essential thing is not in the series of those true or historically verifiable findings, but, rather in the experience that the book makes possible. Now, the fact is this experience is neither true nor false. And experience is always a fiction: it's something that one fabricates oneself, that doesn't exist before and will exist afterward" (2000, 240).[1] He sounds reasonable as he speaks of "the

---

1. This sentence articulates his own kind of "unreason," his being "external" to "French philosophy" and his writing beyond the power and value of the word *truth*. We believe

essential thing." But the value of reasonable understanding is diminished in his work, and the essential thing is not a formulation or a truth. The essential thing happens as his writing incites and provokes readers in such a way that they have their own transforming experiences in connection with it. That means, in relation to *History of Madness* or one of its versions, that readers engage Foucault's account of the formation and reality of unreason as well as his thinking in the lineage of unreason in his account of it. Since in Foucault's terms there is no definitive essence at the core of his work, the readers' experiences—experiences, not judgments—will compose the culmination of their encounters with his work.

The essential thing in his genealogies/archaeologies is thus beyond the stretch of conceptual configurations and historical truths, beyond moralities and other social norms, beyond the confinements of decency. The essential thing in his account of unreason and madness is not agreement with that account. It is found, rather, in the book's inciting readers to think differently from the way they usually think, in their learning to think experimentally in the borders where familiarity dissolves—in the borders of their sensibility where clarity blends with opacity and intelligibility finds its limits, in the borders of their lives where people experience their singular ability to die.[2] The essential thing in readers' encounters with *History of Madness* vis-à-vis madness and unreason happens as they experience with awareness a dimension that is beyond philosophy and as they live in attuned alertness with that awareness.

One of the arts of Foucault's thinking happens when he instigates possibilities for *creative* experiences for people, opens new prospects, intensifies people's sense both of being alive and, being alive, of living with the immanence of continuous destabilization. One of his defining

---

that the following statement is important to bear in mind as we consider his particular manner of thought: "I am an experimenter and not a theorist. I call a theorist someone who constructs a general system, either deductive or analytical, and applies it to different fields in a uniform way. That isn't my case. I am an experimenter in the sense that I write in order to change myself and in order not to think the same thing as before." And further, "[As an author] my problem is to construct myself and to invite others to share an experience of our modernity in such a way that we might come out of it transformed. Which means that at the end of the book we would establish new relationships with the subject at issue" (2000, 240, 241–42).

2. In chapter 1 of *The Passion of Michel Foucault*, James Miller has a particularly revealing account of Foucault's passionate curiosity about extreme boundaries (1993, 13–36).

intentions is to interrupt and unsettle normal situations and feel-good ways of living with questions that, in their setting, are not normal at all. Those are all important things, and they happen as Foucault sees them, not when his thought confronts itself primarily in connection with its "masters."³ It happens when he learns to think in confrontation with real, singular events that he does not understand. How does unreason play in such important things?

A Short Excursus

We will not make a sharp distinction between archaeology and genealogy in Foucault's work. Many interpreters, especially those working at least two decades ago, accentuated the epistemic architecture in his approach to, for example, his history of madness, disciplined knowledge, medical care, and science. His critics, on the basis of these interpretations, found his work overly formalized and identified it with the structuralism popular at that time. Those interpretations lost a sense for what Foucault calls the reality of events, as well as for the significance of discontinuities, displacements, transformations, and power in his works. Foucault describes *Madness and Civilization* (1973b), the first abridged translation in English of *Historie de la Folie*, as both a history and an archaeology of a specific silence that we will discuss.⁴ He says that *The Order of Things* (1973c) is an archaeological inquiry. The subtitle of *The Birth of the Clinic* (1973a) is "An Archaeology of the Medical Gaze." In his book *The Archaeology of Knowledge* (1972), he accepts the word *archaeology*, as he understands it, as defining his approach up to that time. However, the interpreters who make the distinction between archaeology and genealogy sharply differential and find archaeological structures overly formal and static also often find his genealogical studies dynamic in their emphasis on power, institutional relations, and self-formation. We find this severance

---

3. That is, when philosophers think primarily in the contexts set by previous, usually canonized philosophers.
4. The much longer original 1961 French version has the title *Foilie et Dèraison; Historie de la folie à l'âge classique*. The later 1972 publication, *Histoire de la Folie à l'âge classique*, is the one that *History of Madness*, the 2006 translation into English, is based on.

a considerable oversimplification of his thought. He speaks of *Madness and Civilization*, *The Order of Things*, and *The Birth of the Clinic* as developing "axes" that are definitive of his genealogical project (Foucault 1997, 262). In addition to the importance of systematic structures is the importance of dynamic relations of powers in and among those structures, that is, the importance of power issues in rationalities, truths, institutional formations, and reciprocal connections, and especially in knowledge and authoritative disciplines. In his own words, "In writing *Madness and Civilization* and *The Birth of the Clinic* I mean to do a genealogical history of knowledge. But the real guiding thread was this problem of power. Basically, I had been doing nothing except trying to retrace how a certain number of institutions, beginning to function on behalf of reason and normality, had brought their power to bear on groups of individuals, in terms of behavior, ways of being, acting, and speaking that were constituted as abnormality, madness, illness, and so on" (2000, 283. See also Foucault 2006, 575, 577–78). As a crown on his body of irritation over the insistent interpretation of his archaeological works as structuralist, he wrote in his forward to the English edition of *The Order of Things*, "In France certain half-witted 'commentators' persist in labelling me a 'structuralist.' I have been unable to get it into their tiny minds that I have used none of the methods, concepts or key terms that characterize structural analysis. I should be grateful if a more serious public would free me from a connection that certainly does me honor, but that I have not deserved" (1973c, xiv).

MADNESS AND STABILIZING NORMALCY

Madness is a vague and fuzzy word. Its usage in English is not coherent. It can refer to mental illness, the moonstruck lunacy of intense passion in the delirium of love, intense and uncontrolled anger, dementia, abnormal or uncontrolled behavior, dysfunction in daily life, bedlam, and so forth.[5] The word's anarchical intimation and nuance, the frequent lack of

---

5. See, for example, *History of Madness*, 2006, 225ff. Many of the identifiers for madness in the eighteenth century are also valid in the twenty-first century.

reasonable cogency in its usage, however, might compose one of its advantages, a performative advantage, insofar as it refers to nonrational dimensions in the occurrences of people's lives. The word resists the consistency that sensible rationality would require for clear sense unless the word signifies an object of medical rationality and its usage is limited to medical contexts of treatment or cure, or unless it signifies an object of moral judgment that has the intention of correcting or punishing extreme instances of deviation and indecency. But madness, if it is allowed its insolent and untamed inconsistencies, its excess of all statements about it, might well function in attunement with dimensions of living that are beyond sense, truth, value, and constructed order. We will say more about this kind of insolence.

A very different field of reference in comparison with that of madness might bear the name *stabilizing normalcy*, and would include people who are recognized in particular cultures as for the most part being psychologically undisturbed and socially "healthy," who behave conventionally in their social environments, and who are no more than reasonably disturbed by the world around them. Stabilizing normalcy is not often associated with genuine creativity or a kind of nonconformity or deviance that allows new perspectives to energize and generate new ways of seeing, knowing, and behaving.[6] We, the authors, have no doubt that many people suffer terribly with a wide variety of mental health conditions for which medical and therapeutic intervention are appropriate and needed. We also know that everyday normalcy in societies includes contradictions. In addition to communities, law and order, moral codes, professional authorities, senses of identity, and individual security, such normalcy also includes many types of oppression, myopic provincialism, habitual—normalized—cruelty, spiritual stagnation, an elevation of mediocrity in standards of achievement, fear of transformation, and anxiety in the presence of thoroughgoing differences. Decency *and* cruelty? Security *and* stagnation? Stability *and* paranoia? Norms of freedom *and* enslavement? Soaring spirituality *and* unbelievable credulity? Normalcy strikes us as intimate with madness in all its insolence and not as its opposite. One of our claims in

---

6. Mary Oliver: "The extraordinary is what art is about. Neither is it possible to control, or regulate, the machinery of creativity" (2016, 27).

this chapter will be that all manner of sensible, patterned forms of recognition and organized structures of meanings and values constitute the everyday lives of people and that dimensions of processes and events that are beyond those forms and structures, beyond rational sense, and beyond the restraints of grammar and morality also indwell organized formations and constitute their lives. That is, we can see that something like what Foucault calls unreason accompanies stabilizing normalcy. We can see as well that deviation—decisive deviation—from "the normal" is vitally important in the midst of social order. Sharp distinctions, lucid interconnections of concepts, clear norms for behavior and so forth—let's not say "are haunted by" let's say "go hand in hand with"—both chaotic absence of stabilizing order and orders of deviation in particular societies and cultures. Unreason accompanies civilized consciousness. If this claim is accurate, we will be able to understand madness in a lineage of medical/moral concern but think of unreason as an extraordinary dimension in human lives, not as insanity but as neither good nor bad, as a dimension of living that frees, threatens, and unsettles normal, civilized consciousness and provides positive impulses for change and creativity in the midst of everyday stabilities.

A Short Excursus

An anticipatory comment on the word *unreason*. The word can refer not only to madness but to any event, state of mind, or manner of behavior that is beyond reasonable sense or rational authority. It names realities without reason. Although the word is paired with *reason* its difference from reason should not be understood as necessarily an opposite to reason. It is not an opponent; it is just different. When it is definitively objectified, as madness is, for example, by medical science and authoritative judgment, the object called madness or unreason can then be seen as opposite to reason, but that is a situation in which madness and unreason are silenced and co-opted by reason, that is, by the authoritative rationality of the time. The word *unreason* bespeaks a dimension of occurrences beyond reason. *Unreason* is a floating term, an unstable concept that Foucault applies retrospectively in his history of madness to all manner of deviational behaviors that were lumped indiscriminately together during most of the Renaissance. Later, toward the end of the seventeenth century, with the birth of madness as a reality unto itself and the birth of authority regarding it, the word *unreason* had a certain recognizable legitimacy. In all cases Foucault uses the word to apply to existent social divisions, abnormalities, and elements of life. At times he also uses the word to refer to something like a holder for everything unreasonable. It might be used to name a grouping of abnormalities, amoral happenings, or asocial inclinations. And it can refer to attunements with nonrational dimensions of living. Its meaning depends on what counts as reasonable at the time. When Nietzsche or Hölderlin, for example, wrote and thought in attunement with their nonrational, intuitive awareness of dimensions of occurrence beyond reason and meaning, they wrote in a lineage of unreason. Foucault wrote in that lineage, and we understand ourselves to write in it too.

Struggles among stabilizing and destabilizing forces thus seem to characterize everyday living. Interfusing these struggles, as we said in our engagement with Nietzsche, are processes and events that, like the fusions of lineages or what appears as nonsense, happen beyond meaning or structured cognition. In this chapter we will show that dimensions beyond sense, truth, and normative values can bring people to feel their own boundaries, can make evident that our familiarity with ourselves constitutes only a small part of our lives, and that something like unreason interfuses the light of reasonable, meaningful, sensible normalcy in our everyday lives. We will bring Foucault's use of *unreason* to the center of this chapter. We will not attempt to impose sense on the senseless or to stabilize unreason as a concept, but we do want to make a region of unreason more apparent to readers than it might otherwise be, to give attention to whatever is indifferently different from conceptual and grammatical orders, good sense, and normal behavior. Dimensions of occurrence that are beyond schemas, we will say, do not constitute an ontological dichotomy with reason, although those dimensions might indeed seem disconnected from the ordered world.[7] Could the kind of fusions we are talking

---

7. We use the words *fusion* and *interfusion* here to name assemblages of interacting unordered and ordered processes in people's lives.

about constitute disclosive exposure of events on the often-recondite borders of human meaning, reasonable good sense, and normative values? Is our reflective consciousness infused by something like unreason? Does something vaguely like madness in the word's suggestion of exceptional social deviation reflect dimensions that are outside the perimeter of reflective consciousness? Are people's lives crisscrossed by borders—porous borders—that interlace what we consider nonsanity with sanity? Unreason with reason? Abnormal deviations from social morality and behavior with stabilizing normalcy?

We recognize that *madness*, in spite of its many legitimate senses, now normally names a professional understanding of certain types of mental health conditions that are known as mental illness and disorder. *Unreason* has no established, normal, and proper sense.

SILENCE, SILENCING

Stephen Riggins said in an interview with Foucault, "There is in North American Indian culture a much greater appreciation of silence than in English-speaking societies and I suppose in French-speaking societies as well." Foucault responded, "Yes, you see, I think silence is one of those things that has unfortunately been dropped from our culture.... I'm in favor of developing silence as a cultural ethos" (1997, 122). Foucault was silent enough about himself that both James Miller and Didier Eribon, in their biographies of Foucault, spent thousands of hours attempting to crack the silent nut of his personal identity, character, and feelings (1993, 1991). His silence about aspects of his life and sense of himself marked a boundary, a space of disinclination and restraint that reserved something of his own. Funny how the silent distance of such a boundary can draw some people and repel others, and not only the silent distances of people but also the silent distances we experience in connection with stars and galaxies, in open, outstretching seas, or in vast and treeless prairies. Sometimes the sound of wind with the silence can make the distance seem infinite, without horizon. Just distance. Haunting distance without a mark. Ever distance. Sometimes it is merely the silence silencing without dimensions, being nothing that silences. Mere silence. Deep, deep silence, infinitely excessive to the deaths and lives in it. Mere silence too can draw or repel: the silence in an empty house where you were raised that is now void of the sounds and presences, the crises that were so important in their moments, the business of the everyday lives ... finished. Silent. Or perhaps it's the silent space, mere space, the so very silent space that seems to blend with time and leave only eternity. Space without place that draws us toward itself and in that drawing brings us to ourselves in it, to find *it* in ourselves.

We, with Foucault, have in mind wordless silence.[8] Such silence and death seem so close to each other! Foucault, in fact, experienced death as *the* boundary, the great challenge of life, a boundary with which he flirted in his later years. It was a strange flirtation, indeed a happy, exhilarated one, with danger that many explorers and experimenters also experience. Increased alertness, excitement, heart-pumping intensity, with lifeless vacuity so close, so immanently close. livingdying writ large.[9]

Silencing, too, resonates with death. Silencing, often accompanied by forms of slavery and various other kinds of social death, including

---

8. Hard to imagine Foucault wordless, isn't it!

9. James Miller says, "Death, and its significance, was one of Foucault's lifelong obsessions.... He perceived death as the constant companion of life, its 'white brightness' always lurking in 'the black coffer of the body'" (1993, 20). Miller develops Foucault's "passion with death" throughout his book. "Limit-experiences" (Foucault's frequently used term), according to Miller, were for Foucault closely tied to mortality. Miller shows that Foucault, as he grew older and sick unto death with AIDS, continued to enjoy the agonizing pleasure of S and M experimentation and the limit-experiences they occasioned for him. "Death [is] nothing to fear" Foucault said in an interview. Foucault explained that "he'd been walking across the street outside his Paris apartment. He had been hit by a car. And he thought he was going to die. He compared it to a drug experience: it was a euphoric, ecstatic moment. He had a sense that he was leaving his body, that he was outside his own body." A moment later he said to his interlocutor, "Besides. To die for the love of boys: What could be more beautiful?" (1993, 350). There was also deep silence in his passion vis-à-vis death. "'It is in death,' Foucault wrote in 1963, 'that the individual becomes at one with himself, escaping from monotonous lives and their leveling effect; in the slow, half-subterranean, but already visible approach of death, the dull, common life at last becomes an individuality; a black border isolates it, and gives it the style of its truth'" (1993, 20). For Foucault, each individual becomes a single event in death's approach. It is an experience that is quite unutterable even when we talk about it, quite alive and profoundly silent. Perhaps that silence has something to do with death's *lack* of passion and with, we speculate, Miller's persistent fascination with the question, "Who, really, was Michel Foucault?" Perhaps the silence of death's immanence mingled with Foucault's acute sense of personal boundaries and the indifferent and silent absence of identity in a boundary's happening.

oppression and exclusion, happens when people's voices are muted or suppressed in their cultural environment: the silencing, for example, of women in many cultures and social contexts, of the poor, of prisoners, of the indifferently forgotten. Of those who serve unnoticed, only instruments, easily discarded. Of the insane, of those whose signals and signs are rendered meaningless. Often they are as though dead in the insignificance that shrouds them. The reign of everyday mediocrity also often brings with it a silencing of those abnormally creative and intelligent people who in their environments cannot be heard in their visions, insights, or levels of comprehension.

We are not interested in *why* silence and silencing *can* happen. But we do want to know how some silencing practices and institutions developed. Who or what are the agents of silencing? *How* do they happen? Perhaps Foucault's acute awareness of death's immanence and of the individuation that immanence makes possible played a quiet role in his desire to know how silencing cloaks so many people and mutes them. Perhaps this awareness arose for him as he engaged the lineages of unreason in which deviations outside the power of normalcy in addition to limit-experiences beyond rational grasp incited questions normal folks would not think to ask. Perhaps his work on practices of silencing is best understood as a part of these lineages of unreason that can instigate new orders of living, new sensibilities, new bodies of knowledge, innovative art, and unconventional ways of thinking.

The events and Foucault's experiences of them during his two-year internship at Hôpital Sainte-Anne in Paris in the early 1950s formed part of the basis for his critique of medical knowledge and the silencing it occasions and thus formed part of an experiential basis for his writing *History of Madness*.[10] For him it was a transforming experience that, combined with the time he himself spent as a patient in a mental hospital, introduced him to both the silence and the silencing that marked the lives of those authoritatively known to be mad.

He had finished his formal philosophical education and begun his formal study of psychology. He did his informal two-year internship—

---

10. Foucault's discussion of this experience can be found in 1997, 123–24. See also Miller 1993, 62.

"informal" in the sense that he was not supervised by the medical or psychiatric staff, who for the most part ignored him and allowed him to carry out his own study.[11] He was not a psychiatrist and thus lacked the authoritative knowledge to qualify for entry into the circle of those who understood mental illness. He had the run of the psychiatric hospital. Since he was not official staff, he was able to talk with those confined in the asylum without a mantle of confident authority and without the kind of professional knowledge that lost madness to the intelligence that understood it. He was able to listen to them unofficially without needing to place them in a schema of illnesses or abstract categories of deviation from healthy normalcy. We believe that he learned to hear the inmates nonjudgmentally—and that means, in the terms of *History of Madness*, nonrationally—to hear them in their own gestures, signs, and sounds beyond the predictable regularity of grammatical language, beyond moral justification, and beyond the strictures of conceptual clarity. He was able also to perceive a silence between the patients and the trained staff— perhaps he was able to experience this silence outside of the very kind of truth that he pursued as an academic. He did not fully understand this silence. It might have been similar to a silence he experienced before he came out as gay, or when, as a young man and before he fully accepted himself as gay, he was institutionalized with a mental breakdown, or when he later came out and his sexuality was recognized in an order of censored deviations. We believe it was in his time of listening unofficially at Sainte-Anne that he began to conceive of the silencing power that formulated, authoritative knowledge can have. Perhaps during this time he also began to conceive a vague thought of "unreason" that happens beyond the scope of formulation and beyond the force of established authority. How did that silencing power come to be authoritative and institutionalized? How did madness become medicalized insanity? How did authoritative knowledge develop without sensitive alertness to the voices of the mad and to unreason that silently permeates the silencing power?

---

11. According to James Miller, he occasionally "helped conduct experiments in an electroencephalographic laboratory, learning how to analyze abnormalities in epilepsy, and various neurological disorders" (1993, 62).

WRITING OF SILENCING

In his *History of Madness* Foucault wrote, "We need a history of that other trick that madness plays—that other trick through which men, in the gesture of sovereign reason that locks up their neighbor, communicate and recognize each other in the merciless language of non-madness; we need to identify the moment of that expulsion before it was definitely established in the reign of truth, before it was brought back to life by the lyricism of protestation. To try to recapture, in history, this degree zero of the history of madness, when it was undifferentiated experience, the still undivided experience of the division itself. To describe, from the origin of its curve, that 'other trick' which, on either side of its movement, allows Reason and Madness to fall away, like things henceforth foreign to each other, deaf to any exchange, almost dead to each other" (2006, xxvii).[12] We understand this statement to refer to a history of the very kind of silence and silencing that Foucault experienced during his internship at Hôpital Sainte-Anne. There he was introduced to an institution where madness was turned "into a positive science," psychiatry, that silenced unreason "by listening only to the *pathological* voices of madness" (2006, 107; emphasis added.). This silencing was consequent to a history of expulsion as it gradually metamorphosed with the division of madness and reason and converted into silencing practices of institutional confinement sanctioned by well-trained authorities. This transformation follows a time in medieval Western civilization when kinds of people who would later be labeled as mad were a part of people's living together in common. They might be strange or odd or funny—perhaps even prophetic in their inexplicable, often highly mythologized abnormality. People's experience of them—their incoherent sounds, strange gestures, and mysterious or odd facial expressions, or their screams in the night, the terror in their eyes, their hysterical laughter—those experiences might ignite images of a supernatural visionary or of "the Fall and the End of All Things, of the Beast, of Metamorphosis," but no division separated them from their communities (2006, xxxiii–xxxxiv). They were not subject to a definitive and

---

12. These statements by Foucault reflect the quote from Pascal in the epigraph for the preface: "Men are so necessarily mad, that not being mad would be being mad through another trick that madness played" (2006, xxvii).

silencing division. The reality of reason/unreason did not exist. Foucault referred to an undifferentiated *experience*. We highlight the word *experience*. Inexplicably abnormal people were not experienced as mad. They "really" were not mad. They were not the same as the others, but they were nonetheless experienced as belonging to the community even though they were different in some ways. More to our point, they were not silenced and set apart by reason or authoritative knowledge. From this moment, "this degree zero of the history of madness when it was an undifferentiated experience," Foucault proposes to describe the movement as reason and madness fall away from each other, the movement of their very births in which, in their separation, madness, newly born, is silenced, reason is elevated to dominance, and unreason arises in the tricky breach of division.

How could Foucault write a history of the origin of madness, a history of its separation from ordinary rationality and good sense? How was he able to write a history of madness in his alertness to the silence inscribed in the recognition of the insane, of the mentally disturbed? How was he able to go *beyond* the medicalized experience, beyond the border experience of the severance, reason/unreason, and write in the experience of that excess? He was able to describe the severance instituted by cultural lineages and the organizations and discourses that established it. He could see that reason/unreason are together in their severance, in their in-between, in the very enactment of silencing. But to see and hear beyond that divide, he must avoid "a powerful forgetting." Foucault must learn how *not* to "dominate that great division," how *not* to master it. He must set himself apart from those who live in the illusion that they have mastered their madness and freed their madness "by capturing it in the gaols of [their] gaze and morality, having disarmed it by pushing it into a corner of [themselves and] finally [allowing] man to establish that sort of relation to the self that is known as 'psychology.'" For this mastering knowledge about madness, "it had become necessary for Madness to cease being Night, and become a fleeting shadow within consciousness, for [people] to be able to pretend to grasp its truth and untangle it in knowledge" (2006, xxxiv). Rather, Foucault's aim was to avoid appeal to psychiatric or psychological truth, to allow the confused tangle of "madness" and "to allow words and texts, which came from beneath the surface of language, and were not produced to accede to language, to speak of themselves.

Perhaps," Foucault continues, "to my mind, the most important part of this work is the space I have left to the texts of the archives themselves" (2006, xxxiv–xxxv). He left a space of silence, a senseless space, a space that knowledge of madness would happily try to fill, but one that would not let him go and that he did not fully understand.

That aim means that he could never look "for a way out in any psychological *coup de force*, which might have turned over the cards and denounced some unrecognized truth." His aim meant, rather, that "it was necessary to speak of madness only through that other 'trick' that allows men to not be mad, that other trick could only be described, for its part, in the primitive vivacity that engages it in an indefinite debate regarding madness. A language without support was therefore necessary, a language that entered the game, but was to authorize the exchange; a language that constantly corrected itself to proceed, in a continuous movement, to the very bottom. The aim was to keep the relative at all costs, and to be *absolutely* understood" (2006, xxxv). To be absolutely understood, in Foucault's terms, means to speak with language "in a sort of relativity without recourse," language that in both its nuance and its declarations makes no claim to stable truths but "authorizes" an unending exchange with continuous change, continuous movement "to the very bottom" (2006, xxxv).

Crafting and refining that language and understanding would be Foucault's art of thought and description. Although his sentences and paragraphs might make good sense, the good sense is shaded with chaotic experiences of instabilities, fugitive of all order *in* good, well-ordered sense and shaded as well by the experienced nuance of the untruth of truth in an unending debate. His writing is attuned to an indeterminate beyond truth, beyond sense, beyond morality, beyond the division of reason and unreason. It's a quasi-mad authorship, well unfounded in lineages of unreason.

THE SOCIAL REALITY OF UNREASON

How did madness and the power that silenced it come to affect an entire culture? To address this question Foucault's genealogical history of madness begins with the exile of lepers from their homeland, traces the formations of what he called social excommunication and the lineages of expulsion and banishment, as well as the institutions and practices that formed in the power of these lineages, which developed in the late medieval era and into the nineteenth century.[13] These processes slowly produced the imagery and social reality of madness and unreason: they produced institutional practices and cultural sensibilities that played major roles in specifying what constituted madness and in silencing those who were recognized as mad. The corpus of this deadly sensibility was conceived, according to Foucault, in fusions of fear of the incurable disease, leprosy, which people thought to be highly contagious; belief that God's judgment is manifest in leprosy as a punishing curse; practices of exile and scapegoating; and belief that the Christian congregation's practice of ritually casting the leper out of the city is pleasing before God. The expulsion and silencing of lepers carried transcendental, divine significance for the unafflicted. By the power of God's sanction, a sharp division formed between the blessed in the community and the cursed who were sent out of the community and who came to form groups of contaminated, ill-starred exiles who were often free of supervision, even at times free to form their own exilic colonies or to wander as nomads outside the boundaries of the redeemed. Yet by God's grace they bore the indelible mark of mortal condemnation within the promise of salvation after death. "'Dearly beloved,' says a ritual from a church in Vienne . . . , 'it has pleased God to afflict you with this disease, and the Lord is gracious for bringing punishment upon you for the evil that you have done in this world.' The leper was then dragged out of the church by the priest and his acolytes *gressu retrograde* but he was assured that he was God's witness: 'however removed from the church and the company of the saints, you are never separated from the grace of God.' Brueghel's lepers watch from afar, but forever, as Christ climbs Mount Calvary accompanied by a whole people. Hieratic witnesses of evil, their salvation is assured by their exclusion: in a strange reversal quite opposed to merit and prayers, they are saved by the hand that is not offered" (2006, 6).

The lepers personified—they incarnated—both God's grace and God's judgment by virtue of a ritual of exile. The banishment included sin and

---

13. We will not provide a complete summary of Foucault's account of the development—the genealogy—of the asylum's formation and the emergence of unreason. Our purpose is to engage rather than to summarize the formation of unreason's reality as he finds it and the lineages that he identifies as issuing from it.

salvation, spiritual sickness and spiritual cure. The exile might have seemed to be like a cutting out and throwing away of a degenerating part of the ecclesiastical body, but it did not figure a total separation from the church. It was a forced release from the church and its congregation within the shadow of God's ecclesiastically mediated and eternal love, a blessed curse. This banishment—the cursed blessing—figured a division between those accepted by God—the congregation of the saved—and those unfit for the living company of that congregation. Division combined with exile created a powerful form for identifying groups of people. It generated a type of clarity among the saved and the damned but also, as we shall see, among those who were dangerous for the commonweal and those who contributed to a moral and healthy society. The exile of the lepers and the division that it described were social formations through and through, and they constituted a formation with extraordinary force that lingered, if ever so faintly, in the lineages of western Europe until it burst out in sensibilities and practices in which unreason appeared.

We repeat for emphasis: Foucault emphasizes not only the *division* of the sanctified and the unholy—of the whole and the disfigured—but also the continuing force of the *exclusionary division's self-authorization*—its continuing, often vague availability in lineages that played roles in forming what would become the division of reason and unreason and the emergence of madness. The word *division*, in the context of Foucault's thought, names a dynamic form of social practice that separates people on the basis of spiritual/moral/physical qualities—separates the clearly virtuous and normal from those perceived as deviant, lawbreaking, antisocial, or abnormal. "The forms this exclusion took would continue, in a radically different culture and with a new meaning, but remaining essentially the major form of a rigorous division, at the same time social exclusion and spiritual reintegration" (2006, 6). Ecclesiastical authority, divine sanction, and exile were integral to silencing the leper prior to the sixteenth century. It was a silencing created by God's word and embodied by the diseased person: a silencing integral to punishment and revelation, the effect of an act of God's grace. The divine and ecclesiastical content would change, but the formed power of silencing division would continue.[14]

---

14. We note that if people considered this ritual and the beliefs that authorized it beyond the boundaries of reasonable formations and tinged with madness, they would

By the sixteenth century, according to Foucault, "the game of exclusion" continued as leprosy declined and disappeared (2006, 6). In this game, people with venereal disease first joined and then replaced the leper in the leper hospitals, that is, in the containment facilities, that had developed, and "a new leprosy was born" (2006, 7). The site of exile by confinement slowly became a social/medical affair as the power of authority began to shift from the divine to the secular: state and city officials and physicians came to replace priests and nuns in the facilities of containment and confinement, and the horizon of eternal salvation for the socially banished shifted to "a whole network of moral judgments" (2006, 8). Undergirding this shift was a growing acceptance of moral rationality and the social exclusion that it effected by its moral judgment and its authoritative knowledge. The illness of venereal disease fused with immorality and in this combination gave an identity to "hospitals," complete with dungeons, chains, and cells, that held in containment people who threatened the health of bodies and spirits in the normal community. People committed to these institutions became silenced inmate-patients and the objects of, if not healing care, certainly authoritative knowledge and morally... informed? corrupted?... knowledge. By means of increasingly robust, virtuous, moral censure and exclusion, they became silenced patients known as ill in their physical and spiritual degeneracy. The question of healing and spiritual cleansing had not yet emerged. Foucault adds, "It is not in leprosy [or, we can add, venereal disease] that the true heir should be sought, but in a highly complex phenomenon that medicine would take far longer to appropriate. That phenomenon is madness. But only after a long latency period of almost two centuries did this new obsession take the place of the fear that leprosy had instilled in the masses and elicit similar reactions of division, exclusion, and purification, which are akin to madness itself" (2006, 8).

We note that we are in the midst of talking about the emergence of a group of practices, institutions, and lineages in the formation of the mental asylum. In this emergence the exilic freedom of the lepers disappeared

---

find that tincture of madness appearing immediately in the ritual and beliefs. The normal practice—the ritual—and the honored piety of the beliefs would fuse with craziness that is beyond the pale of rationality based on faith. Craziness and religious normalcy would constitute interfused differences, not bifurcated opposites. As this discussion advances, the question of the fusion of reason and unreason will become increasingly significant.

because of the increasing presence of containment facilities for the socially banished. We noted earlier that in the church-originated banishment of lepers, the "victims" were free of continued supervision by the powers that condemned them. Outside the city walls they often were not morally, spiritually, or physically constrained by authorities or supervisors. The sites of containment, those homogenizing buildings that became "receptacle[s] for all that is most vile and sickening in society," those quasi jails, were yet to come (2006, 356). Further, the gaols of morality, as Foucault called them, that characterized the earliest forms of asylums for the mad did not appear until the late eighteenth century. We will soon see that nomadic, anarchical freedom will find its shelter in unreason. It's something of an underground freedom that is created by its difference from moral rationalities and normative systems of order. This freedom is beyond morality, reason, and meaning.

The latency period that Foucault refers to occurred in Europe between the fourteenth and seventeenth centuries and accompanied the developments in the Renaissance that we noted during which secular authority and rationality as well as resistance to ecclesiastical power began to replace the unquestioned priority of the Roman Catholic Church and its authoritative faith. The part of the population that eventually would be recognized as "mad" were recognized in the early part of this period as indefinite objects of curiosity, amusement, irritation, and at times imprisonment in "hospitals"—rather more like warehouses—along with the poor, the infirm, murderers, thieves, the chronically unemployed, and the blatantly immoral. The category of madness had not yet emerged, and the full power of division in the lineage of the lepers and their confinement in lazar houses had yet to come into effect. On its own, unreason was not a "natural" reality whose occurrence defined itself (2006, 102). Rather, before it became a reality, its possibility revealed itself in a social type—in people whose behavior and affect seemed to indicate an absence of reason within the social contexts that defined sound moral rationality. But their behavior figured not simply unreasonableness. It figured the threatening possibility of no reason at all. *No reason at all?! Without sense or morality?* That kind of radical difference needed to be contained and institutionalized. The very thought of a site, a region, a simple and terrifying silence with no reason at all demanded conquering attention at once. The possibility of something like unreason, something threatening corruption and degeneration within society, appeared as though shining through fissures in these people's starkly irrational and illogical behavior. Who or what inspired such behavior? Inspired such disgusting, even frightening foolishness? What then, in the power of the time's imaginary, made sense was to see that the inspiration might have come from "something" without reason, "something" beyond reasonable control. Not only did such disorder come to feel as though it were actively opposed to the sense of reasonable order and moral judgment; it also took on the mythicized, vague imagery of an opponent, an agent of demonic forces, in defiance of Truth. Unreason in the seventeenth and eighteenth centuries, were it not controlled rationally and morally, felt like a threat to order as such and thus to human life and meaning.

If, on the other hand, fools, social leeches, and perverts—if this nonreasonable, immoral segment of the population could be quarantined and neutralized, there would be no need for anxiety about the state of the world. These people who blatantly violated normal decency and behaved outside the borders of reason and good sense, who in their freedom might be experienced as the carriers of demonic cosmic powers, could be both authorized and sanctioned by objectification: they could be branded and quarantined by the ways they were officially recognized and authoritatively validated. Objectification and confinement go hand in hand. Although we might think of punishment in terms of whips and chains, the kind of punishment that Foucault has in mind is found in the neutralization of those who live outside the bounds of reason. Officials and experts could make the appearances of these people into objects of authoritative knowledge and put those objects away, distance them from their homeland, silence them within social institutions, incarcerate them. "It was in society that unreason exiled and silenced itself.... Unreason ceased to be an experience in the adventure that any human reason is, and found itself instead avoided and enclosed in a quasi-objectivity. As a force, it could then no longer feed into the secret life of the spirit, nor accompany it as a constant threat. It was placed at a distance.... Objectivity became the homeland of unreason, but as punishment" (2006, 103). In this homeland of objectification, reasonably normal ways of life could feel safe in moral rationality's social order. It was a punishing order that moral rationality established in part by its power of division in classifying objectification. Unreason appeared contained and domesticated, without even the suggestion of a dimension of occurrences beyond reason, morality, and good sense that could threaten domestic tranquility. Unreason beyond the circumference of rational and moral limitations was not liberated from the tranquility that morality and good sense imposed on it. It—unreason—appeared as a domesticated object of knowledge that lacked any hint of its liberation that was to come.

A Short Excursus

We will see that unreason can play a vitally important role in societies. Its domestication is a foolish project—the more foolish for all the project's success. In this kind of domestication, enormous energy is dedicated to the formation of institutions, knowledge, and practices that ... *stubbornly* is not quite the right word here ... densely and ignorantly attempt to kill the very presence of unreason, to silence it by the forces of normal coherence and systems of stable conceptualization, to isolate rational formations on island-like kingdoms of Truth surrounded by a tumultuous sea pounding their shores, eroding their perimeters, a sea with profound subterranean creatures in its impenetrable dark. Reason is so very limited in its range of sense. It is so often unreasonable in its self-assessments, so dangerous in its confidence. So unaware of its deep-seated kinship with its own absence, with the unreason and mere silence that accompany its careful formulations.

This punishing objectification by recognition, knowledge, judgment, and quarantine emerged and expanded in the seventeenth century and held unreason silent. The apparent absence of reason in people became a reasonable justification to send them to institutions, and this taming containment "opened the way for a discourse about unreason.... Is it not important for our culture that unreason could only become an object of knowledge after it had been subjected to a process of social excommunication?" (2006, 104). In its socialization by means of judgmental recognition, classification, and institutional control by the authorities that knew it, unreason was not at all separable from normalcy and morality. It was a part of decent secular society, excommunicated from social practices, a present pariah silenced by the power that knew it and held it captive. In its silence unreason could happen within the circumference of social orders as their object and in their service. *Reason* referred to the organized discourse of social and moral normalcy and to the values that underpinned and infused it. This discourse—this sensibility—was inclined to institutionalize unreason's disorder *within* a systematized society, to make it available, as we have seen, in a socially controlled environment—not to allow it, as it were, to roam the streets and alleys and live in its anarchic ways within the perimeters of a community's normal acceptance.[15] Unreason's captivity created the conditions necessary to imagine a different kind of institution for the disordered, a healing and compassionate institution for correction and transformation, one in which humane treatment could restore nonreasonable people without a sense of decency to a moral, reasonable, normal, and good life.

The reformers that Foucault had in mind, Samuel Tuke and Philippe Pinel, were motivated by the moral and religious beliefs that people, whether mad or sane, were equal as human beings. The dehumanized objects that some unreasonable people and the mad were forced to become was, they thought, a travesty of justice and mercy. These people were human. They were to be disassociated from the kind of objectivity that turned them into subhuman animals. They should be treated with compassion and respect. The mad were taken out of dungeons, cages, and cells, out of their not simply indecent but horrific imprisonment and, freed from their chains, brought into institutions for decent reform. These reforms were designed to break resistance to authority, to teach people how to conform to patterns of normal morality and public behavior.

---

15. *Discourses*, as Foucault uses the word, refers to sensibilities in action. They are not restricted to written and spoken communications. They include behaviors; the operation of such anonymous agents as institutions, lineages, and cultures; and pre-reflective inclinations and recognitions.

Tuke's and Pinel's therapeutic approaches taught them to be their own agents of supervision and enforcement. Often after normalizing therapy a former patient might seem a bit strange, but in an acceptable way, like the aunt who did not quite fit into the rhythms of normal social life, who lived quietly and unproductively, except for her knitting and her help with household chores, in an attic room in the family house; or the man who laughed inexplicably and inappropriately and on whom manners seemed to hang like an ill-fitting coat, but who could nonetheless pour tea and offer cream and sugar; or the women and men who at one time had been violent and dangerous, who now lived peaceful lives and were able to manage such simple jobs as sweeping streets or making brooms or cleaning stables. Reform, indeed. Certainly the appearance of decency. But the elimination of unreason?[16]

We recall that for Foucault *unreason* currently names dimensions of human lives that are beyond reason, truth, and meaning. Its lineages include behaviors in societies and discourses that are beyond the pale of normalcy, intolerable to good sense, and often anarchic and scandalous. Unreason in Western cultures has incited, not only the fears that can accompany truth and meaning without transcendental foundations. It has also incited with seemingly magnetic power grotesque images that arise from deep within human consciousness: witches and demons, world-threatening eschatologies, evil beyond badness, and diabolically inspired social menace. The presence of people whose lifeways have borne them beyond the boundaries of reason and decency, even beyond the stability of Meaning, has often been experienced as revealing an element of transcendent danger. These perceptions, before madness became a categorized reality, allowed unreason real and often extraordinary power in a culture's world. The sense of life without reason or goodness to give it order, with the images and meanings that accompany its unmistakable threat of instability and insubstantiality, with a protean grounding that performs what cannot be said literally and falls outside the schemas that would make it evident as an object of knowledge and judgment, such a

---

16. See Foucault's discussion of Samuel Tuke and Philippe Pinel (2006, 460–511) for accounts of the socializing and moral training of the mad.

sense was an anxiety-filled... let's call it lust, an anxiety-filled lust for, if not salvation, objectification.

Foucault felt no such lust. He writes and thinks within the force of liberated unreason. Even when he uses transitive verbs with *unreason*— "unreason exiled and silenced itself," for example—the sentences have an almost whimsical, cloud-like quality. If the reader grasps them too tightly, the literal meaning dissolves. Or as Foucault might put it, its truth becomes fiction: one loses the reality it bespeaks. And yet, we repeat for emphasis, the occurrence of unreason in social and cultural contexts can be accompanied by enormous power, not only the power to frighten but also power bred of freedom from the—Foucault might say—monotonous restrictions of normal good sense. An attunement with unreason can incite power for creativity, re-visioning, and inspiration engendered outside the restrictive force of truth, propriety, and the spiritual mediocrity of discursive familiarity. Power, for example, to imagine, contra the functioning culture, a history of madness, a critique of pure reason, a movement of women in restrictive and oppressive societies to free themselves for the development of their independence and ambitions, a revolution in conceptions of sexual mores and of the value of pleasure, a genealogy of morals; power to live in the liminality of the limits of one's imagination, to break the stabilizing forces of social roles, oppressions, enslavements; the power of unreason in its lineages of iconoclasm, truancy from the schools of rational good sense, and deviations from normalcy and canonical conformity. Isn't it wonderful that the exilic freedom of lepers centuries ago transmogrified into living possibilities for creative freedom in the contexts of moralized, rationalized, and religiously controlled societies, a freedom that we find evident in Foucault's description of the occurrences of unreason?

A DARK NETWORK OF OBSCURE COMPLICITIES

The social reality of unreason did not become apparent only in its objectification in authoritative knowledge and in its power to incite creativity and threaten rational order. Foucault's description of networks of obscure complicities in the eighteenth-century correctional institutions is also an account of the social reality of unreason. He points to situations whereby individuals could be established as guilty of something deleterious by forced association with a group of highly differentiated people who were collectively perceived as defective. Secular authorities and the communities that supported them perceived many different deviations from rational order and moral normalcy without regard for individual differences; these were people who figured appearances of unreason broadly and were simply known as "fit for confinement." In this time, as we have seen, thieves, sexual deviants, and particularly odd people, for example, as well as insane individuals, were lumped together in the buildings that effected their confinement and "social excommunication" (2006, 104). A strange aggregation developed that was not based on discriminating attention to different kinds of deviant or norm-breaking behaviors. Varieties of deviance alone sufficed to send individuals into a roiling mix of a community's dregs confined in warehouses for the useless, the criminal, the odd, and the insane. They were all seen as mad in one way or another.

These injudicious institutions created, without explicit intention, a setting that, like the forming of composite rocks, began to meld together different identities, different marks of distinction, different elements—"divergent horizons"—to yield something both new and inimical in the commonwealth (2006, 104). The confining institutions and the imposed identity silenced many lineages and many histories of maltreatment, suffering, family practices, social customs, self-identification, and illness. Unreason began to appear in a transformed guise as madness—as an amalgamation of previously unrelated identities that became subject to classification as a whole. This shift by amalgamation manifested "the enslavement of unreason to something other than knowledge, and insert[ed] it in a dark network of obscure complicities. It was precisely that servitude that was slowly to give unreason the concrete and indefinably complicitous face of madness that is now familiar from our own experience. Inside the walls of the institutions were the debauched and the venereal, alchemists, libertines, those who 'claimed to be witches' and, as we shall see, the insane. Associations became more common and similarities were found, and to the eyes of those for whom unreason was becoming an object, an almost homogeneous field came into being. Out of guilt, sexual pathos, magic and age-old incantatory rituals, delirium and the laws of the human heart, a hidden network of associations emerged, forming the secret foundation of our modern experience of madness. To this domain thus structured, the tag of unreason was to be applied, as men were labelled 'fit for confinement.' That unreason, which the thought of the sixteenth century had considered to be the dialectical point of the reversal of reason, was thus given a concrete content. It was linked to a whole shift in ethics involving questions about the meaning of sexuality, the division of love, profanation and the boundaries of the sacred, and the links between morality and truth. All these experiences, from divergent horizons, were the depths under the simple gesture of confinement. That surface phenomenon hid a system of underground operations all oriented in the same sense: creating in the ethical world a homogeneous division so far unknown. In approximate terms, it can be said that until the Renaissance the world of ethics, beyond the great division between Good and Evil, kept its equilibrium in a sort of tragic unity, that of destiny and of providence and divine will. That unity was now to disappear, broken by the definitive split between reason and unreason. A crisis in the world of ethics therefore came into being, and to the great struggle between Good and Evil was juxtaposed the irreconcilable conflict between reason and unreason, multiplying images of the split. Figures like Nietzsche and Sade bear witness to that. Half the world of ethics thus fell into the domain of unreason, bringing an immense content of eroticism, profanation, magic, ritual, and bodies of visionary knowledge secretly moved by the laws of the heart. At the moment when it was sufficiently freed to become an object of perception, unreason found itself caught up in a whole system of concrete servitude" (2006, 104–5).

Beyond thought, contaminated by an instantiated, dark network of obscure complicities that made it appear like a region of immorality with disease, in a definitive split from reason, unreason appeared as an institutionalized domain of involuntary collusion. That domain was the site of unreason's "concrete servitude" of "obscure complicities." "The debauched and the venereal, alchemists, libertines, those who 'claimed to be witches,' and . . . the insane" populated that domain as involuntarily entwined embodiments of the obscure complicities. We add to this list the unemployed poor who were also institutionalized during that period. The processes effective in the emergence of this domain were diverse and often disconnected in their lineages of fear and moral revulsion vis-à-vis unreason and the perceived deviations, sacrilege, and exile that seemed to manifest it. A "hidden network of associations and similarities" embroiled with experiences from "divergent horizons," mutating without truth or reason to guide them, anonymous in their borders, gave involuntary birth to a new dimension, a new site beyond Good and Evil, beyond reason. Far from a "spontaneous archaeology of cultures," in this emerging experience of unreason "continuity is actually a phenomenon of discontinuity" and seems comprehensible in linear terms only by a backward-looking glance ignorant of "the real problem [which is] transformation of the field of experience." "A new place of exile and predilection" emerged—a new field of experience, an emended sensibility—a site where unreason, in a new division, appeared without challenging reason. Foucault names it "a domain of unreason" where many patterns of deviant behavior are enmeshed in experiences of unreason and "slowly come to belong in a sphere of illness." (All quotes in this paragraph are from 2006, 105.)

When unreason is set apart decisively from reason and appears as sickness, as a malady that might be treated and, hopefully, cured, it is silenced *in its appearance*. That silencing is compatible with objectification but is not the same as objectification. As an object, unreason is within the control of the objectifying discourse, inclusive of institutional policies and practices, the structure of authority active in the objectification, and the dynamic lineages that infuse the force of division. But in its appearance in the eighteenth century as a domain of complicities, as "a field of experience," unreason does not appear as an object of the medical gaze or of any other discourse. Rather, unreason was subject to the shifts in identity effected by institutionalizing a chaos of deviant and hence nonreasonable people who became identified by an imposed and unifying branding. These shifts established what Foucault called complicities, that is, immediate, seemingly codependent associations with other groups and types of individuals in a nuance of unacceptable deviations. Those associations, we have seen, were not necessarily created by anyone, certainly not by the inmates. The network of dark complicities emerged by virtue of practices of containment in particular social and cultural circumstances.

Such phenomena did not happen only in the eighteenth and nineteenth centuries. We are thinking of many possible examples, such as the Nazi national purification mania that, in the name of sane policies and in the illusion of perfecting a pure race, created a combinatory space for Jews, Gypsies, the mentally challenged, the physically disabled, homosexuals, communists, socialists, and Jehovah's Witnesses. The collection brought intimately to bear all of the otherwise unconnected or loosely connected lineages and cultural identities active in those people. The space of detention and "concentration" constituted a domain that found its unity by means of branding all of them "enemies of the state." Many other types of objectification took place, but this particular type of combinatory site created something different from an object. It created a field, not a field of sickness but one for killing in the name of state security. The analogy between unreason appearing as a field of experience and the appearance of "enemies of the state" is rough. But the point is to understand the difference between silencing a population by objectification and the silencing that happens when an assemblage of very different kinds of people becomes a concentrated and unified domain, a forced unity, a cauldron of shared experience and codependency by compelled branding.

Silencing unreason in the seventeenth and eighteenth centuries and silencing enemies of the Nazi state in the early twentieth century share in common both the predominance of appearance without substance and the unreason of the two rationalities. Few passions are more powerful than those that would eliminate immanent impurity and deviations from rock-solid norms, passions that would establish a culture of unmixed uprightness. In the sensibility that we, the authors, share, that kind of passion is absurd—a mad passion integral to a particular rationality. The passion to eliminate unreason by silencing it is also absurd and mad—ill-conceived, we might say. These passions and projects float powerfully in an ether of illusion as rational people attempt to secure their tiny segments of certainty in imagined substructures of universal truth.

APPEARANCE WITHOUT SUBSTANCE

In the previous chapter as we turned to Nietzsche's *Genealogy of Morals* we spoke of moon shadows that appear as interrupted reflections of a reflection. Eternal return, we said, appears in his work as a reflection of an insubstantial beyond that has no sense and that is interrupted by the sense he makes of it. One of Nietzsche's arts is found in the way he develops the nuance of no sense beyond good and evil—much less moral good sense—in the sense of his prose. Foucault has a similar art at work in his *History of Madness* as he elaborates unreason, the hallmark of that book. In this chapter we have engaged unreason in its many appearances: as an undifferentiated experience, as madness, as beyond sense, as socially powerful, as rendered impotent in medical objectivity and as an integral part of society in that silencing objectivity, as bestial and inhuman emotions, as divided from reason, as harboring a kind of freedom, as infesting reason, as a domain or field of experience, as social or moral deviance, as inciting creativity. As a concept, unreason is completely unstable. In Foucault's genealogical history, unreason does not function as a category or classification. Nor is unreason a substantial entity. It lives only in its ephemeral appearances. *It* escapes being an *it*. Even the privative first syllable sensibly negates the word's sense. As we write about it, we sometimes find unreason maddening. And yet Foucault's account of unreason makes sense to us because of his skill in presenting and performing its elusiveness and the powers invested in it.

Like Nietzsche's and Anzaldúa's, Foucault's writing bespeaks an elusive, fugitive, yet forceful beyond that he cannot say directly. Unreason, as it functions in his writing, is similar to a hologram: it is perceptible as the projection of an elusive image that lacks density. A hologram is a three-dimensional image reproduced from a pattern of interference, an image that is formed by the interference of a coherent light source. In the case of unreason, reason is, as it were, that coherent source of light. Try to embrace either a hologram or unreason. It's like embracing a cloud, a shadow, or a pattern of light interference. When unreason is objectified by the attempted embrace of sensible concepts and judgments, its appearance withdraws into silence. It disappears into nothing-to-hold, beyond the defining borders of sense and normalcy. And yet when we speak of unreason's multiple happenings, we are speaking of dimensions of communal, lineage-filled lives. We repeat for emphasis: the instability of unreason's appearances is disclosive of its happening, *and* its happening, beyond embrace as it is, impacts many, many lives.

When we say that reason's coherent, sense-making light is interrupted and something intangible appears in the pattern of the interference—perceptible happenings that seem to appear to escape themselves—we are speaking coherently of nonsense. When we think of moon shadows as analogous to reflections of an insubstantial beyond in speaking of the unspeakable, we are affirming the interruptive nonsense in what we say.

GETTING FREE OF ONESELF, CARING FOR ONESELF

In the introduction to *The Use of Pleasure*, Foucault spoke of the compelling motivation for his work: "As for what motivated me, it is quite simple; I would hope that in the eyes of some people it might be sufficient in itself. It was curiosity—the only kind of curiosity, in any case, that is worth acting upon with a degree of obstinacy: not the curiosity that seeks to assimilate what it is proper for one to know, but that which enables one to get free of oneself. After all, what would be the value of the passion for knowledge if it resulted only in a certain amount of knowledgeableness and not, in one way or another and to the extent possible, in the knower's straying afield of himself? There are times in life when the question of knowing if one can think differently than one thinks, and perceive differently than one sees, is absolutely necessary if one is to go on looking and reflecting at all. People will say, perhaps, that these games with oneself would better be left backstage; or, at best, that they might properly form part of those preliminary exercises that are forgotten once they have served their purpose. But, then, what is philosophy today—philosophical activity, I mean—if it is not the critical work that thought brings to bear on itself? In what does it consist, if not in the endeavor to know how and to what extent it might be possible to think differently, instead of legitimating what is already known? ... But it [philosophical discourse] is entitled to explore what might be changed, in its own thought, through the practice of a knowledge that is foreign to it. The 'essay'—which should be understood as the assay or test by which, in the game of truth, one undergoes changes, and not as the simplistic appropriation of others for the purpose of communication—is the living substance of philosophy, at least if we assume that philosophy is still what it was in times past, i.e., an 'ascesis,' *askēsis*, an exercise of oneself in the activity of thought" (Foucault 1985, 8–9).

"Games of truth," as Foucault used the phrase, refers not only to theoretical and scientific efforts to establish what is true but also to dominating relations of power invested in authoritative knowledge like that of psychiatric and psychological sciences. They are hard games played often in a pre-reflective terrain, at the heart of truths and established facts, where lust for power and passion for the privilege of dominating, defining, or oppressing others rest, rest sometimes anxiously, sometimes with calm brutality. In such cases knowledge, domination, and oppression are inseparable. Other games are played, with a cloak of compassion and with the sincerity of Tuke and Pinel, to overturn regimes of truth that are ignorant of the value of human lives in order to save souls and create communities of charity, mercy, and forgiveness on the basis of revealed Truth.[17] In this context saving souls, showing compassion, silencing, and oppressing go together. Sometimes an odd, perverse mix of Marques de Sade, Saint Dominic, and Saint Francis creates in the name of love harsh restrictions on, in Foucault's terms, bodies of pleasure. Not a witches' brew but a saint's brew of cruelty, asceticism, hope for salvation, life-denial, and domination produces a sanctified game of truth. The stakes in these games are high. Cultures as well as torture chambers and prisons, political and educational systems, rule by holy books and holy people—that is, control by sanctified powers, or control by profane powers without robes, or combinations of both robes and profane powers—participate in these games of making true. Dominations in the context of games of truth are constituted by networks of power/knowledge that can be overturned, or they can mutate with other networks of power/knowledge as they are carried out in institutional structures and practices. Shift the power, and you can refigure truth and the knowledge that it verifies. Or alter truths and knowledge, and you can refigure the relations of power. The rules of these games can figure all manner of interests such as those of various self-identifying races, nationalities, and economic classes. Games of truth can also figure, as we have seen, group anxieties and paranoias.

But Foucault's own game of truth? It has nothing to do with establishing practices of domination. It comes to expression in "an exercise of oneself" in the activity of self-transforming thought, and that activity composes the "living substance" of philosophy as he wants to practice it. He follows the lead of an inclination he calls curiosity that is without substance, articulable truth, or definitive origin and that enables people

---

17. See in this chapter the section "The Social Reality of Unreason." See also Foucault 1997, 281–82.

to put in question their definitive thoughts and knowledge and to get free of themselves. This curiosity is found in individuals' desire to free themselves of themselves, individuals who are ready for transformation and who are willing not to valorize normal propriety, submission to canons of texts and axioms of truth, or the accumulation of knowledge for its own sake. This kind of curiosity leads people astray of themselves and has no interest in legitimating what is already known or inscribed in one's own character. Foucault's kind of curiosity does *not* lead only to *reforms* based on existing practices and institutional formations. Foucault's curiosity and his games of truth take one into foreign territories of experience and, instead of directing people in a particular game of truth, release them for their own practices of freedom, possibly for their *transformations*.

Freeing oneself from oneself has a liberatory aspect, certainly, one that is not founded on "the idea that there exists a human nature or base that, as a consequence of certain historical, economic, and social processes, has been concealed, alienated, or imprisoned in and by mechanisms of repression" (1997, 282, see 281–301). Rather than something quasi-foundational that seeks its self-realization, Foucault emphasizes "an exercise of the self on the self by which one attempts to develop and transform oneself and to attain a certain mode of being" (1997, 282). This process begins *without* a definitive base; it begins *with* uncertainty and questions, *without* guiding knowledge or authorities, the repetition of which gives authorized security. It is *originary*, unfounded and unjustified in its beginning. Usually undramatic in its originality. Simply the beginning of something that inclines people to find out how to bring themselves into processes of transformation. Do you catch a nuance of unreason in Foucault's curiosity?

This process has two interconnected characteristics. People begin to put themselves in question in a variety of ways. That part of the process of liberation might arise from disturbing and deep-seated dissatisfactions with the way they live or with the form of identity they enforce on themselves. Or they find themselves living as though they accept their experiences of discrimination or other types of oppression and do not know why they are acquiescent. They might find themselves bored with being alive or find that they are trapped by circumstances, or find that their passions carry them beyond the boundaries of their lives. Perhaps they are merely tired of being themselves. Or people might move toward the kind of curiosity that Foucault speaks of when they find themselves in a domain of experience they do not understand. They find they want something, and they don't know what it is. Perhaps they want the freedom of uncertainty and the experience of living *in* boundaries instead of with the certainty of being defined by them. As we have seen for Foucault, the intellectual and philosopher, curiosity arose when he experienced the immanence of an unknown and experienced the viscosity of a boundary that unsettled his thinking and what he found worth knowing. He learned how to put himself into texts, to *experience* them as much as possible on their own terms and to expose himself to a new domain of experience. These many different experiences that cultivate an uncommitted curiosity constitute the motivating force for a liberatory movement, the initial steps toward and into what he calls unknown territories of experience. This move can be highly disruptive and disturbing in people's lives. Or exciting and energizing. It might be as quiet and undramatic as growing away from one lifeway and into another until the individuals come to a crisis, a turning point where they turn . . . to nowhere that is familiar. What then?

At this point a second characteristic of liberation can take effect: the formation of practices of freedom that simultaneously allow people, as they get free of themselves, to begin to care for themselves in affirmation of the element of freedom that emerges when they find themselves really in question and beyond the power of rational justification. This latter is a process of transforming self-formation. The transformation need not be like a total makeover of one's self. Friends could certainly recognize familiar characteristics in Foucault as he was transformed by experiencing the silence and silencing of the mad, his "discovery" of unreason, his departure in his way of doing genealogy from many of the influences that played significant roles in his education, such as those of Hegel, Sartre, and Marx, or his deep involvement in the S and M movement in San Francisco. His transformations affected his self and his work through and through. He found no "essential" Foucault, no essence to "get right" or guide him, unless being without an essence were essential.

Foucault wanted to learn to think what he could not think, hear what he could not hear, and see what he could not see. He wanted to develop new ways of knowing, develop a different language and conceptuality in comparison with the canon he found in France's intellectual world. He wanted to become a different intellectual in comparison with the one he had been. In any case, as he attempted *to be* a practice of freedom—a singular event of that practice—he wanted to intensify experiences of differences from himself and not intensify an imagined unity of his life as he toiled in archives, traced down sources, wrote volumes, and experimented with erotic intensity as well as with his self-reflective thought. Other people might find their freedom—their freeing disciplines—in composing music or in painting in ways that release them for radical departures from the tradition they are in. In practices of freedom, people might transform their characters, beliefs, and behaviors in such ways that friends and relatives say, "I don't know you anymore." However the transformation takes place, the beginnings of liberation as Foucault conceives them have no guiding practices, no mores or fundamental meanings to bring light into the dark of uncharted uncertainty. That light comes with the practices of freedom that create new beginnings in new domains of experience and bring to a life something that did not exist and is able to persist.

A thorough process of liberation thus includes both the activity of breaking free from oppression, domination, canonical authority, habituations, and many other patterns of living, on the one hand, and, on the other, self-transformations in "practices of freedom." The implication is clear: breaking free is not enough freedom for Foucault. *Transformation* and *curiosity* are words for living processes but not for mere rebellion, or anarchistic destruction, or static and finished accomplishments. They are words, in the context of Foucault's thought, for engaging one's self and one's thoughts and finding, perhaps with the spur of curiosity, new ways to relate to oneself and the world around them. Curiosity and transformations can lead to living with the kind of understanding—"absolute understanding"—we discussed in the section "Writing of Silencing."[18] It's an understanding that happens as people experience the broadly accepted stabilities in a society as continuously protean—as mutable, plastic formations that often function powerfully and unnoticed and are

---

18. These are the words on which that section was based: "To be absolutely understood" means to speak with "a language without support," "in a sort of relativity without recourse," language that in both its nuance and its declarations makes no claim to stable truths but authorizes an unending exchange, "constantly correct[ing] itself to proceed, in a continuous movement, to the very bottom" (2006, xxxv).

revealed by their interruptions. As one carries out practices of freedom in attunement with Foucault's understanding of curiosity, and as those practices develop into continuing disciplines in people's lives, highly individualized manners of living affirmatively—caringly—form in a world of involution, change, and continuous combinations of creation and destruction. These ways of living are ways of caring for oneself. And in Foucault's life they reflected lineages of unreason and an art of living out of which he was able to conceive many of his projects, including the series *History of Sexuality*.

Several strands of thought in this chapter came together in this section: Foucault's emphasis on formations of relations of power as he developed his archaeological/genealogical history of madness in the lineages of division, exile, and banishment; the silence of madness in the knowledge that understood madness and in the practices that punished it or attempted to heal it; his conception-breaking conception of shifting, inconsistent unreason; his finding in the silence of silenced madness a measure of freedom; his distinction between the productive, creative work in the lineage of unreason, on the one hand, and on the other, madness without an oeuvre; his portrayal of the importance of unreason for the life and vigor of societies; his depiction of not the bifurcation but the intimacy of madness and normal sanity; his conception of games of truth; his conception of practices of freedom. In these practices, as he finds them in his experience, a lineage-formed, conscious event—a self—that cares for itself, develops a way of life, an ethics, born of unreasonreason, always *in* the viscosity of borders of differences, always *in* thresholds of endingbeginning, always on the verge of unspeakable processes beyond philosophy and morality. The performance of his speech and concepts is an art of knowing, of knowing unreason as free and beyond the borders that give it shape and appearance.

In practices of freedom there is no question of "free will" when that term means a domain of undetermined autonomy in human beings. People's and cultures' formations, including will and consciousness, are determined in uncountable ways. But, for Foucault, there is the determined autonomy of individuality: an individual self is a singular, incomplete event that lives its often-incompatible determinations and makes choices in the thick of them. Nothing else and no one else is this event's experience: The searing pain of the whip's lash on her back. The elation one feels while subjecting another into submission. This one's taste of this tea. That one's limit-experience. This one's mourning. His perception of injustice. Her experience of being silenced. Selves with their experiences are all immensely complex events in the world, worldly events that in their singularities can care for themselves, care for others, and choose to begin to live differently from the way they are living. Real events. Individual eventuations. No abstractions, including truths, regardless of their accuracy, can live a person's event. Social orders, knowledge, empowered judgments, various other forces can silence them, speak for their experiences, kill them. But none can exist their existence. Or, of course, die their deaths. Such is the determined autonomy of individuality.

Foucault carries out his own individuality, his practice of freedom, in part by interrupting many certainties and assumed truths. He interferes with the authority of a wide range of unquestioned institutional and cultural practices, and when their proposed solutions are based on unquestioned assumptions, he creates multiple problems with those assumptions. His purpose is to keep them in the air of uncertainty rather than to provide or support a settling solution. Instead of solutions, he wants to create "a malaise" that will keep issues alive and in question for years and out of which creative changes can emerge that were not previously possible (2000, 290). This intention is in accord with his reasoned sense that both unreason and rationalities happen as mutable, dynamic social realities. They are parts of networks of lineages and environmental factors that mix and synthesize to form continuously mutating identities and criteria for meaning and sense. He finds his own truths and meanings, of course, within the powers of the volatile anonymous agencies that are parts of societies' sensibilities.

Foucault did his extensive archival work, wrote his books, and participated in interviews with this understanding of reality. He was curious. He wanted to expose, to unsettle, not to resolve. When he showed the powerful lineages that played their parts in the shaping and continuing lives of "mental institutions"—asylums—for example, he solved nothing. He confronted his readers with exposures of the institutions' complex beginnings, the descents of lineages that actively composed them, and the silencing practices that shocked many people and conflicted with their values. He put in question the confident authority of psychiatry and many of the routine practices of asylums. Normalcy itself became questionable. He exposed seldom-questioned values and the norms of acceptable decency embedded in therapeutic practice. No solutions. Lots of problems. His curiosity and his desire to carry out his own self-care and transformations nonetheless contributed to the creation of a major body of affecting work—an influential oeuvre—that impacted thousands of people, multiple disciplines, and many ways of living without resolving the problems he incited and uncovered.

An important attunement happens in the context of Foucault's pivotal concepts of event, mutability, lineages, relations of power, practices of freedom, appearance without substance, networks of complicity, unreason and its social reality—indeed, this attunement is in effect throughout *History of Madness*. It is an attunement with dimensions of processes and utter silence that are beyond truth, beyond morality, beyond philosophy. *Beyond* in this context suggests unreason's eventuation writ . . . not Large. Rather, writ small. Unreason's eventuation is shaped, not by the language of grand schemes of divine planning or in the enshrined imagery of suprahuman agents but in mortal individualities, in continuously infusing lineages of practice and knowledge, in shifting attitudes and beliefs, in language with unrelenting mutability, in unending exchange with continuous movement, in intervals of silence and emptiness. Beyond definitive shapes, amorphous unreason enters our world forcefully as nothing we can grasp.

For Foucault, attunement to indeterminate beyond accompanies his sense of the instability of truths and meanings that the attunement generates. This attunement was a cause of joy for him, the joy of finding out how to think differently from his previous thinking; the joy of finding new, transforming domains of experience; and above all, finding out, in the absence of preestablished essences, how to conceive what he believed was true as though it were written to become fiction. He did not think of the truths of history that he uncovered as stable. He did not write to establish any stable truths but to motivate readers to find their own voices in relation to the subject at hand, to, say, asylums, prisons, educational institutions, political regimes, religious rituals, sexuality. We believe his joy came in the processes of finding his own voice in fields of experience that were new to him and in his releasing individuals to their own events and experiences. He wanted to effect among his readers and audiences, at best, multiple changes that would form a sometimes-disorderly chorus of voices and perspectives within social orders. Foucault found a way of living, an ethics, that maximized limit-experiences in his life; it is an ethics that releases people to their pleasures, to their freedoms, and motivates them to find their own limit-experiences. His joy, we believe, happened in resonance with the dimension of indeterminate beyond that is shadowed in protean unreason with its lineages of productive madness, institutional change, and new, liberating ways of caring for oneself.

Anzaldúa's Nepantla

Where do we find ourselves?

We encountered the liberatory force of beyond in the thought of Nietzsche and Foucault. We noted that beyond is a happening without such border-creating and controlling schemas as moral hierarchies, systems of meaning, or chronological time, which are, all of them, nothing in themselves in spite of their extraordinary power to measure and to set orders and limits. Multiple lineages happen beyond the identities they compose and often carry with them elements quite contrary to those identities. Modern systems of justice, for example, that have lineages of cruelty, torture, and revenge, or, for a second example, self-sacrificial love that carries out lineages of fear of mortal, amoral life. Dynamic lineages constitute anonymous agencies in the forceful roles they play in the formations of humans' inner lives, in their "souls," in Nietzsche's terminology, as well as in the formations of institutions, systems of punishment, and moral hierarchies.

Nietzsche's and Foucault's genealogical work have three aspects that are especially relevant to an understanding of the liberation they make possible: first, exposure of the fluid, mutationally formed capacities and senses that we often consider constant and stable (universal factors in human nature, for example, or senses of dignity and reverence, or cherished values that we invest with the power of universality); second, the transfiguring power of experiences that are attuned to beyond in our feelings, perceptions, habits, recognized kinships, practices of connecting with others and ourselves. This kind of attunement makes possible the transformational ability to think and to live differently, to affirm being alive, and to laugh with joy and without cynicism, disappointment, or nihilism when we live consonant with the dimensions of our lives that are beyond the limits of conception, beyond affirmations of our most esteemed values, and beyond the most significant meanings in our lives; and third, the porosity of borders that becomes apparent in Nietzsche's and Foucault's genealogical work. Lineages are not stable identities in themselves. They are porous in the sense that they form a dynamic weave of interfusing practices and values. They are mutational and permeable.

The complex interplay and infusions of lineages are strikingly apparent in the writings of Gloria Anzaldúa. Her attentiveness to the often-silenced lineages of her heritage and to the workings of the very formations of power in her ways of living and thinking that she was striving to overturn is a reminder of the many forms in which genealogical sensibilities can appear. As we noted in the introductory chapter, reading Anzaldúa brought us both to a more heightened sense of beyond philosophy than we would otherwise have had. Her unique voice combined with her distinctive sense of beyond and her artful writing style resonated deeply within us while at the same time causing us to hesitate at thresholds of our understanding. These movements rattled our preconceptions.

Anzaldúa's voice heightened the polyphony of our understanding of beyond as it accompanied the polyvocality of Nietzsche and Foucault. We found that any effort to compare by identifying similarities or differences or to look for a linear sequence—for instance, Nietzsche introduced a way of thinking that Foucault built upon, but they missed a dimension foregrounded by Anzaldúa—muted our attunement to beyond. We hope readers will come to understand practices of reading, both Anzaldúa's and our own, as being more like the unfurling pages of the Codex Tezcatlipoca, née Codex Fejérváry-Mayer, where there can be different reading practices.[1] As with the codex, at times it is illuminating to read from top

---

1. This is one of the few Aztec codices that survived the colonialization of the Americas. Spanish colonizers systematically destroyed much of the population as well as the culture of the Aztecs. The name *Codex Fejérváry-Mayer* denotes the Hungarian collector, Fejérváry, who "owned" the codex in the eighteenth century and the English antiquarian, Mayer, who bought it. Maarten Jansen and Gabina Aurora Pérez Jiménez, whose work has

to bottom; at other times reading from outer margins to inner content is more revealing.

Anzaldúa wrote her becoming through her myriad efforts to give voice to unsayables. "Intento dar testimonio de mi propio proceso y conciencia de escritora chicana. Soy la que escribe y se escribe / I am the one who writes and who is being written. Últimamente es el escribir que me escribe / It is the writing that 'writes' me. I 'read' and 'speak' myself into being" (2015, 3).[2] Through the resonances of her writing, we turn our attention to Anzaldúa's beyond.

CARVING BONE, CREATING FACE: AUTOHISTORIA

Becoming open to Anzaldúa's thought is a process of becoming open to beyond philosophy. She writes in flesh and blood, out of pain and desire, from intuition and "an awareness and intelligence not grasped by logical thought," words quickening in her engagement with los espíritus. "You stop in the middle of the field, and, under your breath, ask the spirits—animals, plants, y tus muertos—to help you string together a bridge of words" (2015, 117–18). Anzaldúa's writing interweaves spirit, body, mind, intellect, intuition, politics, and art. She writes (with) her life. "When I write it feels like I'm carving bone. It feels like I'm creating my own face, my own heart—a Nahuatl concept. My soul makes itself through the creative act. It is constantly remaking and giving birth to itself through my body. It is learning to live with *la Coatlicue* that transforms living in the Borderlands from a nightmare into a numinous experience. It is always a path/state to something else" (1987, 73).

---

focused on Mixtec codices, have suggested that the codex be renamed to better reflect its Indigenous origins, calling it Codex Tezcatlipoca, the Nahuatl name of the god Tezcatlipoca, who is one of the creator gods and is shown in the center of the first page of the codex. As Aztec cosmology always brings together the female and the male, we use the abbreviation née, which could be interpreted as encompassing the male (né) within it.

2. We follow Anzaldúa in her *plurilingüe* practices of translation. While she often provides a literal or contextual translation, at times she refuses to translate or highlight her code-switching. When we quote from her, we honor her self-translational choices. And when we discuss terms she uses in her writing, we will follow her practice of not marking them as foreign by italicizing them. We will, however, provide definitions of some of her key concepts.

Anzaldúa writes to transform. Herself, of course. But you and me if we bodily ingest her words/worlds. As she explains, "writing is not about being in your head; it's about being in your body" (2015, 5). One does not simply read Anzaldúa but rather engages her. To listen to her voice is to experience her admonition to change. If we read her simply to understand, we have not heard her or attended to her unsayables. This exchange is costly; engaging Anzaldúa means being engaged in transformation—hers, ours. "We can transform our world by imagining it differently, dreaming it passionately via all our senses, and willing it into creation" (2015, 20).

Her writing is intensely personal at the same time that it is turned out from herself to such issues as oppression, racism, homophobia, and lineages of forceful, often preconscious symbols and psychological associations. Anzaldúa understood and acutely experienced the contradictions inherent in liberatory efforts. When the very concepts we use to understand and express ourselves or the words we use to give voice to silences are themselves carved from the formations that limit and oppress us, how do we transform our understanding? When what counts as proper thinking and acceptable forms of theorizing captures our tongues, how do we shift? How do we think, write, feel, create differently? How do we, Anzaldúa admonishes us, produce without being re-produced by the very structures we are questioning? How do we gather together words in ways that express differences, that queer the writing and recast problems?

Anzaldúa's response is not singular but multivocal—*vocare*, to call. The *plurilingüe* of her texts are crafted to call attention to the multifaceted power of language. "'Drought hit South Texas,' my mother tells me. '*La tierra se puso bien seca y los animales comenzaron a morrirse de se.' Mi papá se murío de un* heart attack *dejando a mamá* pregnant *y con ocho huercos*, with eight kids and one on the way. . . . *El siguiente año* still no rain. *Mi pobre madre viuda perdió* two thirds of her *ganado*. A smart *gabacho* lawyer took the land away *mamá* hadn't paid taxes. *No hablaba inglés*, she didn't know how to ask for time to raise the money" (1987, 8). While she knows only too well the many ways the power of language can limit and silence, she also knows that it can have liberatory power: "My use of both languages, my code-switching, is my way to resist being made into something else. . . . This resistance is part of the anticolonial struggle against both the Spanish colonizers and the white colonizers" (2000, 246).

Readers are thus asked to attend to their own linguistic practices and to examine how their code-switching practices, or lack of them, resonate with hers. As we hear her voice we are reminded of how our own tongues have been tamed.

Refusing to tame her wild tongue, she speaks multivocally. She brings to her writing her border tongue, her living language—*Pachuco*, Tex-Mex, Chicano Spanish, North Mexican Spanish dialect, Standard Mexican Spanish, Standard English, working class and slang English (1987, 55). Her writings enact the multivocal lineages of her experiences and give her a unique fluency. They also remind readers to attend to how some confluences of lineages silence while others are silenced. "Chicanos and other people of color suffer economically for not acculturating. This voluntary (yet forced) alienation makes for psychological conflict a kind of dual identity... I have so internalized the borderland conflict that sometimes I feel like one cancels out the other and we are zero, nothing, no one. *A veces no soy nada ni nadie. Pero hasta cuando no lo soy, lo soy*" (1987, 63).

Anzaldúa calls for a response—convocar, to summon, to call. She calls to tus muertos, to los espíritus, to the sea and the animals and the plants. Convocado; she is called. "As you go about your day, the potential story calls to you. At first la llamada is just an intangible longing, a vague yearning for form. Soon it becomes a beat pulsing subliminally. It won't take no for an answer" (2015, 96). She calls to her readers through images and stories, myths and emotions—and words that make us tremble. "I dwell on the imagination's role in journeying to 'non-ordinary' realities, on the use of the imaginal in nagualismo and its connection to nature spirituality."[3] Her desire is not to "describe realities but to create them through language and action, symbols and images" (2015, 7). She writes in attunement with beyond. To engage Anzaldúa is to be called to shift, to cocreate. To open ourselves to her in ways that we can be part of the journeying to "non-ordinary" realities.

Anzaldúa's autobiographically informed writings illustrate the differences and conflicts of the assemblages of lineages and sensibilities that inform her life. She identified as an American mestiza, a person of mixed

---

3. The word *nagual* comes from the Nahuatl word *nahuālli*, a human who has the power to transform spiritually or physically into an animal form.

races, especially Indian and Spanish. As she grew up the dialect she spoke was not recognized as an independent language and had no printed literature. She was a queer woman who grew up in a family and a culture that were homophobic and misogynist. Her body was physically marked by difference. She was a dark-skinned woman, la prieta, who grew up shadowed by "the myth of the superiority of the white races" (2015, 127). Poverty figured in all aspects of her upbringing. She worked in the fields as a migrant worker when she was a child and until she finished college. She had in her lineages conqueror and conquered, Brown and White, Christian and non-Christian, much violence and exploitation with multiple forms of destructive, disheartening prejudice, and, as we shall see, many divine figurations—los espíritus, Coyolxauhqui, La Llorona—that originated millennia ago, and la muse bruja that animated her work. She was physically marked by disease, a hormonal disorder that accelerated puberty and affected her stature, as well as the onset of type 1 diabetes when she was an adult. She was often defined and adversely impacted by the negative social connotations of her differences. "I was always angry," she said in an interview, "and I am still angry" (2012, 268).

Anzaldúa's response was to write from her differences, from the many moments of conflict that circulated in her lineages, and to find in those divergences and tensions catalysts for transformation. "Being lesbian and raised Catholic, indoctrinated as straight, I *make the choice to be queer* (for some it is genetically inherent). It's an interesting path, one that continually slips in and out of the white, the Catholic, the Mexican, the indigenous, the instincts. In and out of my head. It makes for *loquería*, the crazies. It is a path of knowledge—one of knowing (and of learning) the history of oppression of our *raza*. It is a way of balancing, of mitigating duality" (1987, 19). It is in her differences, Anzaldúa tells us, that she begins to feel, think, experience, imagine differently. "I had to figure out how to imagine/create/discover certain concepts/theories" (2015, 6). Throughout the chapters of this book, our readings are inspired by the very queries that stirred Anzaldúa's creativity: How do we speak vis-à-vis the unspeakable? How do we provoke new ways of thinking and living? How do we think, live, feel outside the realm of the familiar, the expected, the normed?

The lineages that figured in her life were dynamic, conflictual, interactive. Describing herself, she explained: "I am a seventh generation

American and so I don't have any real 'original Mexican' roots.... My ancestors have always lived with the land here in Texas. My indigenous ancestors go back twenty to twenty-five thousand years and that is how old I am in this country" (2012, 274). Anzaldúa is more richly anchored as an American than either of us—one fourth generation, the other merely second. Yet despite the absence of "real 'original Mexican' roots," her Indigenous Mexican heritages loomed large in her life. "Las raíces that sustain and nourish me are implanted in the landscape of my youth, my grandmother's stories of la Llorona, my father's quiet strength, the persevering energy of de la gente who work in the fields. I lived the first seven years of my life in a house with dirt floors. Los ranchos de me tierra (Jesús María y Los Verjeles) *cradled me and gave me strong Mexican indigenous roots embedded in preconquest tierra*" (2015, 67; emphasis added).

The Mexican-American border split her family. "The ones of our family who ended up north of the border, in the U.S., were the Anzaldúas with an accent, whereas the ones who lived in Mexico dropped their accent after a while. As the generations then went by, we lost contact with each other. Nowadays the Anzaldúas in the United States no longer know the Anzaldúas in Mexico. The border split my family, so to speak" (2012, 274). Yet both her deep connections with divisive borders and Latin American lineages were very much a part of the occasions of assemblages that formed her. "I must forsake 'home' (comfort zones, both personal and cultural) every day of my life to keep burgeoning into the tree of myself. Luckily, the roots of my tree are deep enough in la cultura Mexicana and strong enough to support a widespread branch system" (2015, 67).

She discovered that the root system of the tree needed expansion and interconnection with other root systems until the defining elements in her life began to shift to an altered nurturance and a new sensibility began to form, a renewed Gloria Anzaldúa who found bridges connecting her with many cultures, some of which she had ignored and others that she had disliked intensely. Through this process a different identity emerged. "My spiritual reality," she said, "I call spiritual *mestizaje*, so I think my philosophy is like a philosophical *mestizaje* where I take from all different cultures—for instance, from the cultures of Latin America, the people of color, and also the Europeans" (2012, 277). Nepantla, as we will see, was a central dimension of Anzaldúa's transformative journey. In an interview included in the fourth addition of *Borderlands/La Frontera*, she explained that she used the term *Nepantla* to refer to the unraveling of what people call "reality." "And I now call it Nepantla, which is a Nahuatl word for the space between two bodies of water, the space between two worlds. It is a limited space, a space where you are not this or that but where you are changing. You haven't got into the new identity yet and haven't left the old identity behind either—you are in a kind of transition. And that is what Nepantla stands for. It is very awkward, uncomfortable and frustrating to be in that Nepantla because you are in the midst of transformation" (2012, 276). She found a new freedom from the very boundaries that defined her as mestiza. It was a freedom that emerged from her undergoing the soul-shaking rigors of nepantla as she found her own identity as chicana-in-question and her world enormously expanded. She wrote her book *Light in the Dark/Luz en lo Oscuro* (2015) in this new sensibility.

Ask yourself, why do we provide a biography for Anzaldúa?

She was so aware that she wrote in and about her bios, her corpos! She referred to her work as autohistoria and autohistoria-teoría, describing her writing as a hybrid genre. "Conectando experiencias personales con realidades sociales results in autohistoria, and theorizing about this activity results in autohistoria-teoría. It's a way of inventing and making knowledge, meaning, and identity through self-inscriptions" (2015, 6). We have spoken of her biographically because her work emerges explicitly from her self-history, her autohistoria, as text and context. Through her autohistoria, she came to understand that body, life, spirit, and beyond in nepantla happenings are inseparable in the sense that they compose one happening.[4] Her philosophical understandings emerged from corporeal experiences. Her autohistoria-teoría comes from the flesh. "For me," she said, "writing is a gesture of the body, a gesture of creativity, a working from the inside out. My feminism is grounded not on incorporeal abstraction but on corporeal realities. The material body is center, and central.

---

4. As James Maffie elaborates, "Nepantla-processes are nepantla-middling or nepantla-reciprocating. They consist of nepantla motion-change ... we need to resist the temptation to *reify* nepantla that comes with treating *nepantla* as a noun designating (or adjective modifying) a state of being, state of affairs, condition, relationship, arrangement, place, or thing. I worry such common translations of *nepantla* as 'the middle' and 'the center' support this temptation, and I urge us to eschew them" (2013, 362).

The body is the ground of thought. The body is a text" (2015, 5). A site of beyond was Anzaldúa's body, her cuerpoespíritu, a dimension of her corporeal happening.

"In nepantla you sense more keenly the overlap between the material and spiritual worlds; you're in both places simultaneously—you glimpse el espíritu—see the body as inspirited. Nepantla is the point of contact where the 'mundane' and the 'numinous' converge" (2015, 128).

ENFLESHED GENEALOGICAL SENSIBILITIES

"I speak and write from what grounds me," Anzaldúa explains, "my physical body, the body of a female, a Chicana tejana, embedded in an indigenous Mexicana culture rich in symbols and metaphors, a body immersed in many cultures, a queer body" (2015, 182). Anzaldúa's genealogical sensibilities are corporeally textured. They are outspokenly enfleshed.

The fleshiness of Anzaldúa's tracing of lineages is neither discursive nor nondiscursive. Hers is a fleshiness that refuses a mind/body division and in that refusal finds resources for transformation. "It dawns on you that *you're not contained by your skin*—you exist outside your body and outside your dream body as well. If the body is energy, is spirit—it doesn't have boundaries. What if you experienced your body expanding to the size of the room, not your soul leaving your body. What if freedom from categories occurs by widening the psyche/body's borders, widening the consciousness that senses self. . . . The last thing you want to uphold is the Cartesian split, but thus far you haven't a clue how to unknot el nudo de cuerpo/mente/alma" (2015, 134–35).

Flesh. An odd word to use for one who desires to unknot in order to entwine—cuerpomentealma. Remembering that the roots of the Old English *flǣsc* include *vita* (life) as well as kin (flesh of my flesh), we can follow Anzaldúa down the path of Coyolxauhqui, beyond the divide of body and mind, with an appreciation of the dynamic and fluid imporings of corporeality.[5] Flesh happens as a *phusis* of becomings.[6] Listening

---

5. In Aztec mythic history, Coyolxauhqui, "Face painted with Bells," is the oldest daughter of Coatlicue and Mixcoatl and is the leader of the Centzon Huitznahuas, the southern star gods. Huitzilopochtli, the Aztec god of war, cut Coyolxauhqui into pieces, throwing her head into the sky, where it continues to reveal itself as the moon.

6. We evoke *phusis* here in its sense of lively upwelling, the arising of things in their imporings, happenings without norms or values.

to Anzaldúa we come to understand that we happen through our fleshy becomings with others and learn to appreciate our mutual vulnerabilities, our viscous porosity. "I listen to waves impact the shore, waves originating from beyond the far edge of the sea, perhaps caused by a storm in a distant corner of the earth or the ice melting in the Arctic. Our actions have ripple effects on all people and the planet's environment. We are accountable for all the wars, all human disasters—none of us are blameless. We ourselves have brought this great turmoil upon ourselves. We are all wounded, but we can connect through the wound that's alienated us from others. When the wound forms a cicatrix, the scar can become a bridge linking people split apart" (2015, 21).

We use the term *enfleshed* to describe Anzaldúa's genealogical sensibilities. *Enfleshed*, with its connotations of giving bodily form, to making real or concrete, signals the deep interconnections of lineages of humans and the institutions they build, from empire to corporation. These lineages carve themselves into the flesh and shape bodies and desires, habits and comportments, attitudes and norms. *Enfleshed* moreover signals that the complex lineages of human enfleshment are deeply intertwined with other lives and ecologies. Enfleshed genealogical sensibilities are attuned to the ways in which centuries of enslavement and conscripted labor not only carved scars into the bodies and psyches of those who were bonded but also molded those who were their oppressors. Such sensibilities understand the ways that the land upon which we walk, the beings with whom we share the landscape, the systems of life of which we are a part are themselves formed by these practices of colonialization, borders forcibly shifted, the scars of plantations etching the flesh of human bodies and the land itself.[7] "How do we survive these wounds and struggles? The path of knowledge requires that we apply what we learn to all our daily activities, to our relationships with ourselves, with others, with the environment, with nature" (2015, 91).

---

7. Anzaldúa's home, the Rio Grande valley, is a complex example of such practices. Its Indigenous populations were colonized first by the Spanish and then again by the United States. In both cases, the lifeways and identities of the Indigenous peoples of the region were subsumed in the prevailing cultures of the conquerors. Even its name, Rio Grande, was an imposition of both waves of colonialization of the Mexican landscape. See, for example, Alejandro Lugo, 2008.

Enfleshed genealogies remember the reciprocal vulnerability of things in the making. Not my body, your body, but the complex imporings of environments, institutions, norms, sensibilities, elements. Anzaldúa's enfleshed genealogical sensibilities call into question the naturalization or normalization of the body, its purity, its wholeness, its stasis. Anzaldúa's autohistoria-teoría manifests the becoming of things. "Nothing is fixed. The pulse of existence, the heart of the universe, is fluid. Identity, like a river, is always changing, always in transition, always in nepantla. Like the river downstream, you're not the same person you were upstream. You begin to define yourself in terms of who you are becoming not who you have been" (2015, 135). Corporeality is a nexus of flux, a temporality beyond identity, normativity, or mastery. Her enfleshed genealogical sensibilities remind us to be attuned to the hinges and folds, the excesses and unthinkables, the ineffables that shape identities. "This perspective from the cracks enables us to reconfigure ourselves as subjects outside the us/them binary.... Our perspective's stability relies on liminality and fluidity" (2015, 82). This is an attunement with beyond.

Granted, Anzaldúa at times talks about her body, but our choice of speaking rather of flesh and enfleshment serves as both a caution and a reminder. Bodies are too often thought of as bounded and autonomous, separate from others yet visible to them. They carry many marks and signs. As we've emphasized in the previous section, Anzaldúa's body carried the effects of a childhood lived in poverty—skin, muscles, and bones affected by long days in the fields, by the chemicals used to kill unwanted organisms and to accelerate the growth of others seeping through her pores and affecting her health. While we do not wish to obscure such bodily effects or the ways in which visible identities are shaped and impacted by social norms, we follow Anzaldúa's path and seek to trouble the habits of ossification that can happen when bodies are thought of as matter separate from mind or spirit, or when materiality is seen as separate from discourse, or when culture is seen as bifurcated from nature.

Enfleshed in our usage evokes the viscous porosity through which skin is not simply a barrier but also an opening to others, to those who would caress us as well as those who would wound us. Anzaldúa's attunement to the fleshiness of writing permeates her texts. "Everything that writers do—whether it's fictions or images—has to go through the body. Readers are also affected physically. Every word you read hits you physiologically—your blood pressure changes, your heart beat changes; your cells, your bones, your muscles are moved by a beautiful poem, a tragic episode" (2000, 77). Whether it be the words on the page or the air that we breathe, we live and die because of our openings to the world. We *are* because of complex exchanges of flesh—food, water, air, pesticides, heavy metals. While we might think of ourselves as "spacious, singing flesh" (Cixous 1976, 889) attuned to the ways our openness permits joy and wonder, Anzaldúa's writings are a reminder that our openness can also make us open to pain and to despair. We are all these happenings and more. Our flesh is shaped not only by the materiality of earth, air, fire, and water but also by legacies of lineages, such as those that associate brown skin with inferiority, queerness with abnormality, femaleness with subservience. And these same lineages not only shape individuals and their interrelations, they give flesh to the institutions that regulate us and materialize in how we transfigure the flesh of the world.

Anzaldúa's enfleshed genealogical sensibilities offer a persistent reminder of the anonymous agency of such materializations. A becoming that is always influenced by, infused with, the particularity of lineages. In *Borderlands/La Frontera*, she reminds us that "the work of the *mestiza* consciousness is to break down the subject-object duality that keeps her a prisoner and to show in the flesh and through the images in her work how duality is transcended" (1987, 80). Flesh is neither passive nor immutable, but alive (*vita*) in relationality and exchanges. Attuned to her body, Anzaldúa is reminded of her interfusions with the bodies of others and with the environment; she is reminded that her body is neither singular nor fixed but in a constant flow of relationality. "Our bodies are geographies of selves made up of diverse, bordering, and overlapping 'countries.' We're each composed of information, billions of bits of cultural knowledge superimposing many different categories of experience. Like a map with colored web lines of rivers, highways, lakes, towns, and other landscape features en donde pasan y cruzan las cosas, we are 'marked.' Life's whip makes welts and thin silver scars on our backs; our genetic code digs creases and tracks on our flesh. As our bodies interact with internal and external, real and virtual, past and present environments, people, and objects around us, we weave (tejemos), and are woven into, our identities.

Identity, as consciously and unconsciously created, is always in process—self—interacting with different—communities and worlds. Identity is relational" (2015, 69).

Anzaldúa's enfleshed genealogical sensibilities inform the movements of her writing and enable her to create new possibilities for enfleshment, new enactments of corporeality. "In our very flesh, (r)evolution works out the clash of cultures. It makes us crazy constantly, but if the center holds, we've made some kind of evolutionary step forward. *Nuestra alma el trabajo*, the opus, the great alchemical work; spiritual *mestizaje*, a 'morphogenesis,' an inevitable unfolding. We have become the quickening serpent movement" (1987, 81).

Speaking in tongues, Anzaldúa reminds us of the ever-shifting relation between affect and cognition, of ethos and episteme, of habits of thought and habits of action. Knowledge is of and from the flesh. "Back on the timber bridge, the wind shifts, whipping your hair away from your eyes. La Llorona's wail rises, urging you to pay heed. All seven ojos de luz blink 'on.' Your body trembles as a new knowing slithers up like a snake, stirring you out of your stupor. You raise your head and look around. Following the railroad tracks to the horizon, you note the stages of your life, the turning points, the rips in your life's fabric. Gradually the pain and the grief force you to face your situation, the daily issues of living laid bare.... As your perception shifts, your emotions shift—you gain a new understanding.... By using these feelings as tools or grist for the mill, you move through fear, anxiety, and anger, and blast into another reality. But transforming habitual feelings is the hardest thing you've ever attempted" (2015, 131). Embodiment, affect, spirituality, cognition happen together. Cuerpomentealma. Anzaldúa reminds us so forcefully that we cannot simply think our way out of oppressive systems. While oppressive institutions, beliefs, norms, practices color our thoughts and infuse our concepts, they also leak into our affects and attunements—anger and anxiety, hope and fear—they are chiseled into our flesh and mold los espíritus. When we are attuned to Anzaldúa's reminders we can begin to carve bone and create our own face, our own heart.

Anzaldúa reminds us of the limits of cognition and of the deep attunements in-between, beyond cognition: the imporings, each seeping into the others, of affect and concept, cultural attunements and institutional inclinations, episteme and norms, multiple ancient lineages with modern ones. The anonymous agency of this imporing gives shape to the order of things and carries us with it, giving rise to habits of thought and fueling habituated actions, affective dispositions, and desires. Neither mine nor yours, but effected through what Foucault called the dynamic "positive unconscious of knowledge" (Foucault 1973c, xi). Forms of feeling, thinking, knowing, attending, inhabiting, acting happen in the space of sensibilities. They inform not only what and how we know but what we desire and hold good.

Anzaldúa helps us to see the corporeal dimension of beyond, to appreciate that we must become undone in every way—conceptually, affectively, habitually, passionately—in order to give rise to new sensibilities. As Anzaldúa describes it: "You shed your former bodymind and its outworn story like a snake its skin. Releasing traumas of the past frees up energy, allowing you to be receptive to the soul's voice and guidance. Taking a deep breath, you close your eyes and call back tu alma—from people, ideas, perceptions, and events you've surrendered it to. You sense parts of your soul return to your body. Another inhalation, more tendrils of spirit reenter the places where it went missing. The lost pieces draw to you like filaments to a magnet. With a tender newly formed sense of self you stand, wobbly. Sensing los espíritus all around, you face east, the direction of the visionary, offering a dream of the possible. Challenging the old self's orthodoxy is never enough; you must submit a sketch of an alternative self. As a modern-day Coyolxauhqui, you search for an account that encapsulates your life, and finding no ready-made story, you trust her light in the darkness to help you bring forth (from remnants of the old personal/collective autohistoria) a new personal myth" (2015, 139).

Colonial lineages, heteronormative histories, androcentric inheritances infuse our habits of thought. Indeed, they permeate our flesh in myriad ways. They infuse what disgusts us as well as what pleasures us, inform whom we love and whom we hate. They give rise to expectations, senses of life's purpose, as well as to hope and despair. They are carved into the flesh of institutions as well, informing how we structure business practices or design prisons or deploy militaries. While giving voice to silenced experiences is certainly an important step, one we find throughout Anzaldúa's corpus, her writings are designed to create and transform.

Her writings are performative. They are designed to incite us, to bring us creatively, transformatively to our senses. A key movement of her creativity is beyond. Nepantla.

NEPANTLA

"I call the space where I struggle with my creations 'nepantla.' Nepantla is the place where my cultural and personal codes clash, where I come up against the world's dictates, where these different worlds coalesce in my writing. I am conscious of various nepantlas—linguistic, geographical, gender, sexual, historical, cultural, political, social—when I write. Nepantla is the point of contact y el lugar between worlds—between imagination and physical existence, between ordinary and nonordinary (spirit) realities. Nepantla concerns automatically infuse my writing: I don't have to *will* myself to deal with these particular points; these nepantlas inhabit me and inevitably surface in whatever I'm writing. Nepantlas are places of constant tension, where the missing or absent pieces can be summoned back, where transformation and healing may be possible, where wholeness is just out of reach but seems attainable" (2015, 2).

The many profound and pre-reflective influences flowing in Anzaldúa's life were harbored in a spiritual space that had its specificity by virtue of the often conflicting and oppositional imporing effects of those influences. Nepantla, an assemblage of different dynamic formations of cuerpomentealma, of different, often ancient and often contemporary cultures (such as the conflicts of Mexican, Anglo, and Indigenous cultures that Anzaldúa experienced). Nepantla, a zone of questionability where sensibilities—that is, where basic senses of meaning, identity, and purpose—come into unresolved conflict. Nepantla, a dimension beyond good/evil, true/false, male/female, I/they.

Nepantla is for Anzaldúa a space where she experienced not in certainty but in question the basic ideas, tenets, and identities inherited from her families, languages, education, and different but nonetheless internalized cultures that formed the rhizome-like roots of, in Anzaldúa's words, her tree of life. Nepantla is a dimension of happening where people struggle to find equilibrium between the outer expression of change and their inner relationships with it, a dimension where they do not know with clarity who they are or are becoming. In this dimension, what counts in one's life falls apart without the texture of identity. A person is lost and aware of unsayables at the same time. Or we could say that the processes of schematized time, its reliable structures, are suspended in the happening of nepantla processes, in the transpiring of concrescence. Crucial, liminal, like an obscure threshold, something other than time or meaning happens in the processes of nepantla. It is a dimension without schema or meaning, a dynamic occasion beyond. The happening of beyond, of nepantla, is the occasion of a central movement in Anzaldúa's philosophical reflections.

Many images circulate in the work of Anzaldúa. They are imaginal movements to new attunements. She returns time and time again to borders, a liminal space for the creation of what she called a new mythos, a self-transformation, that will change "the way we perceive reality, the way we see ourselves, and the way we behave" (1987, 80). The space of nepantla becomes a central dimension of her spiritual activism. As she explains, "Bridges are thresholds to other realities, archetypal, primal symbols of shifting consciousness. They are passageways, conduits, and connectors that connote transitioning, crossing borders, and changing perspectives. Bridges span liminal (threshold) spaces between worlds, spaces I call nepantla, a Nahuatl word meaning tierra entre medio. Transformations occur in this in-between space, an unstable, unpredictable, precarious, always-in-transition space lacking clear boundaries. Nepantla es tierra desconocida, and living in this liminal zone means being in a constant state of displacement—an uncomfortable, even alarming feeling" (Anzaldúa and Keating 2002, 1). Anzaldúa's exquisite attentiveness to lineages, to the resonances of their vibrating tensions and contradictions, attuned her to dimensions of beyond. "Perceiving something from two different angles creates a split in awareness that can lead to the ability to control perception, to balance contemporary society's worldview with the nonordinary worldview, and to move between them to a space that simultaneously exists and does not exist. I call entering this realm 'nepantla'—the Nahuatl word for an in-between space, el lugar entre medio. Nepantla, palabra indígena: un concepto que se refiere a un lugar no-lugar" (2015, 28). The no-place of nepantla was her transformatory core.

Bridges reflect the in-between movement from and to the in-between of nepantla. *Light in the Dark/Luz en lo Oscuro* was Anzaldúa's story of "the thresholds between worlds" that she experienced following what she calls the path of conocimiento.[8] Conocimiento, with its intricate enfoldings of affectcognition, fleshspirit, cuerpomentealma, is a complex journeying within the overlapping worlds of sense that she inhabits, worlds that emerge from complex and often conflicting lineages—American and Spanish and Mexican, conqueror and conquered, Aztec and Christian, White and Brown. These lineages carry with them complex weaves of borders, dividing in their different ways mind from body, rationality from spirituality, culture from nature, humans from environments. Anzaldúa's path is a reminder to us all of the complexity of lineages, of lifeways, of institutions, of philosophies. And of all the borders within and between them. For we are, each of us, a weave of lineages, of borderlands, that often discordantly collide. We share many lineages with each of you, but our differences are part of the weave as well. Our lineages entwine in ever-shifting configurations of differences, none of which is ever all-encompassing. Rather than choose one side over another or get caught up by a sense of chaos, becoming open to the space of the in-between can attune us to beyond, to nepantla. "Nepantla is the site of transformation, the place where different perspectives come into conflict and where you question the basic ideas, tenets, and identities inherited from your family, your education, and your different culture" (2015, 127).

Our lineages in all their complexity and the ever-changing warp and woof of their weave provide the bridges, the in-between spaces for the movement beyond our familiar lifeways. What some of the lineages exclude, silence, oppress are sites for resistance. But the profusion of lineages also provides openings to possibilities for other lifeways. Their fault lines and cracks serve as thresholds to such possibilities. A threshold is a place of porosity, a happening of endingbeginning, of unmakingmaking. A place in which we might experience the fluidity of porous differences. Thresholds are moments of passing through that can transform us and in which we can be open to new thresholds. Some thresholds are thrust upon

---

8. Anzaldúa's understanding of conocimiento, which we expand upon below, encompasses but goes beyond the traditional Western conception of knowledge. It is robustly embodied and happens through "opening all your senses, consciously inhabiting your body" (2015, 120).

us. Others we choose to inhabit. Each of us faces thresholds. The question is how we attend to their liminal force.

Anzaldúa's response in *Light in the Dark/Luz en lo Oscuro* is to urge us to learn to dwell in these liminalities, to become nepantleras. Nepantleras are those who "trouble the nos/otras division," Anzaldúa explains, "by living on the slash between 'us' and 'others.'" Nepantleras live in fluidity and recognize "that we're all complicit in the existing power structures, that we must deal with conflictive as well as connectionist relations within and among various groups." Moreover, "las nepantleras upset our cultures' foundations and disturb the concepts structuring their realities. Las nepantleras nurture psychological, social, and spiritual metamorphosis" (2015, 82–83). The cracks between worlds, the many tensions and discontinuities of our complex lineages, are thresholds of possibility where "the binaries of colored/white, female/male, mind/body are collapsing" (2015, 119). These are liminal, in-between places where we are neither oppressor nor oppressed. Where we are beyond. Nepantla. A site of transformation, transition, and transposition. The journey Anzaldúa calls for and to which she is called has neither telos nor resolution. We are, in this journey, in continuous processes of unfolding, of becomings.

We, you and I, write, live, experience with and through complex lineages and sensibilities, but not all of us inhabit/are inhabited by the same weave. Some of us, like Anzaldúa, carry complex lineages that weave worlds of sense from non-Western, Western, and Indigenous sensibilities. "I was born and live in that in-between space, nepantla, the borderlands. Hay muchas razas running in my veins, mescladas dentro de mi, otras culturas that my body lives in and out of. Mi cuerpo vive dentro y fuera de otras culturas, and *a white man* who constantly whispers, 'Assimilate, you're not good enough,' and measures me according to white standards. *For me, being Chicana or any other single identity marker is not enough—is not my total self.* It is only one of my multiple identities." The differences in our lineages can be a source of tension, but they can also be a path beyond if we are willing to live artfully on the slash in-between. "Along with other border gente, it is at this site and time, en este tiempo y lugar where and when, *I help co-create my identity* con mi arte" (2015, 64). Identity is like a river, a flow, a becoming that is in a constant state of flux. Attunement to our complex lineages can serve as a reminder of the porosity and complexity of what we often take as unchangeable—race or gender or sex or sexuality. Attunement to the unthinkable.

We are, none of us, without the whispering of multiple lineages. But how do we listen? How can we attend to the often-subtle differences? How do we become open to unsayables? Is there a *poiesis* of disclosive indirectness? The query at the heart of this book and the question we hear resonating in Anzaldúa's writings is, *how* do we find ourselves beyond the dominant lineages in our identities and beyond normalities and enter into the art of self-transformation?

THE COYOLXAUHQUI IMPERATIVE

For Anzaldúa, the happening of self-transformation is a difficult, often pain-filled process. It involves "falling apart," the dimension of nepantla in which formations of one's identity and sense of self are impacted and shaken until they disintegrate, pull apart. Falling apart is a dismemberment that opens one to the possibility of new happenings of the complex weave of our lineages, openings to transfigurations and reconstructions of identity. A happening where we might experience the unthinkable. "To re-image identity in new ways requires that we change the focus of the lens trained on our faces and shift our perceptions. It requires letting go of the old identifications and behaviors. The who-we-are is currently undergoing disintegration and reconstruction, pulled apart, dismembered, then reconstructed—a process I envision symbolized by Coyolxauhqui" (2015, 74).

Transformations, Anzaldúa reminds us, are a form of crisis; they are difficult, taxing experiences. "En este lugar we fall into chaos, fear of the unknown, and are forced to take up the task of self-redefinition. In nepantla we undergo the anguish of changing our perspectives and crossing a series of cruz calles, junctures, and thresholds, some leading to a different way of relating to people and surroundings and others to the creation of a new world" (2015, 17). Nepantla is a dimension in which basic senses of meaning, identity, norms, purpose fall apart. It is a happening in which one does not know with clarity who they are or who they are becoming. It is a frightening, paradoxical time, for we can only change if we can see the parts of ourselves that make us tremble. "Seeing through these cracks makes you uncomfortable because it reveals aspects of yourself (shadow beasts) you don't want to own. Admitting your darker aspects allows you to break out of your self-imposed prison. But it will cost you" (2015, 132).

Anzaldúa describes the experience of nepantla as one in which the authority of her primary self-identity fades as she becomes open to the flood of multiple lineages and their influences. The porosity of borders intensifies as who-she-is steps, voluntarily or not, aside and grants—concedes—the in-pouring of the often obscure, seemingly infinite reach of lineages and sensibilities. Time as she might count it fades as she moves into untimely processes that give rise to occasions of transformation and transmutation in the flow of shifting lineages. She describes such processes as "dwelling in liminalities" and reminds us that "the Coyolxauhqui imperative is an ongoing process of making and unmaking. There is never any resolution, just the process of healing" (2015, 71, 20).

Falling apart is a key element of Anzaldúa's response to oppression. As she explained: "Knowing that something in you, or of you, must die before something else can be born, you throw your old self onto the ritual pyre, a passage by fire. In relinquishing your old self, you realize that some aspects of who you are—identities people have imposed on you as a woman of color and that you have internalized—are also made up. Identity becomes a cage you reinforce and double-lock yourself into. The life you thought inevitable, unalterable, and fixed in some foundational reality is smoke" (2015, 138).

The process of falling apart, of being wounded, Anzaldúa tells us, is a painful process of being dismembered, being torn asunder. It is where the wounding occurs like fire that consumes the very sensibility of her life. Through this untimely process of disintegration and reintegration of lineages, wounding can issue in a rebirth of cuerpomentealma, new sensibilities. She frequently emphasizes that these processes are outside her control. Her coemergent experience of "the healing [that] occurs in disintegration" and the birthing of new sensibilities are parts of an assemblage of mutating processes over which she has no ascendency in the self she thinks of as her own (2015, 29). She can fight the darkness and disintegration. Or she can affirm the wounds and begin a process of reconciliation with the disintegration. The stance she takes will have crucial effects on her forming, changing identity. But the ancient and deeply rooted symbols and images have lives of their own in nepantla. The happenings of the transformation are not hers to control.

These wounds, if affirmed, can become bridges that allow changes of attitude, increased alertness to the many often-conflicting dimensions of what is happening, or inclinations toward healing conciliation. In her transforming sensibilities, Anzaldúa might find that conciliatory attitudes emerge in the wounds where anger and resentments have flared, in, for example, her connections with White women and men whose actions and attitudes range from well-intentioned but insensitive points of view to aggressive, oppressive actions. She might become more alert to people in countries that she previously ignored. She might become more nuanced in her awareness of the legacies of the Spanish conquistadores who left a heritage of cruel oppression, slavery, erasure of Indigenous cultures, and genocide as well as cultures that formed the language and informed many of the spiritual practices in Latin American societies and cultures. Will she have increased compassion for those who have ignorantly lost touch with the powerful influences available in ancient Indigenous traditions and symbols? Is such compassion one motivation for writing *Light in the Dark/Luz en lo Oscuro*?

We have said that Anzaldúa's account of nepantla and her experiences of it coemerge and that *nepantla* symbolizes a worldly, corporealspiritual event. In some instances, however, the language sounds as though she is speaking of an intensely private event. At other times, she says, "It's not race, gender, class, sexuality, or any single aspect of the self that determines identity but the interaction of all these aspects plus as yet unnamed features. We discover, uncover, create our identities as we interrelate with others and our alrededores/surroundings. *Identity grows out of our interactions, and we strategically reinvent ourselves to accommodate our exchanges.* Identity is an ongoing story, one that changes with each telling, one we revise at each way station, each stop, in our viaje de la vida (life's journey).... We must challenge the present concepts, creating frameworks that span the fissures among us and link us in a series of interconnected webs (telarañas)" (2015, 75; emphasis added). In other words, she finds that both falling apart and, as we shall see, reconstitution take place in her life of interconnected webs (telarañas) and interactions with both human and nonhuman others. She is both alone in her own event (no one can have her experiences; no one can live her life for her) and thoroughly interconnected with others and her surroundings. *She* becomes an occasion of many, many interactions. She knows that shifting sensibilities must come from outside as well as within the system. As she transforms, she affects and is affected by the world around her in new ways. Perhaps even her anger will change and a new perception of such borders as body/mind, woman/man, Mestiza/American will shift in a new openness to new relationships that remove the slash nos/otras if, as she says in *Borderlands*, we meet halfway. If you and we have the courage to become nepantleras and live on the slashes. If we are willing to navigate the cracks between worlds, perhaps the boundaries of ordinary clarity will seem relative and limited, sometimes protective and overassured. Perhaps in this fiery, smoky liminality a transformed sensibility will emerge that will effect changes in our interconnected world. And through that imporing emergence, this happening of beyond, perhaps new concepts, new ways of thinking, inhabiting, seeing, experiencing will materialize.

For Anzaldúa the process begins with words.

GESTURES OF THE FLESH: LINEAGES, WRITING, AND CUERPOESPÍRITU

"For me," Anzaldúa says, "writing begins with the impulse to push boundaries, to shape ideas, images, and words that travel through the body and echo in the mind into something that has never existed. The writing process is the same mysterious process that we use to make the world" (2015, 5). How does that writing process work? How can we create with words? How can something that is beyond the boundaries of sense be given form through writing? Writing, she says, begins with the impulse to push boundaries. This impulse to push boundaries initially arises from beyond the bounded identity. Anzaldúa refers to this dimension as "a vague and undetermined place created by the emotional residue of an unnatural boundary" (1987, 3). The impulse forms in the wounds of falling apart as borders that have been constructed to hold at bay many lineages and influences are breached. The fissures that open up in the place of borders give rise to complex interplays of lineages with their assemblages of widely diverse sensibilities and different ways of living. In other words, the impulse to push boundaries and to shape new images and words emerges in the dynamic, interfusing impacts of the lineages that Anzaldúa experienced as her familiar self and world fell apart.

We are speaking of that strange phenomenon that we have found in other of our featured philosophers: dimensions of beyond, dimensions of processes without schemas can arouse dispositions that are inclined to putting in question all types of normativities that we hold as though they were *not* mortal. Beyond can have the further effects of prompting individuals to free themselves from parochial habits of unexamined self-restrictions—of making those restrictions optional—and of opening new prospects for different options that come with urges to imagine the world differently, to push boundaries, and, as Anzaldúa says, to shape ideas, images, and words that travel as vague imaginal desires through the body. Beyond can engender a physical desire to form things that have never existed inclusive, especially for Anzaldúa, of one's own character and sense of self. The human capacity to make images and words, the reflective imagination, has in Anzaldúa's experience a unique power of connecting with the influences of shifting, mutating lineages and their liminal processes. Attuned to that liminality, perhaps one can become attentive to unsayable dimensions of experience that, in their indirection, provide entryways to transformed lifeways. Lifeways that are themselves always lively infusions of many lineages, many happenings of cuerpoespíritu.

Cuerpoespíritu: the inseparability of what Anzaldúa calls the spirit world and the natural world and of the non-voluntary forces that play significant parts in her self-transformation. In order to do justice to her understanding of cuerpoespíritu, we have spoken of lineages, sensibilities, occasions, assemblages, and processes. These concepts have the reach and the allowance of pre-reflective depths that we find necessary to understand Anzaldúa's experiences. They also function well in relation to the unbounded chaos of nepantla. As one direct example of what we mean, consider her statement: "It is at this site and time, en este tiempo y lugar where and when, *I help co-create my identity* con mi arte. Neither art nor a person's identity is an entirely willed activity. Other forces influence, impact, and construct our desires—including the unconscious and collective unconscious forces and residues of those that came before us, our ancient ancestors" (2015, 64). Deploying our concepts, we would alter and extend this passage in the following manner: Other forces influence, impact, and construct our desires. These forces include the mutating lineages and sensibilities that are infused with inheritances from our ancestors and that emerge in the places (lugares) where borders have been constructed to hold them at bay.

As such borders are breached in the workings of Anzaldúa's border arte imagination, the fissures give rise to complex occasions of mutating lineages with their assemblages of multiple inheritances and sensibilities. These infusions of lineages happen without order, flooding Anzaldúa's familiar world, opening her to the possibility of new happenings of identity.

We believe that Anzaldúa found her challenge to write in her cuerpoespíritu—her cuerpoespíritu that she did *not have* so much as it, in its vast reach, had her. "Nepantla concerns automatically infuse my writing: I don't have to *will* myself to deal with the particular points; these nepantlas inhabit me and inevitably surface in whatever I'm writing.... It is the writing that 'writes' me. I 'read' and 'speak' myself into being. Writing is the site where I critique reality, identity, language, and dominant culture's representation and ideological control" (2015, 2–3). We understand Anzaldúa's writing as an upwelling, a *poiesis* in which something new emerges. And in this emergence, the world we are of and we shift. Perhaps if we attend carefully to the resonance of her words, we will be taken up in their unruly creative power such that the force of her writing, and perhaps ours, writes us. We, you and we, shift, and as we shift, reality shifts.

We have asked before, how can we critique identity, language, or norms when the dominant culture's representation and ideological control infuse our minds, hearts, words, desires? Anzaldúa's texts offer a light in the darkness, a *poiesis*, an attunement to mundo neuvo, to the processes of beyond. "Today with the sea's scent rising up and the cypress's fragrance wafting down, I ask the tree for an inspiration. I ask it to help me imagine and open to el cenote, that underground well of memories and shamanic images ... I must think in images, hunt for symbols, and engage in conceptual interpretations of those images—that is, I must translate images as symbols for concepts and ideas. I must do it not by controlling the images as my conscious mind wants but by surrendering to them and letting them guide me" (2015, 24–25). *Poiesis*, extended authorship, a bringing forth beyond—are those possibilities for those of us subjected by academic normalization? How do "the lechuza eyes of your naguala open, rousing you from the trance of hyper-rationality induced by higher education?" (2015, 135).⁹ How do we find our cenote sagrado, our divine well of transformation? ¹⁰

BORDER ARTE CONOCIMIENTOS

Recognizing the many lineages that thread through her bodymindspirit, her cuerpoespíritu, Anzaldúa writes toward a becoming. "Soy la que escribe y se escribe/I am the one who writes and who is being written" (2015, 3). Writing functions for her as a path in-between, a way to give voice to silenced lineages. "I 'speak in tongues'" she tells us, "understand the languages, emotions, thoughts, fantasies of the various sub-personalities inhabiting me and the various grounds they speak from. To do so, I must figure out which person (I, she, you, we, them, they), which tense (present, past, future), which language and register, and which voice or style to speak from. Identity formation (which involves 'reading' and 'writing' oneself and the world) is an alchemical process that synthesizes the dualities, contradictions, and perspectives from these different selves and worlds" (2015, 3).

We are, none of us, without the whispering of multiple lineages. In-between those lineages are fissures, sites of rupture that can create a disturbance, a movement beyond. But how do we listen? How can we attend to the often-subtle differences? How do we find ourselves beyond the dominant lineages in our identities and normalities and enter into the art of self-transformation?

Anzaldúa beckons with conocimiento, with its movement beyond. "Beyond the subject-object divide, a way of knowing and acting on ese saber you call 'conocimiento'" (2015, 119). Conocimiento is a form of

---

9. Lechuza is an owl. *Naguala* is a Nahuatl term for a magician or for a human who has the power to transform either spiritually or physically into an animal form, a trickster.

10. *Cenote sagrado* is located in the northern Yucatán Peninsula in the Mayan city of Chickén Itzá. It was a site of great significance to the Mayans. *Cenote sagrado* is a formation, a deep pit that provides connections to subterranean water bodies, an entryway to *Xibalbá*, the Mayan underworld.

knowingacting that goes beyond divisions such as reason/spirituality, mental/bodily, theory/activism, self/other. We have seen that in Anzaldúa's experience, we, each of us, are extended occasions of all manner of lineages. We are fleshy assemblages, certainly material and tangible, but also at once spiritualimaginal. Cuerpomentealma. What Anzaldúa comes to understand is that removing the slashes is a path of conocimiento: "Spirit and mind, soul and body, are one, and together they perceive a reality greater than the vision experienced in the ordinary world" (2015, 24). The imaginal acts can be corporeally affective and, for a small example, change the way people breathe, as in an exciting dream, or, for a very different kind of example, allow other imaginal beings to speak as one cannot speak to one's self. They can transform people's being in the world, the sensibilities that engender their inclinations, values, and meanings. The silent language of spiritualimaginal processes is one of symbols, images, and affective intuitions—liminal figurations and senses outside the restrictions of grammar, good sense, rationality, or analysis. That means, for Anzaldúa, outside the human world. The power of imagination links with inhuman regions in the human cuerpoespíritu, occasions of strange processes in assembled lineages of symbols, images, and unspeakable dimensions of language. For, as we have seen, the roots of human life go deeper than human life, far deeper than a person's identity; those roots are indifferent to personhood and to their effects on the identities that they nourish or destroy. Anzaldúa's experiences are performances of these excesses in her own life, and the performances brought her into a new sense of kinship in the world: "Today I walk to the ocean, to my favorite tree, what I call la Virgen's tree. Most days, I put my arms around the tree and we have una 'platica' (talk), but today I straddle and stretch out on la Virgen's gnarly protruding roots, thick as a horse's back, absorbing the tree's energy, in kinship with it. Al espíritu del árbol I pray for strength, energy, and clarity to fuel este trabajo artistico. In return le hago una promesa: to offer it un milagrito" (2015, 67).

Conocimiento is a key component of Anzaldúa's enfleshed genealogical sensibility. It is an imporing of mental, emotional, instinctive, imaginal, spiritual, bodily awareness that can give rise to subversive knowledges that disrupt conventional ways of understanding. Conocimiento, Anzaldúa tells us, "comes from opening all your senses, consciously inhabiting your body and decoding its symptoms.... Attention is multileveled and includes your surroundings, bodily sensations and responses, intuitive takes and emotional reactions to other people and theirs to you, and, most important, the images your imagination creates—images connecting all tiers of information and their data. Breaking out of your mental and emotional prison and deepening the range of perception enables you to link inner reflection and vision—the mental, emotional, instinctive, imaginal, spiritual, and subtle bodily awareness—with social, political action and lived experiences to generate subversive knowledge" (2015, 120). Conocimientos, the flashes of insight, the new attunements, the affective shifts come from all our senses and are "reached via creative acts—writing, art-making, dancing, healing, teaching, meditation, and spiritual activism—both mental and somatic" (2015, 119).

Anzaldúa's conocimiento is a happening across many borderlands. The United States and Mexico, certainly, but always also the many borderlands of sex and sexuality, of bodily ability and disability, of spirituality, of culture. To emphasize only one, a Chicana theorist, or even some, a Chicana queer theorist, of Anzaldúa's borderlands is to fail to appreciate the complexity of her thought and the fluidity of her conception of self. "As a *mestiza* I have no country, my homeland cast me out; yet all countries are mine because I am every woman's sister or potential lover. (As a lesbian I have no race, my own people disclaim me; but I am all races because there is the queer of me in all races.) I am cultureless because, as a feminist, I challenge the collective cultural/religious male-derived beliefs of Indo-Hispanics and Anglos; yet I am cultured because I am participating in the creation of yet another culture, a new story to explain the world and our participation in it, a new value system with images and symbols that connect us to each other and to the planet. *Soy un amasamiento*, I am an act of kneading, of uniting and joining that not only has produced both a creature of darkness and a creature of light, but also a creature that questions the definition of light and dark and gives them new meanings" (1987, 80–81).

One practice of conocimiento is what Anzaldúa called *border arte*: the practice of transformative becoming through creative attunements in our myriad lineages. The border artist, she tells us, "connects to that nepantla state of transition between time periods, connects to the border between cultures"; they "are engaged in 'reading' that nepantla, that border, and that cenote" (2015, 55). Border artists live *in* the border, the in-between, and from that position, trouble the slash that divides and separates. "Transformations occur in this in-between space, an unstable, unpredictable, precarious, always-in-transition space lacking clear boundaries" (Anzaldúa and Keating 2002, 1). This troubling creativity is attuned with beyond. From this liminal, unbounded domain, border artists might find a path to new ways of thinking, feeling, desiring, inhabiting. "We enter the silence, go inward, attend to feelings and to that inner cenote—the site of imagination, the creative reservoir where earth, female, and water energies merge. We surrender to the rhythm and the grace of our artworks. Through our artworks we cross the border into other subjective levels of awareness, shift into different and new terrains of mestizaje" (2015, 58).

The practice of border arte is a reminder that we cannot simply reason our way out of oppression. Border arte can incite a critical reassessment of the very categories of thought. In those instances, people begin to experience how certain lifeways are rendered nonsense through dominant sensemaking. People can then come to understand how our very desires, even those for truth and justice, are woven outof threads that bind us to cruel and erratic practices. By representing other worlds of sense—other sensibilities—border arte can help us recall marginalized lifeways. It can provide us with different ways of seeing and bodying forward. Border arte can catalyze new ways of thinking, being, desiring, inhabiting that resist and transform oppression. Anzaldúa emphasized the link between art and creation, *poiesis* and political transformation. Unveiling through new disclosures, "la nepantlera, artista-activista, with consencia de mestiza offers an alternative self. As intermediaries between various mundos, las nepantleras 'speak in tongues'—grasp the thoughts, emotions, languages, and perspectives associated with varying individual and cultural positions" (2015, 82).

Through our artworks we can articulate our attunements with beyond. Or is it that the happening of beyond shines through our artworks? How do we listen to the images that speak to and through us? For Anzaldúa, it does not happen in a flash of blinding inspiration. It is in the continuous movement of the stirring of our borders, of attunements to their fissures, to the unsayables that opens us to change. Anzaldúa's border arte conocimientos often return to narratives of identity, to the need to continuously re-vision them and create together anew:

>   And as I grew   you hacked away
>   at the pieces   of me   that   were different...
>   Oh,   it was hard,
>   Raza   to cleave flesh from flesh   I risked
>   us both   bleeding to death...
>   there's no-
>   thing more you can chop off   or graft on me that
>   will change my soul.   I remain who I am, multiple
>   and one   of the herd, yet not of it. (1987, 173)

Speaking of her writing process, she explains that she writes in ways to engage readers in the processes of questioning their "unconscious values, views, and assumptions about reality, about culture, about everything." To push against the boundaries of what is acceptable and traditional, she developed a border arte style in which "there are lots of gaps between passages—its style is elliptical and spiral." She writes in such a way that "the reader has to fill in a lot of the gaps" so that the meaning of the arte is neither in the text, nor in the author's intent, nor in the reader, but rather in the anonymous agency in-between where reader, writer, text coemerge, cocreate, co-alter (Anzaldúa and Keating, 2009, 188–90).

"Decolonizing reality," Anzaldúa reminds us, "consists of unlearning consensual 'reality,' of seeing through reality's roles and descriptions.... To change or reinvent reality, you engage the facultad of your imagination. You must interrupt or suspend the conscious 'I' that reminds you of your history and your beliefs because these reminders tie you to certain notions of reality and behavior" (2015, 44). In *Borderlands/La Frontera*, Anzaldúa describes la facultad as "the capacity to see in surface phenomena the meaning of deeper realities, to see the deep structure below the surface." She tells us that "it is an instant 'sensing,' a quick perception arrived at without conscious reasoning. It is an acute awareness mediated by the part of the psyche that does not speak, that communicates in images and symbols which are the faces of feelings, that is, behind which feelings reside/hide. The one possessing this sensitivity is excruciatingly alive to the world" (1987, 38). Furthermore, la facultad involves the capacity for shape-changing form and identity. In her writings and imaginings la facultad includes the ability to accommodate mutually exclusive, discontinuous, and inconsistent worlds. It allows one to hear and perhaps even to become "that voice at the edge of things" (1987, 50).

"Art and la frontera intersect in a liminal space where border people, especially artists, live in a state of nepantla" (2015, 56). Border arte engages imagination in ways that can create openings to dimensions beyond and sets to stirring those borders that have seemed so stable, so intractable. Identities, values, lifeways, normativities that seemed so "inevitable, unalterable, and fixed" become smoke (2015, 138). Border arte can arouse dispositions that are inclined to trouble all sorts of borders. In the imporing, shifting borders, we might become aware of silences that shift our sensibilities and enable us to begin to cultivate new desires, habits, lifeways. "The border artist constantly reinvents her/himself. Through art s/he is able to re-read, reinterpret, re-envision, and reconstruct her/his culture's present as well as its past" (Anzaldúa and Keating 2009, 183).

Anzaldúa's mestizaje sensibility was a central element of her continuous self-reinvention. She illustrates this strategy of resistance and transformation in her account of redefining herself: "Tussling con remolinos (whirlwinds) of different belief systems builds the muscles of mestiza consciousness, enabling it to stretch. Being Chicana (Indigenous, Mexican, Basque, Spanish, Berber Arab, Gypsy) is no longer enough; being female, woman of color, patlache (queer) no longer suffices. Your resistance to identity boxes leads you to a different tribe, a different story (of mestizaje) enabling you to rethink yourself in more global-spiritual terms instead of conventional categories of color, class, career. It calls you to retribalize your identity to a more inclusive one, redefining what it means to be una Mexicana de este lado, an American in the U.S., a citizen of the world, classifications reflecting an emerging planetary culture. In this narrative, national boundaries dividing us from the 'others' (nos/otras) are porous and the cracks between worlds serve as gateways" (2015, 141).

Border artists recognize the myriad types of borders. Some borders demarcate countries and cultures. Others divide people into genders. Others create gulfs between reason and emotion. Yet others separate humans from ecosystems. Border artists are skilled at bridging many types of borders and guard against the "psychological propensity to set up orders of rank" (Nietzsche 1967, 90): this identity, for example, provides more or better resources than that, this faculty is more objective than that. The inclination to ossify must also be resisted. New configurations of identity, while initially productive, can create new divisions, new rankings that themselves have to be dismantled. Border artists understand that their work is never finished. Instead of conjoining opposites, border artists must fully accept—even love—being multiply split and beyond conjunctions. They must write and think in the liminal thresholds of the many boundaries that live in cuerpoespíritu and let themselves find attunement with nuances and hues without promise of clear and defining lines of difference and identity.

Anzaldúa's aim is not simply to transform herself but in the process to show those of us who are willing to listen, who are willing to follow her journey, how transformation happens. "My job is not just to interpret or describe realities but to create them through language and action, symbols and images. My task is to guide readers and give them the space to co-create, often against the grain of culture, family, and ego injunctions, against external and internal censorship, against the dictates of genes" (2015, 7).

BEYOND TOGETHER

While Anzaldúa's writings at times seem intensely personal, her connection to community is clear. "In fact, border artists are engaged artists. Most of us are politically active in our communities, making community-based art. If disconnected from la gente, border artists would wither in isolation. The community feeds our spirits and the responses from our 'readers' inspire us to continue struggling with our art and aesthetic interventions that subvert cultural genocide" (2015, 58–59). Nepantleras create not just for creation's sake but for the sake of transformation-with-others. Their engagements with others provide recognition, ways of understanding, articulating, living. Attunement to the responses of others, to the ways the differences in their lineages, their experiences, their lifeworlds animate the creative movement is a key component of border arte liberatory work.

For Anzaldúa *transformation-with-others* means the creation of coalitions, not around sameness but around our differences. For if we embrace sameness we are never challenged to change, to shift, to transform. "Diversity of perspectives expands and alters the dialogue," for Anzaldúa, "not in an add-on fashion but through a multiplicity that's transformational" (Anzaldúa and Keating 2002, 4). In dialogue with difference we can together expose the cracks in the dominant sensibility and begin to see through them to the fictions of belief systems. "The fissures disrupt the neat categories of race, gender, class, and sexuality" (2015, 86). As borders are unsettled, possibilities for experiencing beyond arise. This experience can incite refigurations. "We revise reality by altering our consensual agreements about what is real, what is just and fair. We can transshape reality by changing our perspectives and perceptions. By choosing a different future, we bring it into being" (2015, 21).

Liberatory work happens in solitary engagement with the mutational force of one's lineages as well as through our engagements with others. Sensibilities, for Anzaldúa, are crafted not only by means of the attunements of individuals with their particular lineages but also through the transformatory potential we find in exchanges with others, with groups of nepantleras. But we must be careful to avoid creating closed communities, communities of sameness and simple agreement. We must rather honor people's otherness in our cultivation of communities of engagement. As Anzaldúa explained, if we say only people of color are welcome, we continue to walk the color line. To refuse to include men holds fast the gender line. To refuse such inclusions can block challenges to established configurations of identity and obscure openings to more expansive configurations of identities. Nepantleras, for Anzaldúa, do not hold fast to borders; they seek links in-between. "Where others saw borders, these nepantleras saw links; where others saw abysses, they saw bridges spanning those abysses" (Anzaldúa and Keating 2002, 4). Perhaps we might call these communities-beyond-communities.

Certainly, conflicts can arise from the configurations of different identities, from coalitions of people from different locations. But to see conflict as merely negative is to miss its productive capacities. "Conflict, with its fiery nature, can trigger transformation depending on how we respond to it. Often, delving deeply into conflict instead of fleeing from it can bring an understanding (conocimiento) that will turn things around" (Anzaldúa and Keating 2002, 4). Nepantleras are accustomed to struggle, dissension, collision, incompatible differences, loneliness, and profound confusion. But they are, in their sensibilities, predisposed to a citizenship that is without a final and static identity, one that welcomes differences, one that is always on bridges and in thresholds and within processes of transformation. Anzaldúa calls it becoming a "world citizen." "Bridging the extremes of cultural realities, las nepantleras stand at the thresholds of numerous mundos. As world citizens, las nepantleras learn to move at ease among cultures, countries, and customs. The future belongs to those who cultivate cultural sensitivities to others" (2015, 85).

BEYOND PHILOSOPHY

Border arte, through its engagement of the human capacity to make images and words, its engagement with reflective imagination, has in Anzaldúa's experience a unique power of connecting with the influences of lineages and their liminal processes. Through such power we can find ourselves beyond ourselves. "Imagination, a function of the soul, has the capacity to extend us beyond the confines of our skin, situation, and condition so we can choose our responses. It enables us to reimagine our lives, rewrite the self, and create guiding myths for our times" (Anzaldúa and Keating 2002, 5). Border arte includes both "the soul del artista y el alma del pueblo" (2015, 62). Border arte is at once deeply personal as well as responsive to others. As border artists recreate themselves, they are at the same time engaged in the creation of new communities, new coalitions. Perhaps border artists can weave a story or speak of their life in such a way that holds in its indirection a threshold—a liminality—that opens to unsayables, that allows a disorientation that is itself apocalyptic. That telling and imagining would be a physical gesture in which cuerpomentealma in its lively infusion enacts its extensive range of existence, enacts enfleshed freedom, we might say, that is unavailable in the force of the more traditional, atomic imagery of bodies. Extended bodies gesture themselves—indicate themselves—not simply by signs and signals, but as living, lineage-born, creative imaginal events.

The forces, details, and intimations of lineages differ and shift in their processes of beyond. Anzaldúa's historical spiritmindsoulbody is different from that of people who live in different webs of lineages. It is different from that of Nietzsche or Foucault, to be sure, but from ours as well. In this part of the book, we have been interested in the ways Anzaldúa experienced and understood her world of corporeal spirituality and not in the truths or possible normative values she found in her singular experiences of nepantla. We have emphasized enfleshment, the beyond of nepantla, Anzaldúa's way of experiencing cuerpomentealma, her way of writing, her understanding of the connections between writing and profound transformations in her sensibility, her prioritizing of experiences of myths and of imaginings over systems of concepts and abstract signs, her accounts of extended enfleshment, and her manner of bringing these experiences into her border arte. We see these emphases as highlighting the ways she found her life to happen. In her border arte, she encouraged readers to turn to their own lives, their blind spots and silences. Perhaps through her work we can gain a renewed appreciation for our experiences of falling apart.

Her work makes clear some of the limits in professional philosophy and the importance of plowing new ground for philosophical thought by engaging on their own grounds works that could well appear at first as needing philosophical pruning and cleansing. What is at stake in the desire to carefully demarcate that which is *not* philosophical or at least not "good" philosophy? Aren't the important issues often found outside the limits of reason, good sense, and propriety? Aren't two of the most important questions "Where are we now?" and "Where do we seem to be heading?" In feeling these questions, readers might experience the need to question the extent to which they feel at home in philosophy. Or they might rethink philosophy's "home."

Let us ask again: How do we write, think, feel, create, respond differently from the way we do at home? How do we undergo transformations? How do we open thinking to new possibilities and move beyond the lineages that subject us, lineages that create bifurcations? Good/evil, male/female, Western/non-Western, mind/body, reason/emotion, culture/nature. Can we write in attunement to dimensions beyond such dualisms?

Can such attunements loosen the hold of their defining power? Can such writing serve to catalyze our transformations so that we find ourselves moving beyond the borders the dualisms enforce?

We who write out of American or Continental philosophical traditions can no more leave Western philosophy behind than we can shed our bodies. But just as our bodies are in a state of constant change, practices of philosophy are neither fixed nor hegemonic. Anzaldúa calls us to consider the dimensions of poetic and aesthetic awareness and language that are beyond the pale of philosophy as philosophy is often conceived. This poetic and aesthetic awareness and language constitute thresholds for happenings of beyond. In the remainder of this book, we explore the question of how shifts in sensibilities enabled through aesthetic lineages can attune us to dimensions beyond philosophy. We call this *border art philosophy*.

In both form and content, Anzaldúa speaks out of the freedom engendered by her experiences of beyond. Nepantla. "So, don't give me your tenets and your laws. Don't give me your lukewarm gods. What I want is an accounting with all three cultures—white, Mexican, Indian. I want the freedom to carve and chisel my own face, to staunch the bleeding with ashes, to fashion my own gods out of my entrails. And if going home is denied me then I will have to stand and claim my own space, making a new culture—*una cultura mestiza*—with my own lumber, my own bricks and mortar and my own feminist architecture" (1987, 22).

In part II, inspired by Anzaldúa and informed by encounters with beyond found in her work and the work of Nietzsche and Foucault, we turn to what we call *border art philosophy*.

Border Art Philosophy

LIBERATORY PHILOSOPHY AND BEYOND

Our attunement to what we have named "dimensions of beyond" has been cultivated through our reading of three very different writers. As we engaged their work, we came to understand ways of writing that opened both out of and into silences and unutterables. We were alert to the ways each of our thinkers catalyzed transformations in their attunements to dimensions of beyond that they variously named Dionysian and Apollonian powers, unreason, and nepantla. When we speak of transformations in this context we are speaking of enfleshed transmutations of people's desires, intentions, and orientations in the world. We are speaking of changes in the tones of our lives, of the way being alive feels, of sea changes in our images of ourselves and the world around us, of metamorphoses in our ways of thinking and writing, as well as transformations of institutions and political systems. We are speaking of profound experiential and social transformations out of which people come to think, feel, desire, and act in ways that were not previously possible.

The kind of transformation we are talking about happened for Nietzsche as he, in the figure of Zarathustra, found himself able to laugh, dance, and sing in a full sense of life without God or Meaning. He was also able to think and to create his own version of genealogical knowledge in his sense of an indefinable dimension—a no-thing—beyond good and evil, beyond good and bad. Foucault discovered that he could live, think, and perceive in the lineage of unreason and in attunement with a dimension of occurrence beyond truth and all other ordered schemas, and not just live but live with persistent, dynamic curiosity, excitement, and joy. Anzaldúa came to see through agonizing processes of falling apart and the continuous destabilizing of all senses of identity in her experience of nepantla that she could live with a sense of belonging and gratitude in a world more open, more available than any world she had previously known.

So we have been writing about transformation, not reformation. *Reformare*, from the Latin *re-*, back, and *formare*, to form or shape. To restore to form. To improve or refine. To remove faults. *Trans*, from the Latin for across or beyond. Foucault, in speaking of his work, explains that his "books are experiences, in a sense, that I would like to be as full as possible. An experience is something that one comes out of transformed.... I write a book only because I still don't exactly know what to think about this thing I want so much to think about, so that the book transforms me and transforms what I think.... I am an experimenter in the sense that I write in order to change myself and in order not to think the same thing as before" (2000, 239–40). Anzaldúa writes to carve and chisel her own face, to create herself and create new cultures "con mi arte" (2015, 64). She does not aim to reform herself but to transform. "As we walk through the flames of transformation. / May we seize the arrogance to create / outrageously / soñar wildly—for the world becomes / as we dream it" (2015, 157). Nietzsche phrases his process of transformation this way: "Whoever sticks with it and learns to ask questions here will experience what I experienced—a tremendous new prospect opens up for him, a new possibility comes over him like a vertigo, every kind of mistrust, suspicion, fear leaps up, his belief in morality, in all morality falters—finally a new demand becomes audible. Let us articulate this *new demand*: We need a *critique* of moral values, *the value of these values themselves must first be called into question*—and for that there is needed a knowledge of the conditions and circumstances in which they grew, under which they evolved and changed ... [and one finds that] morality [is] the danger of dangers" (1967, section 6, 20).

We, Charles and Nancy, write to experience such transformations—in this case, the transformatory power of experiences of dimensions of beyond in the thinking of Nietzsche, Foucault, and Anzaldúa. In doing this work we realized that readers could only begin to fathom dimensions of beyond in their writing through creative engagements with those dimensions in attunement with which they wrote and to which their work creatively gestures. For if one reads their texts only with the aim of identifying their methods, defining their terms, or penetrating their meanings, the work miscarries. The more readers only try to clearly grasp what they say, the further removed they are from experiencing beyond. Their texts offer much more than what readers can grasp with clarity. They offer experiences. What we find in each of our authors, and what we, if we have been successful, have offered in our readings of them, are limit-experiences, nepantla-like happenings, experiences beyond the confines of the sense people can make of them. Those experiences wrench us from ourselves, and we are no longer just our selves. "Which means that at the end of a book we would establish new relationships with the subject at issue: the I who wrote the book and those who have read it would have a different relationship with" the subject at issue (Foucault 2000, 242).

Our personal attunements with beyond emerged out of the paradoxes of liberatory work. Each of us has been drawn to the work of those who are concerned with uncovering and addressing practices of tyranny and oppression. We have witnessed over the past few decades, in addition to the liberatory impact of Marx, Nietzsche, Dewey, Beauvoir, Fanon, and other transformatory thinkers, a rise of many forms of what Nancy has labeled "liberatory philosophies": feminist philosophy, critical philosophy of race, queer theory, decolonial philosophy, to name a few. But at the core of liberatory philosophy lurks an enigma, one found at the very limits of reforms—the possibility of what seems to be impossible, the possibility of processes of transformation that emerge in attunements with dimensions of occurrences that are beyond formations.

Think about the values woven so tightly into the fabric of so many liberatory efforts: progress, freedom, democracy, justice. Consider how many resources have been devoted to defining and securing them. Books written. Campaign slogans crafted. Wars waged. Here we find ourselves confronting the paradox of liberatory philosophy. How can we who wish to engage in liberatory work avoid getting caught up in and by the very practices of power that we wish to critique? How do we avoid simply creating "a new disposition of the same power with, at best, a change of masters"? (Foucault 1977, 216). Do we ask, perhaps, for the impossible?

Ours is a repetition of an oft-repeated quandary of liberatory work. *"For the master's tools,"* Audre Lorde admonishes, *"will never dismantle the master's house. They may allow us temporarily to beat him at his own game, but they will never enable us to bring about genuine change"* (1984, 112). What can we do if our goal is to avoid decent reforms? Even the very act of opposition, does it not risk what Nietzsche confronted in his polemic with the ascetic ideal? Does it not risk continuing and intensifying the meaning and reality of what we set ourselves in opposition to and thereby keep in motion the very practices of power it is set against? How do we create in ways that are non-reformist? "It's not enough to denounce the culture's old account," Anzaldúa reminds us, "you must provide new narratives that embody alternative potentials. You're sure of one thing: the consciousness that's created our social ills (dualistic and misogynist) cannot solve them—we need a more expansive conocimiento. The new stories must partially come from outside the system of ruling powers" (2015, 140).

Foucault, as we have seen, also found that to reach beyond the seemingly endless processes of reforming the masters in the philosophical canon of his time, he needed to separate himself—liberate himself—from "acceptable" philosophy and turn toward experiences that took him not only from that regional discipline but also from himself. He needed to let himself undergo exposure in the disclosive power of such phenomena as the generation of unreason and the silence of the mad. In the impact of such experiences, he found a new vocabulary, a new manner of thinking, and a transformed self.

Liberatory: to set free, to release from restraint or bondage. From the Latin *liberatus*, past participle of *liberare*, to set free, to be unrestricted. We know only too well the limits of simplistic notions of freedom. As if we need only cast off physical shackles, open previously barred doors, and those who had been subjected would be set free. Liberatory movements have learned a painful lesson time and time again: we who are to be set free are rebound by new shackles hewed out of the same lineages of beliefs and values that had initially captured us.

Let us ask again: *How* are we when we engage in liberatory philosophies? Where are we when we do such work? We don't just have a problem in mind—injustice or oppression, confinement in life-denying moralities, bondage to imagined deities, unfree labor or the prison-industrial complex—we have a goal in mind. Something like justice, say, or perhaps equality, and, of course, freedom. Perhaps a new way of knowing and evaluating. Perhaps a transformed sense of community and government. "Give me liberty or give me death"—Patrick Henry (1775). So much ink and blood have been spilled over these ideals. "We hold these truths to be self-evident: that all men are created equal" (*Declaration of Independence*, US 1776). We have heard them advocated so often, how can we not be inspired? "I want to be remembered as a person who stood up to injustice . . . who wanted to be free and wanted others to be free"—Rosa Parks (Parks and Reed 1994, 86). They taste like, well, like progress.

Liberatory philosophies often diverge in approach and aim. Many attempt to expose oppression, reveal its source, and right the wrongs through fair and just solutions. They provide principles (equality, autonomy, equity, rights) and carefully detail the implications of values (respect, conformity, responsibility, fairness). The work is difficult and complex, but we can see the social changes they have effected, can we not? Consider how far we've come in the United States over the last decade—same-sex marriage, a Black president, the transgender bathroom directive.[1] Progress? Decent reforms?

We liberatory philosophers come to this work with conceptions of good and bad, right and wrong, justice and injustice. But we discover—well, at least some of us do—that such goals are framed and given meaning within the very practices, institutions, and orders of sense we are trying to reform. That is, we can't simply "reform" if that means taking the same forms and norms and expanding them or rearranging them—the forms of moral imperative, for example, or the forms of dogmatic certainty to shape new values and beliefs. For then we will find—or, worse, won't even realize—that our efforts only reinforce or simply reformulate the very structures that serve to oppress. If our liberatory theories, our narratives of freedom, circulate within practices of reason, conceptions of possibility, and normed behaviors that produce or reinforce systems of

---

1. The fact that Trump was able so easily and so quickly to reverse many of the efforts of liberatory movements—from transgender rights to environmental protections—is a reflection of the general absence of the transformation we advocate.

oppression, we silence experiences of the inconceivable, the unimaginable, the unthought. "What then does this language—the given language of freedom—enable?" Saidiya Hartman challenges, for "once you realize its limits and begin to see its inexorable investment in certain notions of the subject and subjection, then that language of freedom no longer becomes that which rescues the slave from his or her former condition, but the site of the re-elaboration of that condition, rather than its transformation" (Hartman and Wilderson 2003, 185). "Re-elaboration of that condition." You see, don't you, that the practice of liberatory philosophy is shot through with paradox?[2] We are often caught up in the very values, institutions, desires we wish to critique. They circulate in our thoughts, inform our habits, infuse our flesh, affect our desires.

So how do we twist free from the frameworks, structures, institutions that so enfold us even in our reformatory efforts? Might attunements to dimensions of lives that are beyond—free of our certainties, free of the force of our good sense and values—provide one response to this query? These would be attunements that do not necessarily destroy values and meanings but rather twist free of their dominating force and allow people to open to experiences that are beyond what they can think and discursively know. As we have seen with Foucault, Anzaldúa, and Nietzsche, attunements to beyond animate their work. They animate as well our efforts to work with them.

Liberatory. Rather than tracing the Latin roots of *liberty*, perhaps we can look to the ancient Greek term for freedom or liberty, *eleutheria*, ἐλευθερία, to serve as a light in the dark. Perhaps we can begin to understand the meaning of *liberatory* that we see in their work by remembering that Eleuthereus was one of the names of Dionysus, not the reformer but the liberator. Perhaps, like Nietzsche, in the exuberance of the Dionysian spirit and its lineages we might find dimensions that are beyond good and evil, beyond philosophy.

A genealogical approach in liberatory philosophy, whether informed by the doing of genealogies or by genealogical sensibilities, can be understood through this conception of liberation, *eleutheria*. We who perform

---

2. We note as well how often freedom from particular religious and moral bondages shifts into new religious and moral bondages, how what is called spirituality undergoes changes in content here and there but remains basically the same out of church as it was in church.

genealogically inspired liberatory work also attempt to expose oppression and reveal its source. However, we differ in aim from many practices of liberatory philosophy. Rather than identifying principles or values that can guide our work, often seeing them as the firm ground of our work, we aim to trace the lineages of values from which their value itself derives. Rather than having a sense, whether clear or hazy, of the society or practice or telos to which liberatory work is to aspire, we question the legacy of the vision of such goals, such teloi. Our work is guided by the intention to undo the unquestioned authority of values and purposes. Undo, from the Old English *undon*, to unfasten and open, to unfasten by releasing from a fixed position; to cancel, discharge. To loosen the hold, to trouble the ground. With genealogical sensibilities, we are able, at least on good days, to see the disfigurement inherent in the "good" of many social orders or the bondage woven into particular languages of freedom. But then, one might protest, this undoing, this genealogical loosening, serves what purpose? Is the worry that it is an aim without a particular goal, without fixed measure? Well, yes, and yet, no. Genealogical sensibilities intend to loosen the hold of the life-denying values of the social order, to abort the reproduction of a social order that frames some ways of living as not fully normal by its very order, the lives, for example, of queer folk, Black folk, disabled folk. Yet to do so by attending to the impossible, to the unutterables that dislodge the particular goals and fixed measures of political and ethical good sense. Liberation. *Eleutheria*. Beyond.

Pause and ask again: How are we when we engage in liberatory philosophies? Where are we when we do such work? In the undoing of values, we may become undone—desires shift; identities and politics that seem natural, certain, self-evident unravel in the in-between, in what we call the dimensions of beyond. We are in a place of undifferentiated becoming, what Anzaldúa calls nepantla. *Not* a no-place, a utopia. Rather, a place of no-thing yet to be something. A terra incognita, not (yet) known. The performativity of genealogically informed liberatory philosophies follows no fixed rules, not even a lesbian rule. Liberation is found in the porosity of such liberatory philosophies, in their lack of doctrinaire solidity, in the ways they set the soil to stirring, in the ways they nurture and encourage liberation in their Dionysian excesses. In the stirring we might find ourselves undone. *Eleutheria*. This means, does it not, that liberatory philosophies must be creative and that creativity happens in the thoughts' and language's performativity? As Derrida suggested (did he learn this from his reading of Nietzsche?), creativity happens "in the writing (or if you prefer, in the future production) of a language and of a political practice that can no longer be comprehended, judged, deciphered by [established] codes" (1988, 139). Foucault submitted truth to experiences that might diminish truth's value. He liberated experience from the power of truth and found his own liberation, as we have seen, in developing a kind of knowledge that in its pursuit and performativity changed him in relation to the subject matter and created the possibility for his readers to experience a new relation with the issues at hand. This performativity in its attunement to a dimension of reality that is beyond truth allows—encourages—transformative change. At its best, liberatory thinking liberates the thinker by its transformative power.

But if there is no rule, not even a rough guide, do we not risk getting lost? Are we not infused with the desire to know what to do? Don't just describe how certain kinds of power work on us; tell us how to get out of the grip of those powers! Don't just advocate being beyond good and evil; give us the positive position. Tell us what to do. Explain the normative impact of the genealogical description. How will it change what I choose to do? How will I act, think, desire, live? Always the desire to make the movement concrete and certain. But the harder we work to grasp the answer, to stabilize truths, to know just what to do, the more we lose the force of attunements with beyond. We find ourselves caught fast in a logic/logos, in ways of thinking, acting, desiring that reject, whether consciously or not, beyond without Meaning, reject any experiences of beyond that provide no normative foundations or universal and reasonable sense, reject any experiences of beyond that do not provide desirable goals.

We are saying that we need to focus, not on stances or positions, but on temperaments and dispositions. On willingness to question the value of values themselves. On openness to the unthinkable. On attunements to influences and exchanges, to lineages and vectors of power. On acceptance of the pain of falling apart and the necessity of learning to live in the midst of change with a new responsiveness to uncertainties that render not-knowing animating rather than paralyzing. "An ethical query emerges in light of such an analysis," Judith Butler claimed. "How might we encounter the difference that calls our grids of intelligibility into question without trying to foreclose the challenge that the difference delivers? What might it mean to learn to live in the anxiety of that challenge, to feel the surety of one's epistemological and ontological anchor go, but to be willing, in the name of the human, to allow the human to become something other than what it is traditionally assumed to be?" (2004, 35) We offer a response: a willingness to be undone. Attunements to beyond without Meaning. Not a conception of freedom hewed from incontrovertible values. Rather an ineffable sense of freedom bestowed by absent beyond.

Where do we find ourselves now? We have traced the complex circulations of beyond through the work of Anzaldúa, Nietzsche, and Foucault. We have identified the attuned movements with beyond in their work as well as the singularly different lineages and processes in their work. Their openings to beyond differ yet attune us to incalculable, uncountable ongoing corporeal processes of transformation and simultaneous and unsynchronized infusions in porous tapestries of lineages and environments.

Where do we find ourselves now? Perhaps you, responsibly and justifiably, are with us in attunement with a non-agential dimension beyond the domain of responsibility, justification, and intentionality. We hope that you, like us, have become disturbed, elated, surprised, provoked, excited, unsettled. That you too find yourself in a movement in which you break away from your self, a movement in which the limits of your identities are challenged or surpassed, in which rigid beliefs and values are destabilized and rendered porous and the inflexible grids of universalized certainty dissolve. A movement in which you, like we, experience the unfamiliar and experience an uncanny place far from home. Echoing Foucault, "Maybe the target nowadays is not to discover what we are, but to refuse what we are" (1982, 785).

BORDER ART PHILOSOPHY

> Art, all art, not just painting, is a foreign city, and we deceive ourselves when we think it familiar.... We have to recognize that the language of art, all art, is not our mother-tongue.
>
> —Jeanette Winterson, *Art Objects*

The paradox of liberatory philosophy cannot be explained away, unraveled like a Gordian knot, or even cleaved and separated into components to be simplified and resolved. Careful analysis, to be sure, has its place. The path to transformation is paved by an understanding of the ways dominant conceptions of liberation, freedom, or, indeed, justice are themselves tied to particular sensibilities, in this case to Western worlds of sense, and, in being so tied, are interlaced with the very oppressions that they strive to address. But such understanding is only a first step. If conceptions of freedom and justice, if the very norms that guide us toward good actions and just societies are infused with sensibilities that give rise to the oppressions we strive to undermine, then we cannot *think* our way out of the problem. We cannot reason or argue our way to liberation by using frames that define what constitutes a rational argument or delimits what counts as good philosophy when those very frames emerge from oppressive sensibilities that incline people toward the oppressive practices that we are trying to transform. Inclinations and feelings, often pre-reflective, as we saw in the first part of the book, infuse and inform thought and arguments. The best we can hope for in the context of oppressive sensibilities is a re-formation of the oppression. We see, for example, that segregated schools, lunch counters, and water fountains are unjust. We ban them. That's progress, isn't it? Yes. But the "progress" is qualified. Changing the laws that established segregating practices and institutions constitutes an improvement. But changing the laws alone is not sufficient to change the attitudes, beliefs, and practices—sensibilities—that are racist. These continuing sensibilities result, for example, in the far higher rates of incarceration and unemployment of Black men in comparison to White men in the United States.[3] Civil rights aren't very civil when the injustice that they aim to correct is woven into the very fabric of racist attitudes and of dominant sensibilities that include indifference to economic injustice and the rights of minorities. Liberatory philosophy that addresses such problems is in need of attunements to those dimensions of life that are beyond the power of such sensibilities, attunements that disorient us, dislodge us, and open thresholds of experience beyond the lineages of oppression. Beyond the very sensibilities out of which intolerable meanings, values, lifeways emerge. We need paths to dimensions of

---

3. A 2013 study conducted by the Pew Research Center found that in 2010 all Black men were six times as likely as all White men to be incarcerated in federal, state, and local jails.

beyond where there are no paths and where resonance with the inconceivable makes transformation possible.

In what, then, would such a practice of liberatory philosophy consist? Not in a fixed stance or an imposition of concepts, a principle of action or a model to live by, but rather in practices in which people undergo transformational processes in their dispositions and sensibilities. We might say that it involves processes of reorientation, an undergoing that, in going under, might give rise to transformations of sensibilities. Such a reorientation involves an attunement to unimaginables that engender previously undreamed conceptions. A process inclusive of people's willingness to be affected in ways that put at risk their values, their cherished beliefs, even their identities. A falling apart that might open to, open us to shifts in ways of living, thinking, feeling. A continuous undergoing, rather than a fixed goal. A creative becoming. A *poiesis*.

If what is liberatory is not in theory or in history or in carefully designed methods but in the *experience* that transforms us to think, feel, conceptualize differently, then an option for liberatory philosophers is to write from experiences of the dissolution of thought and the falling apart of both identity and certainty through which we might become open to new fields of experiences. This is a process of writing that interrupts, that opens to a fissure, a cenote, a void, a silence—where we are in question, *are in* the force of the question of our selves and our ways of living. These are practices attuned to undoing, to experiences of liberation, that appeal to an opening within experience itself. To processes that open (us) to transformations.

We have discovered in each of our three thinkers such ways of writing, creating, and cultivating dispositions that are attuned to unutterables. Anzaldúa called such processes of writing *border arte*. Inspired by Nietzsche, Foucault, and Anzaldúa, we propose practices of what we in part I called *border art philosophy* as key aspects of liberatory philosophy. Border art philosophy, as we understand it, is a creative process. It is composed of ways of writing, reading, and responding that are attentive to silences, disruptions, unspeakable losses, unthought dimensions of thinking. These are efforts to write and respond from within experiences that are beyond thorough comprehension, not something we can grasp or dominate. Not something we can control (*comprehendre*, Latin, "to seize"—*con*, "with," and *prendere*, "to take"). These are efforts that are beyond, in Judith Butler's words, our grids of intelligibility but with which we can become resonant. Border art philosophy engages ways of writing and responding that are open, opening us to us-in-the-making, porous, attuned to affective dimensions, longings and laughter, suffering and astonishment. These are ways of doing philosophy that can shift sensibilities that in turn shift ways of doing philosophy. Border art philosophy is not a fixed mode of theorizing but rather one involving ways of writing, reading, responding that enact their own creativity and, in the doing, can catalyze transformation. Border art philosophy involves practices in attunement with that which is beyond the possible, what we, the authors, and you cannot yet do or think. It is a practice of philosophy that is difficult and opaque, that is always in process, and that takes courage and persistence. A doing of philosophy that is attentive to and often formed by the shades of nuance and the subtleties of tone that give creative potential to words to wordlessly say what cannot be narrated but what can nonetheless be disclosed.

The phrase *border art philosophy* resonates with our and Foucault's, Anzaldúa's, and Nietzsche's attunements to lineages and to the many types of borders these experiences and lineages enact—geographical, conceptual, affective—borders of place, thought, influence, and feeling. As we engaged their work, we experienced with them movements beyond the borders of philosophy, beyond the borders of conceptual understanding, beyond such opposites as good and evil. These movements occurred in the enfleshed experiences within the force of which our authors wrote. And they occurred in the flux of their multiple heritages where the liminality of in-between dissolves the clarity of boundaries, where tried-and-true differences meld, where there is neither truth nor lie. Border art philosophy for us includes recognition of eventuations that are formed by mutations of lineages, the melding of such influences as cultures, class structures, religions, and so forth. These imporing processes constitute anonymous agencies in people's lives and provide diverse thresholds of endingbeginning. As we have emphasized, lineages are not simply kin lines from the past. They are dynamic, ongoing, and mutating activities that are without guiding schemas. They constitute ceaselessly melding borders, the homeland of border art philosophy.

Border art philosophy is thus multilineal in cultivating a rich sensitivity to the complexity of lineages and other anonymous agencies that make up current sensibilities as well as our individual senses of self. It is attentive to the movements of distinctions, demarcations, and divides that create borders and boundaries: reason and unreason, mind and body and spirit, good and evil. Border art philosophy opens the way for an attuned sensitivity to the ways these distinctions and oppositions function in societies and cultures, sensitivity to their imporings and impacts, to the openings their movements permit and those not allowed. Border art philosophy scrutinizes those lineages that are dominant in order to understand their powers, their dissonances, and their gaps. It carries with it attentiveness to the ways the selves of even those of us most committed to liberatory movements harbor lineages from the oppressions that we fight so hard against.

The practice of border art philosophy is a movement that happens in the liminality of being *in the border*, not simply on the border. Its movements are not between: being between this culture and that, for example, between this sensibility and that. There is a viscosity to being in the border, where the sharp lines between differences and distinctions quiver and inflow. In the liminality of being in the border, we find ourselves solicited. *Solicited*, from the early fifteenth century, "to disturb, trouble," from Middle French *soliciter* (14c.), from Latin *sollicitare*, "to disturb, rouse, trouble, harass; stimulate, provoke," from *sollicitus*, "agitated," from *sollus*, "whole, entire," + *citus*, "aroused," past participle of *ciere*, "shake, excite, set in motion." Being in the border affects a trembling in which forms of thinking, feeling, acting come into question, seem to melt into one another, quiver in uncertainty, and we come to find ourselves troubled and in question. As Foucault reported, "In attempting to uncover the deepest strata of Western culture, I am restoring to our silent and apparently immobile soil its rifts, its instability, its flaws; and it is the same ground that is once more stirring under our feet" (1973c, xxiv). In these imporing movements, we are in the happening, shaped and shifting in the anonymous agency of in-between. We find for ourselves that

To survive the Borderlands

you must live *sin fronteras*

be a crossroads (Anzaldúa 1996, 5).

Remaining *in* borders constitutes a potentially creative experience. Border art philosophy involves cultivating the uncertainty that comes with experiences of being in borders. That experience with its instabilities can be frightening. One needs to be willing to want the instability, to affirm it, to think in its solicitation. With that affirmation, the fusing differences as they blur—in their anonymous agency—can provide glimpses of what was once obscure and perhaps also provide, if not words, then occasions for styles, nuance, and resonances—forms of communicated attentiveness—that give a measure of apparency to unsayables. The happenings of viscous movements when we are in borders might allow us to bring to light the unseen. As if it were sensible. Almost palpable. But not quite. Being in borders, being in-between, cannot make unreason reasonable, but perhaps in its fluid movements being in-between might open up fissures in the bedrock of good sense, dislodge our contentment with reasonable beliefs and systems of ideas, and generate possibilities for previously unconceived ways of thinking and communicating. Perhaps we will find ourselves, the happening of our very selves, in excess of our normalcy.

We have spoken of border art philosophy, but what of the doing, the formation and articulation, the *poiesis* of border art philosophy? How do we enact the silences? How do we give voice to pre-reflective dimensions of experience? Develop habits of attunement to beyond?

There is no definitive answer, no method. There are, however, practices of engagement, ways to maneuver, that can develop when we are attuned to experiences of being in borders. We have suggested practices of border art philosophy that take the form of genealogy and genealogical sensibilities. We have spoken of this approach to border art philosophy in terms of lineages. One approach is to cultivate an intimate awareness of the interconnected, interpenetrating, and mutating groups of lineages, processes that include developments of normative practices and changes in hierarchies of authority and values. Such practices of border art philosophy in their attentiveness to lineages can give rise to a philosophy more concerned with genealogies that expose the ways truths and the value of truth itself have developed than with uncovering truths, more focused on creating openings in transformative thought than with constructing arguments, more attuned to experiences than to creating justifications. This attentiveness engages the sensibilities that engender systems of belief rather than simply evaluating the belief systems themselves. Border art philosophy also nurtures an experiential, involved attunement with those lineages that are silenced or ignored. To rouse one "from the trance of hyper-rationality induced by higher education," genealogically informed border art philosophy engages lineages of ideas and concepts, certainly, but also music, dance, and myth in addition to lineages of authoritative hierarchies, formations of institutions, identities, punishments, subjections, rejections of physical desire, etc. (Anzaldúa 2015, 135). Genealogically informed border art philosophy traces the shadowy contours of worlds of sense not only as objects of attention but also as aesthetic experiences on the part of the thinker at the silent edge of borders, in the borders of silence.

These practices of border art philosophy can push us beyond the arguments, descriptions, values, mastering concepts, favorite issues, and even truths that characterize thinking. The impulse of border art philosophy is found in the experiences beyond schemas that attunements in the in-between of borders can incite. A phrase, thought, feeling, orientation, or new prospect gets under our skin and excites a movement. If we can attune ourselves to the movements that happen when we are in borders and experience ourselves in radical differences from our familiar world of meanings, values, and perceptions, we might have an occasion for genuinely liberatory creativity. These opportunities are events that cannot be mastered or commanded. Rather, they constitute occasions of insight that we do not create and occasions of movements that we do not authorize. We are affected by and caught up in movements that as they engender possibilities break us away from ourselves. These are experiences that happen when the engagements are intense, and openings to many types of transformations become possible. "Nietzsche was a revelation to me," Foucault wrote. "I felt that there was someone quite different from what I had been taught. I read him with a great passion and broke with my life, left my job in the asylum, left France: I had the feeling I had been trapped. Through Nietzsche, I had become a stranger to all that" (1988, 13). Such experiences, we have said, wrench the subject from itself and take people out of the conviction that they are autonomous subjects. They show us that in being subjects we are living connections *in our eventuations* with images, cultures, peoples, places, a vast range of often-conflicting values, and liminal thresholds into which we cannot see clearly. These experienced elements in our extensive individuation happen in and through lineages and their continuous mutations, languages, environments, societies, and intricate relations of power. They—experiences beyond schemas—can rattle the cages of our certainties, not by substituting those certainties with new certainties, but by holding certainty in question: not eliminating certainty, but experiencing our certainties in question.

Border art philosophy, as we understand it, offers neither a fixed telos nor a guarantee of "success." Our efforts to set the ground to stirring may miscarry or even be redeployed in unexpected and, indeed, oppressive ways. We asked how we might be attuned to the risks of such uncertainty. How might we find an ethos, communal ways of living, with alertness to the risks of uncertainty and, equally important, the risks of certainty?

Uncertainty is an elemental feature in Foucault's thinking. His thought, as we have seen, lives in borders where the boundaries of truth are continuously exceeded by experiences in domains without rational formations. Within his context of expectation, the risk of uncertainty provides an opportunity for individuals to find ways to care for their ever-changing selves in their worlds of chaotic orders. In this unsettled world of knowledge and evaluation, we face such issues as these: How might we recognize values that are carriers of lineages whose consequences we want to avoid or neutralize? How might we be able to do something with the ways we are "done by norms"? We offer practices of attunement that turn us beyond normal and normalizing patterns of living. We look for ways to appropriate Foucault's ascesis, his discipline of listening to silences. We engage him to learn more about living in a genealogical sensibility. We cultivate alertness to the borders in which we think and evaluate without certainty and without ever knowing the full range of consequences that arise in the wake of our actions. And we pay particular attention in our encounters with him to his art of nuance, style, silence, and suggestion as he speaks of unspeakables and the fictions of experience.

Anzaldúa's border arte approach was to weave together creativity-spirituality-knowing. She developed practices like that of conocimiento, which she referred to as "a form of spiritual inquiry," one that she found to be deeply embodied. "Conocimiento comes from opening all your senses, consciously inhabiting your body and decoding its symptoms" (Anzaldúa and Keating 2002, 542). She digs deep into the cenote of her lineages, unearthing forgotten myths as resources for inspiration, for different living. She pays attention to the sites of pain and knows that witnessing the pain can be a source of new understanding and an opportunity to reconstruct her life. She attends to the "always-in-progress, transformational processes" of her *autohistoria* and the ways the permutations shift what she can see and the stories to which she can give voice. She cultivates attunements and ways of living that might transform those oppressions that rule when identities become primary and values are unquestioned. Certainty was never the goal of her arte.

Nietzsche's "whole new prospect" to which we have referred arose when an art of asking questions replaced the value of certainty. As he cultivated that art and the genealogical knowledge that resonated deeply within it, he experienced the limits of rational clarity, well-developed moral goodness, and ordinary common sense. He experienced those limits as well as the restrictions of fabricated, powerful spiritual comforts that religions and Western metaphysics provide. Nietzsche's life was a process of transforming the anxiety inherent in the death of God and all the ramifications of that death to joyful affirmation of being alive. One aspect of his border art philosophy is found in communicating that joy in his knowledge and writing through well-honed indirection, alertness to the feelings that pervade philosophical formulations, and skill in developing performative styles. Inside his work the reader finds anguish, depression, courage, disappointment, hope, and, of course, joy. Not unchallenged certainty or desire for it.

Anzaldúa's path is one example of the *poiesis* of border art philosophy, as are the differently figured paths of Nietzsche and Foucault. There are many others in the twentieth century who found their own paths in border art philosophy, such as Gaston Bachelard, Simone de Beauvoir, Maurice Blanchot, Hélène Cixous, Jacques Derrida, Luce Irigaray, Achille Mbembe, Hortense Spillers, and Sylvia Wynter. The paths in attunement with the dimensions of beyond that we have engaged are neither uniform nor fixed. They shift and change. Those who try to turn them into a methodology ossify them, silence them. They must "soñar wildly—for the world becomes / as we dream it" (Anzaldúa 2015, 157). Nietzsche, Foucault, and Anzaldúa help us understand that liberation will never occur as long as we remain anchored in a sensibility of certainties through which oppressive practices are formed and made sensible as well as unquestionable. As long as liberatory philosophy operates within the contours of oppressive systems—what Nietzsche would name herds—we can expect, at best, decent reforms.

Endingbeginning. Transition. In this part of the book, each chapter has its own topic, and one does not flow naturally into the other. We understand some of the chapters in the context of "beyond philosophy" to compose particular alertness to what we think of as the threshold quality of thinking and events that happens beyond the range of good sense, such as we find in Kandinsky's art and discuss in chapter 7, or in livingdying, which we discuss in chapter 8. In chapter 6, on the other hand, we take a close look at the importance of cultivating ecologically informed genealogical sensibilities in order to avoid crafting liberatory actions that risk creating situations that further the oppression those actions were intended to eliminate. In chapter 9 we encounter sensibilities and normativities in their instabilities and unpredictabilities. We write these chapters in attunement with *beyond* as we have developed the word in the contexts of all three thinkers. This attunement, as we show in chapter 9, opens the way to an emphasis on decisiveness and, in Foucault's sense of the term, hyper-activism.

In all of the chapters we write in a sensibility that is positively attuned to the liminality of events—of things—as we raise such topics as liberation, forms and practices of oppression and silencing, anonymous agencies, viscous porosity, extended agency, in-between, the middle voice, erotic love without objectification, livingdying, sensibilities, and normativities. The writing in this part of the book expresses genealogical sensibilities as we have described them in part I and, we hope, brings unspeakables to disclosive immediacy. We will have carried out our intentions of writing border art philosophy if you find through your reading and beyond your agreements and disagreements with us experiences that you have not had before, or that you seldom have, perhaps a desire to be an agent of liberation for yourself and others. Perhaps you will experience a sense of transcendence without Transcendence, meanings without Meaning, and affirmation without Affirmation.

Playing with Fire

FIRE IN THE DARK

We live in dark times. Times of denial of the destructive impacts of lifeways that have become so normalized that few can imagine living differently. Denial comes in multiple guises and habits. One nexus of denial is found in the ways so many individuals, communities, businesses, and countries respond to the ever-growing signals of anthropogenic climate change and warnings of coming disasters. As we write, the NASA Global Climate Change site offers what they call "vital signs of the planet": carbon dioxide up 411 parts per million, the highest levels in 650,000 years; global annual temperature up 1.8 degrees Fahrenheit since 1880, with the majority of the warming occurring in the past 35 years, with eighteen of the nineteen warmest years in the 138-year record occurring since 2001; sea level rising 3.2 millimeters per year, with the global average sea level increasing nearly seven inches over the past 100 years (NASA 2018). We have seen countries across the globe already dealing with devastating impacts from sea level rise, extreme weather events, and precipitation changes. These threaten food security and water availability, livelihoods, the health of humans, and the survival of species and ecosystems.

Yet we've made so little progress in facing this peril of our own making. Indeed, some people don't even accept that there is an issue, much less one that demands a response. The opposite of good reason and common sense seems to be gaining a foothold: our future president, in 2012, tweeted,

"The concept of global warming was created by and for the Chinese in order to make U.S. manufacturing non-competitive" (quoted in Marcin 2017). The now president Trump, despite seven more years of compelling data, has continued to deny the reality of climate change. In a 2018 interview he continued his evangelization of denial: "There is a cooling and there is a heating and I mean, look—it used to not be climate change. It used to be global warming. Right? That wasn't working too well, because it was getting too cold all over the place. The ice caps were going to melt, they were going to be gone by now, but now they're setting records, so OK, they're at a record level" (Trump 2018). Such statements are archetypal examples of the operation of what we call a sensibility of denial.

As we have articulated in the previous chapters, our conception of sensibility is both indebted to and moves away from more commonplace uses of the term. In speaking of sensibilities, we emphasize attention to feelings and affect, but we also emphasize the pre-reflective generation of meaning and value. Sensibilities predispose us in some directions and not in others; they cajole us to hold tightly to some values while silencing others. They encompass not just ways of knowing but also affective responses, habitual dispositions, bodily comportments, forms of desire. Sensibilities, in our usage, are active, mutational dimensions constitutive of our societies and cultures. Sensibilities, with the nuance we are deploying, include those habits, beliefs, practices that constitute the pre-reflective agency of the interrelations, organizations, and environments of groups of people. People in their intersubjectivity are informed by multiple shifting sensibilities. They are often, in their multiplicity, both fragmentary and in tension. Transformations can be sparked by such fissures and frictions.

Some live comfortably with a sensibility of denial even when the facts demand a response. The response we advocate is intense work to facilitate the emergence of new sensibilities. Our desire is to ignite the fire of Anthropocenean sensibilities.[1] We are not interested in new labels or the

---

1. We use the term *Anthropocenean* rather than *Anthropocene* because it is not our intention to take a stand on the classification debates. Those who wish to classify (when, why, how) are typically attempting to demarcate an epoch in which humans have had significant impacts on the Earth's geology and ecosystems. Such classifications are difficult in that we humans have always been changing and being changed by the environments we are in and of. Our concern is not with classifications but with the potential of

debates as to their attributional accuracy—Anthropocene, Capitalocene, Chthulucene, Androcene, Corporatcene, Plasticene, Petrolcene, or Elachistocene.[2] We are interested in new ways of being affected, attentiveness to becomings-with that transform the ways we live with our extensive environment. Anthropocenean sensibilities, we submit, would require us to live differently from the ways we live, to embrace new lifeways. Perhaps embracing the myriad meanings of "humans as a geological force" will enable us to appreciate that human lifeways are intricately intertwined with such things as ocean currents and precipitation patterns or that global business practices infuse the flesh of fish and humans alike. And perhaps such insights will have the potential to create a rupture in current ways of thinking and habits of acting. Embracing those meanings might constitute a strong first step toward transforming our sensibilities of denial. Perhaps such infusions and ruptures might provoke an attunement to what is unthinkable in sensibilities of denial, and in that provocation usher in an onto-ethical transformation in which an appreciation of the nature and extent of human impacts on global environmental processes might serve as the catalyst for a radical transformation in behavior and attitudes. This transformation might well include shifts of habits, affective dispositions, and ways of conceiving—in other words, the emergence of new sensibilities of the magnitude required to live differently. We might see this new, culture-changing emergence as a new coming of desire that could serve to transform our imaginary, evoke shifts of habits, refashion affective dispositions, and interrupt ways of conceiving. Anthropocenean sensibilities demand an appreciation of the inherent interconnectivity among things, removing sharp borders (humans/environments, nature/culture) and encouraging attention to the porosity of interrelationality, the rich interactions through which subjects and environments are co-constituted. Sensibilities that interrupt sedimented habits of conceptualization and provoke new ways of living together.

In this discussion we bring together resources from disparate places: Anzaldúa's efforts in *Light in the Dark/Luz En Lo Oscuro* to put

---

Anthropocenean sensibilities to serve as a reminder of the complexity of these infusions and in doing so to effect a transformation in habit, attitude, and comportment.

2. For a helpful discussion of the nomenclature debates, see Schneiderman 2017.

Coyolxauhqui back together with the tools of nepantla and conocimiento; Foucault's genealogical approach to self-transformation; Derrida's deconstruction of doxa and certitude; and Butler's resolve to engage the risk of ethics. Their voices serve as the tinder for kindling a fire in the dark on the path to new sensibilities. Anzaldúa provides the first step in this journey when she writes about identity transformations: "Knowing that something in you, or of you, must die before something else can be born, you throw your old self onto the ritual pyre, a passage by fire. In relinquishing your old self, you realize that some aspects of who you are—identities people have imposed on you as a woman of color and that you have internalized—are also made up. Identity becomes a cage you reinforce and double-lock yourself into. The life you thought inevitable, unalterable, and fixed in some foundational reality is smoke" (2015, 138).

In our perceptions, habits, economies, and policies, many of us are living in the dark cage of denial. The shift we are talking about requires significant changes in who we are individually *and* collectively, a passage by fire, a deathly experience that makes possible lifesaving lifeways.

A FIRE-FORGED SPECIES

Passage by fire. The dance of fire serves as a reminder of our deep interconnections in the world. People happen as worldly interconnections, and our ways of living are not only between things. They are also in-between. In our ways of passing through the world we all, each of us, live immediately *in*-relation with all manner of such anonymous agencies as climate zones and climate changes, diets, modes of dwelling, physical transformations, the given flora and fauna. Like flames enflaming—dancing—in their transformations, at once together and passing on in passages in-between.[3] Attentiveness to fire's movements recalls us to the *becomings with* that constitute our ways of being worldly (Haraway 2007).

We humans are a species forged in fire.

What set the genus *Homo* apart in its becoming different with other animals? Neither bipedalism nor increase in cranial volume nor tool use nor language development was unique to *Homo*. The current scientific

---

3. See chapter 7 for a discussion of being in-between.

understanding is that "it is the mastery of fire which distinguishes the genus Homo from other members of the animal kingdom.... The appearance of a species which has learnt how to kindle fire meant that, for the first time the flammable carbon-rich biosphere could be ignited by a living organism" (Glikson 2014, 76, 77).

We are a species transformed by fire.

Fire allowed humans to migrate to harsh climate zones. "Fire opened the night by providing light and heat. It protected caves and shelters. It rendered foods more edible, leached away toxins from cassava and tannic acid from acorns, and killed bacteria that caused salmonella, parasites that led to trichinosis, and waterborne microbes" (Pyne 2001, 24).

Cooking made new diets accessible, giving us relatively small teeth for our body size. Harvard biologist Richard Wrangham argues that the unprecedented increase in brain size found in our long-ago hominid ancestors was due to fire, in this case the use of fire to cook food, which enabled the body to extract more of the calories in the food, from 30 percent more for grains and tubers to 78 percent more for protein. Cooking breaks the connective tissue in meat and softens the cell walls of plants to release their stores of starch and fat. Hominids who played with fire were thus able to eat less and spend less time foraging and literally chewing. Cooking allowed easier digestion of proteins, relieving early humans from energy-consuming chewing and thereby enhancing the brain blood supply. It is from this stage that hominins grew taller and leaner, shedding much of their original hair cover, allowing perspiration, cooling, and the long-range chase and hunt of animals (Wrangham 2009).

In previous chapters we have developed accounts of porosity and imporing, what Nancy has labeled the viscous porosity of things in their happenings, to serve as reminders of the enfleshed interweaving of complex lineages, of bodies, of sensibilities (Tuana 2008). These terms are designed to serve as reminders of openness and exchanges. We have spoken of how values and their orders are porous and of how transvaluations can happen because of shifts in sensibilities, authoritative knowledge, or political climates. We have traced the porous webbings of lineages that interlace what is considered nonsanity and sanity. We have spoken of how to bring to bear enfleshed genealogical sensibilities to the movements in-between nos/otras in ways that will remove the slash. Here we bring such genealogical sensibilities to openings and exchanges: the dance of fire and human evolution; the influences and inflowings of power and devastation in coal fields; exchanges between lifeways and waterways. Perhaps attunement to such infusions will ignite a passage of fire and set in motion a light in the dark, fiery sparks that might serve to activate a transformation of our sensibilities of denial.

Fire infuses the imaginaries that informed people's awareness of themselves and the elements in the world that nourished them. Fire mythologies from far-flung people present fire as a potent power stolen for humankind. Prometheus, Inti, Jaguar, Loki, Mātars'van, Raven, Grandmother Spider, Crow. But the heroes of these myths are complex creatures who figure the often-dangerous, life-giving gift of fire and who themselves abide immediately in the magical, tricky passage of fire to the yet to become *Homo sapiens*. They indwell the coming of fire and the fire itself in its blazing fate. These figures are not simply connected with *Homo sapiens*. They are in-between in the gifting. Consider Coyote of the Native American tribes of the Pacific Northwest and First Nations. Coyote, the trickster, fooled the fire beings, stole fire and its secrets, and brought them to humankind. Coyote is both hero and deceiver, both clever and reckless, forever getting himself and the people around him into trouble. Coyote is he who transgresses boundaries and through that transgression brings chaos and change. The gift of fire is always a complex gift—it settles into imaginaries as at once both beneficial and harmful, indispensable to life yet a catalytic danger.

Corporeal exchanges like the coming of fire into the lives of *Homo sapiens* are not inherently positive or negative. They are the happenings of concrescences, of fusions and coalescences. Some corporeal exchanges are beneficial to some in some instances. Some are harmful to some in some instances. Fire can literally save our lives, but we can also perish in its flames. Through our viscous porosities, our openness with the world, we can be physically and psychically nourished as well as injured. We never leave fire's passage unchanged.

We are a species that has transformed the earth with fire.

The harnessing of fire by humans elevated the oxidizing capacity of the species by many orders of magnitude through release of solar energy stored by photosynthesis in plants. Beginning from these beginnings, we have continued to release energy stored by photosynthesis, diving deep into the planet to release the energy of the fossil carbon of ancient biospheres. "Global CO_2 emissions from fossil fuels and industry have increased every decade from an average of 3.10.2 GtC yr^{-1} in the 1960s to an average of 9.40.5 GtC yr^{-1} during 2007–2016. In 2011 fossil fuel burning released 9.5 ± 0.5 GtC to the atmosphere, 54% higher than in the 1990 Kyoto Protocol reference year" (Global Carbon Project 2017, 424). Between 2015 and 2016 coal burning was responsible for 40 percent of the global CO_2 emissions from fossil fuels and industry, oil 34 percent, gas 19 percent, and cement 5.6 percent (Global Carbon Project 2017, 429).

Might our experiences of anthropogenic climate change—sea level rise, more frequent severe weather events, heat waves, increased flooding and droughts—be the fissures in our current sensibilities that provide openings to new ways of responding, new attunements to habits of thought and action that are silenced by our current sensibilities? Perhaps the play of fire could fuel the emergence of Anthropocenean sensibilities.

Anzaldúa's path of conocimiento, happenings of knowingacting *in* borders, with its intricate concrescences and dynamic fusings of affectcognition, fleshspirit, cuerpomentealma can take us to regions of experience beyond reason and deepen the fissures in our current sensibilities. Might the fire of Anzaldúa's path serve to ignite this transformation from sensibilities of denial to Anthropocenean sensibilities? Take us "beyond the subject-object divide" to ways of recognizing and knowing that arise out of people's interfusion with the elements and processes of their environments? (Anzaldúa 2015, 119) Offer paths to ways of thinking and living that we cannot now conceive?

"We stand at a major threshold in the extension of consciousness," Anzaldúa explains, "caught in the remolinos (vortices) of systematic change across all fields of knowledge. The binaries of colored/white, female/male, mind/body are collapsing. Living in nepantla, the overlapping space between different perceptions and belief systems, you are aware of the changeability of racial, gender, sexual, and other categories rendering the conventional labelings obsolete. Though these markings are outworn and inaccurate, those in power continue using them to single out and negate those who are 'different' because of color, language, notions of reality, or other diversity. You know that the new paradigm must come from outside as well as within the system" (2015, 119). Anzaldúa's path into new paradigms for human agency, her path of conocimiento, leads out of and away from sensibilities of denial that have no sense of human agency infused in its environment with its environment. Her path out of cultures formed by binaries, her efforts to remove the slash—human/environment—may provide a catalyst for Anthropocenean sensibilities. Hers is a fiery path of transformations in which *Homo sapiens* may begin to awaken to an extended agency-with-their-environment. Not agency here, environment there. Rather agencyenvironment.

A new way of thinking, living, responding will not happen through modifying the content but not the form of our current practices: "Man" is the master of his fate and must be held responsible for his actions; humans as a species have become an agent of geological change and must be held responsible by enforcing principles of climate justice. The same trope writ large. The master's tools. Our call for movements that might open us to Anthropocenean sensibilities is an appeal beyond the current frames. To think what is not (yet) thinkable. Perhaps attunement to the imporing in-between that embodies worldly happenings, to the silent, nonhuman indifferences in the processes of rapid environmental change will trouble thought and in that troubling open thinking to the unthinkable.

EARTH ON FIRE

We have spoken of genealogical sensibilities, of how Anzaldúa's enfleshed genealogical sensibilities attuned her to infusions, moving her away from sharp bifurcations and turning her rather to the deep interconnections of lineages and of things. Anzaldúa wrote in red and black ink: *Tlilli, Tlapalli*, the Nahuatl couplet that, in bringing together the black and red ink of the codices, serves as a reminder of border art philosophy, of the art of speaking of the unspeakable, the imaging of disclosive indirectness.[4] She directed our attention to how oppressive practices circulate in the complex and mutable ways we humans structure our societies, build our institutions, imagine possibilities and impossibilities. And she noted how

---

4. "Tlilli, Tlapalli / The Path of the Red and Black Ink" is chapter 6 of *Borderlands/La Frontera* (1987).

these same practices etch the bodies of humans and nonhumans alike, seeping deeply into flesh and soil alike, reminding us of the inextricable interconnections between identities-communities-worlds. Perhaps by becoming attuned to the anonymous agency of such imporings we might be undone in ways that give rise to new possibilities. Perhaps in the tierra desconocida of nepantla, in the midst of its unknown, we might find paths to new sensibilities, Anthropocenean sensibilities. Alongside the path of red and black ink, let us here follow the incendiary lineages of coal.

Dense foliage from forests became buried underneath soil. As the layers of soil and new foliage became layered on top of the old, the growing pressure of the soil compressed the plant matter, and heat and pressure produced chemical changes that removed oxygen and left carbon deposits. Coal. Each layer of coal is referred to as a coal seam. Those thick enough to be profitable are mined. Coal seam fires are a hazard of coal mining. While some are naturally occurring, the increasing exposure of coal due to mining has expanded both the size and prevalence of coal seam fires, with thousands of fires across the world, indeed in every country that mines coal (Kuenzer and Stracher 2012).

Coal seam fires are the most persistent fire on earth, able to burn for thousands of years. Burning Mountain in Australia, the oldest known coal fire, has been burning for about six millennia. The fires are a persistent although too often hidden threat to human and ecosystem health. As the coal burns, carbon monoxide, carbon dioxide, hydrogen sulfide, mercury, methane, and various toxic trace elements such as arsenic, selenium, and lead vent from the ground, threatening the health of local inhabitants, human and nonhuman alike, and can lead to ecosystem deterioration (Finkelman and Stracher 2011). They also contribute to greenhouse gas accumulations, adding to rising temperatures, which in turn threaten to trigger more fires (Turetsky et al. 2014).

Perhaps tracing the blazing fire of coal's lineages with enfleshed genealogical sensibilities might help unsettle current habits of thought and attune us to sensibilities that enable us to apprehend the fire of coal's destruction in all of its seams and crevasses. We know coal's lineages incorporate environmental destruction. Strip mining scars the land as well as the ecosystems it rips apart. Underground coal mines leach toxic compounds into the air and water. But do we remember that coal's lineages incorporate racist lineages? The infusions of racist exploitation and environmental exploitation have long histories. In the United States, for example, coal and racism are intricately woven together. The 2012 study *Coal Blooded: Putting Profits before People* examined 378 coal-fired power plants in the United States and documented both the negative impact of these coal-fired plants and the disproportionate negative impact on Black and Latin American communities due to the siting of plants in neighborhoods with high percentages of people from one or both groups (NAACP 2012). The study found that of the nearly six million Americans who live within three miles of a coal power plant, "39 percent are people of color—a figure that is higher than the 36 percent proportion of people of color in the total U.S. population. Moreover, the coal plants that have been built within urban areas in the U.S. tend overwhelmingly to be located in communities of color" (NAACP 2012, 15). Jacqueline Patterson, the environmental and climate justice director for the NAACP, explained the consequences of these facts: "An African American child is three times more likely to go into the emergency room for an asthma attack than a white child, and twice as likely to die from asthma attacks as a white child. African Americans are more likely to die from lung disease, but less likely to smoke.... And these are people who are living within three miles of the coal-fired power plants" (quoted in Toomey 2013).

This is indeed one dimension of environmental racism and is the type of lens through which we might interrogate the disproportionate impacts of climate change on people subjected to racist oppression.[5] While not minimizing this aspect of the linkage of environmental harm and racism, it is too superficial to remain the only dimension of

---

5. Other than its inclusion in quotes, we are intentionally avoiding the phrase *people of color* for the ways in which it flattens differences between the people so included as well as those excluded and silences and reinforces the privileging of White people as "colorless" (and thereby "raceless"). It is also a term that does not travel well, for who counts as a "person of color" in one country will not always so count in another, which itself signals one of the reasons a racial and racism dimension is such a problematic omission from climate justice concerns. For those who trace the differential impacts of climate-induced migration, this dimension will be crucial to consider as there may be times in which the very meaning of a group's racial or ethnic identity shifts as they shift spatially, as well as the way racist practices are often location specific yet subject to shifts due, in some instances, to shifts in migration.

attention. From this perspective we would achieve, at best, reform but not transformation, as it does not mine the deep and long histories of the infusions of racist exploitation and environmental exploitation. It does not travel deeply enough into the ways racism was and is often literally incorporated into institutions and social practices, as well as into the flesh. Such a journey requires enfleshed genealogical sensibilities attuned to the fleshly labors that built nations and the fortunes of both individuals and states, labors that were woven into the emergence of both colonialism and capitalism.[6] It would require setting a fire along the seams of such exploitation in order to unearth its current incorporations. Let us trace some of the paths of this incorporation. We will find it has been long burning.

To incorporate. A verb. From the late Latin *incorporates*, past participle of *incorporare*, "unite into one body, embody, include," from Latin *in-*, "into, in, on, upon," + verb from *corpus* (genitive *corporis*), "body." Meaning: (1) To put (something) into the body or substance of (something else), blend; absorb, eat, also solidify, harden; (2) To legally form a body politic with perpetual succession and power to act as one person, establish as a legal corporation.

To give a sense of how we might travel along the path of conocimiento, the path of red and black ink, and drill more deeply into the infusions of racism and environmental exploitation, let us examine the practice of coal mining in the US South after the Civil War and reflect on how racism and environmental exploitation were incorporated in coal mining. The war ended chattel slavery as a legal institution in the United States, but it did not end its influence on the sensibilities of many white Southerners or mitigate its impact on the bodies of many former slaves. The North was not immune from internalized racism, but in the South, it was bred in the bone. Years of justifying the cruelties of chattel slavery created unbroken convictions in White Southerners of their superiority and deep fear and resentment of the specter of freed slaves. The ideology of the inherent superiority of Whites over Blacks and the often-deployed justification

---

6. This history is being unburied by the work of historians such as Edward E. Baptist, Sven Beckert, Ada Ferrer Greg Grandin, Walter Johnson, Jason W. Moore, Adam Rothman, Calvin Schermerhorn, and Ned and Constance Sublette.

of the enslavement and often brutal treatment of millions of people were deeply embedded in the psyche of many Southerners.[7] The legal emancipation of people who had been treated as property did little to undermine the moral order that was used to justify chattel slavery and often creates flares of resistance to the Northern effort to force a new political structure upon the South. Not only did the Thirteenth Amendment fail to transform Southern sensibilities, but there was often little change in the ways land would be worked, cotton picked, or coal mined. Instead, a series of willful duplicities, sensibilities of denial akin to current climate change denial, created a new system of enforced labor, whether through exploitative sharecropping arrangements or the convict lease system. The bodies of slaves were treated as a source of fuel, something to be put to work and to be consumed into the work of earning a profit. That slaving economy of treating some people simply as economic resources to be used to turn a profit was carried on post–Civil War, first through unfree labor practices and later, and arguably to this day, through unlivable wages.

The reincorporation of Black Americans into unfree labor in the postwar South takes many forms. Our focus is on the criminalization of Black life that was designed to exploit it in coal mines. Vagrancy laws served this purpose. Although Mississippi was the first state to enact vagrancy laws in 1865, Alabama, Arkansas, Florida, Georgia, Louisiana, North Carolina, South Carolina, Texas, Tennessee, and Virginia were not far behind. Such laws not only identified as a vagrant anyone who was deemed insufficiently employed but also included as a vagrant anyone whose lifestyle was deemed inappropriate: "rogues and vagabonds, idle and dissipated persons, beggars, jugglers, or persons practising unlawful games or plays,

---

7. Of the more than 12 million African people who were abducted, enslaved, and transported across the Atlantic, approximately half a million were transported to the United States between the mid-seventeenth century and Congress's 1808 ban on the importation of slaves, with approximately 18% murdered or dying because of the harsh treatment of the Middle Passage. However, by 1860, the Black population in the United States increased from approximately 400,000 in 1808 to 4.4 million in 1860, of which the vast majority (3.9 million) were slaves. This increase is due in large part to the practice of forced "breeding" through forced sexual relations between slaves and between slave women and free men (Berlin 1992; Sublette and Sublette 2015). For studies of the legacy of slavery on pre- and post–Civil War Southern sensibilities, see Deyle 2005; Fox-Genovese and Genovese 2008; Genovese 1998; Genovese and Fox-Genovese 2011; Irons 2008; and Robinson 2017.

runaways, common drunkards, common nightwalkers, pilferers, lewd, wanton, or lascivious persons, in speech or behavior, common railers and brawlers, persons who neglect their calling or employment, misspend what they earn, or do not provide for the support of themselves or their families or dependents, and all other idle and disorderly persons, including all who neglect all lawful business, or habitually misspend their time by frequenting houses of ill-fame, gaming houses, or tippling shops, shall be deemed and considered vagrants under the provisions of this act" (Mississippi 1866). Southern objectification of the newly freed Blacks as disorderly in both body and mind served as a vehicle for control. But their objectification led not to containment in asylums or even in prisons but to incarceration in farm fields and coal mines.

The broadness of vagrancy laws allowed widespread misuse, which was used to arrest and fine freed Blacks. Most of these laws had a provision that failure to pay the fine could result in convict leasing. But whether because of forged charges like vagrancy or other wrongs like theft or assault, real or imagined, a system of forced labor ensued that benefited plantations as well as corporations such as railroad companies and ironworks. This system of enforced labor resulted not only in deplorable working conditions but also in high levels of deaths for those so sentenced. It was the energy of slaves by a slightly different name.[8]

Alabama's convict lease program fueled the coal industry. During the Civil War, much of the coal supplied to the Confederacy came from Alabama's coal fields, the southernmost tip of the Appalachian coal field. During that time, slaves were often taken off plantations and forced to work in the mines. Forced labor in the coal mines shifted in name only after the Civil War, when hundreds of freed Blacks were convicted of crimes like vagrancy, then leased to companies like the Tennessee Coal, Iron, and Railroad Company, one of the largest exploiters of convict labor, whose headquarters moved to Birmingham, Alabama, in 1895.

A report in *The Engineering and Mining Journal* from 1909, for example, declared: "Coal operations in Alabama promise to be steady for some time. The distribution of convicts among the coal companies will bring about some development... there is considerable free labor still to be had

---

8. Here we are indebted to Blackmon 2008.

for the mine work in the State, and it is being taken up more and more" ("Metal, Mineral" 187). The energy of slaves.

The experience of this "considerable free labor" working in the mines was described in *Homegoing: A Novel* by Yaa Gyasi. While a fictionalized account, it provides a glimpse of such exploitation. In it we learn of the fate of H, who was arrested on the charge of "studyin' a white woman" and who, when he was unable to pay the fine, was sold by the state of Alabama to work the coal mines outside Birmingham. The daily experience of convict laborers is described by Gyasi. Once H and the other prisoners traveled, through tunnels of exploded rock, the three to seven miles required to reach the coal face where they were to work: "H shoveled some fourteen thousand pounds of coal, all while stooped down low, on his knees, stomach, sides. And when he and the other prisoners left the mines, they would always be coated in a layer of black dust, their arms burning, just burning ... more than once, a prison warden had whipped a miner for not reaching the ten-ton quota ... whipped him until he died, and the white wardens did not move him that night or the rest of the next day, leaving the dust to blanket his body, a warning to the other convicts" (2016, 161).

According to Douglas Blackmon's findings, in Alabama nearly 20 percent of leased prisoners died in the first two years, with the mortality rate rising in the third year to 35 percent and in the fourth year to nearly 45 percent (2008, 57). Their remains were incorporated into the ground around the coal mines, leaving depressions scattered across the field where many hundreds, possibly even thousands, of those who died in the mines were buried. And of those who did not die before they "served out their sentence," many were sentenced to the diseases and early deaths caused by coal dust that settled in their lungs and became incorporated into flesh. Coal workers' pneumoconiosis, black lung disease, is a common aftereffect of breathing in coal dust. The coal dust would have been thick in the mines worked by convict laborers. Little if any ventilation and very narrow passages would have contributed to high concentrations of coal dust breathed in hour by hour, day by day. Dust that enters the lungs becomes part of the body as it can neither be destroyed nor removed by the body. The particles become incorporated into the tissues and structures of the lungs and pulmonary lymph nodes. The coal dust, so incorporated, catalyzes the release of various proteins and enzymes that cause inflammation and fibrous growths. As the growths and lesions lump together, lung tissue is destroyed, leading to severe shortness of breath, chronic cough, heart problems, and premature death. *Racism is incorporated into flesh.*

This bodily incorporation of coal dust was one of the consequences of the incorporation of the bodily labor of Blacks into the flourishing of the postwar economy in the South and into the wealth of corporations like the Tennessee Coal, Iron, and Railroad Company, the profits of which were merged with the United States Steel Corporation in 1907. Racism was in this way literally incorporated into the environmental harms caused by coal mining, from the impacts on groundwater to the release of methane to acid mine drainage. Just as we cannot ignore the impact on the average family wealth of Blacks in the United States in the twentieth and twenty-first centuries of the loss of so many Black lives to convict labor, we cannot ignore the way in which corporate wealth is in turn grounded in both racism and environmental exploitation. To ignore these incorporations or to understand them only as separate and separable phenomena is to overlook the long history of their infusions.

Following the path of red and black ink through enfleshed genealogical sensibilities can provide helpful lenses for tracing complex lineages to unsettle habits of thought. We start to see the ways that treating people as pools of labor, resources to be exploited for the advancement of some at the expense of others, is a hardened seam of current sensibilities. If we see only rising greenhouse gases as the cause of anthropogenic climate change, we miss the larger frame and risk simply repeating it. Slavery by a different name. Enfleshed genealogical sensibilities disclose the complex infusions of flesh—incorporations of coal dust and lung tissues, of racism and environmental exploitation. Perhaps in the fiery imporings of our attunements to such lineages we can begin to shift.

FIGHTING FIRE WITH FIRE

"To be innovative and subversive," Anzaldúa reminds us, "a writer must write what readers haven't been taught to read yet—a different and unfamiliar literary form—present an experience not yet articulated or portray a familiar one from a radically different perspective" (2015, 110).

As we follow the path of red and black ink, where do we look for answers? How do we live out of the lively lineages to which we have become attuned? Can we perhaps return to the past to reclaim new futures? Can the allure of the past be a trustworthy guide? Might we find in such a return suppressed sensibilities? Do such returns constitute paths to new lifeways, or are they repetitions of the same? Can being in the border of pastpresent offer resources for transformation? Can we respond from in-between?

To animate these questions, consider the impacts of anthropogenic climate change in the Bolivian Amazon. Shifts in precipitation patterns have led to food insecurity as crops in various regions have been adversely affected by both flooding and droughts. In the highlands, the two main glaciers that provide drinking water are shrinking, affecting both food production and water security. Between 1986 and 2014, the glaciers of Bolivia shrank by 43 percent (Cook et al. 2016). The Chacaltaya glacier disappeared completely in 2009, five years earlier than projected.

Adapting to the impacts of climate change on the Bolivian population will be particularly difficult, as more than 60 percent of the total population lives below the national poverty line, the majority of whom are subsistence farmers.[9] Water security is a major issue, as the loss of glaciers has significant effects on water supply as well as hydropower. The rapid glacial melt in the Bolivian Andes over the last thirty years has affected the availability of water in cities and rural areas alike (Hoffman and Weggenmann 2013; Ramirez et al. 2001; Bradley et al. 2006). The Tuni and Condoiri glaciers, for example, which provide 30 percent to 40 percent

---

9. The lineages of poverty in Bolivia track along similar paths as we have seen with coal and racism. Colonialism's wealth extraction in Bolivia, as in most colonialized areas, required a ready reserve of cheap labor. Silver mining, for example, relied on the imposition of the *mita* system upon indigenous populations, namely, forced labor draft of indigenous men between eighteen and fifty years old. Their toils in silver mines often resulted in devastating health impacts, as mercury was widely used in silver mining. The silver that flowed from mining centers in Latin America resulted not only in Spain becoming a leading global power but also in the undermining of Andean indigenous communities (Robins 2011). Unfree labor practices continue to be ubiquitous in Bolivia. The 2006 Anti-Slavery International Report found that despite Bolivia's legal abolition of slavery and compulsory labor, between 35,000 and 60,000 men, women, and children, the vast majority of whom are indigenous peoples, are forced laborers through forms of debt bondage, particularly in the sugar cane industry, in the Brazil nut industry, and on ranches (Sharma 2006).

of the potable water for the more than two million people who live in the neighboring cities of La Paz and El Alto, have shed more than a third of their ice mass since 1983. In addition to providing drinking water, glacial meltwater is crucial for agriculture, industry, and hydropower (Kinouchi et al. 2013). These glaciers are melting so quickly that they are expected to disappear by 2045.

Bolivia, along with other nations in South and Central America, accepted privatization of transportation, electricity, and water resources as conditions of International Monetary Fund and World Bank loans in the 1980s. As a result, the cost of water rose exponentially. The people of the Cochabamba valley began to fear loss of control of all water resources. Even the rain collected and distributed for centuries by Cochabamba's municipal water company and by communal water systems that had never been part of the governmental water system were coming under the control of the US-based Bechtel Corporation. These changes led to protests in opposition to water privatization led by then labor leader now president Evo Morales. The Water War resulted in the ousting of the Bechtel Corporation, the proclamation of access to water as a human right, and the related banning of its privatization throughout Bolivia.[10]

Morales crafted the Water War and the subsequent Gas War based on a platform that claimed as a collective cultural right indigenous practices of "traditional use and distribution of water." "These water movement activists mobilized essentialized discourses of usos y costumbres, emphasizing indigenous uses of water in order to create a strategic platform for local and regional struggles to reclaim water from private hands" (Fabricant 2013, 161). Such organizing to reclaim and nationalize resources fused with demands for indigenous rights and a return to an indigenous cosmovision. Although many of the protestors were urban mestizos who did not self-identify as indigenous, the discourse usos y costumbres emphasizing indigenous uses of water became an effective tool to unite activists despite differences in race, class, and social sectors in efforts to negotiate for collective water rights.

---

10. The 2010 film *También la Lluvia* (Even the rain), directed by Icíar Bollaín, depicts some of the complexities of the Cochabamba Water War.

A similar platform has been developed in Bolivia in response to climate change. The Bolivian Platform for Climate Change, La Plataforma Boliviana Frente al Cambio Climático, proposed a response that was designed to mobilize climate adaptation measures through deploying indigeneity. This was done by utilizing Andean indigenous cosmovisions and so-called "ancient" indigenous practices to justify resource reclamation and sovereignty. Organizations formed to reclaim traditional pre-Columbian landholding patterns based upon kin relations and collective work patterns, the ayllu. Ayllus were typically extended family groups that were self-sustaining units, that farmed or traded for all their needs, that owned a parcel of land, and in which the members had reciprocal obligations, including the care and education of children and work in the community fields. In return everyone participating in this labor received support from the community for such tasks as house construction or other essential physical needs. This return to "past" indigenous structures and practices was promoted by various international development organizations such as Oxfam in the belief that climate change adaptation and risk management practices based on indigenous models would be more acceptable to Bolivians.

"The border artist," Anzaldúa reminds us, "constantly reinvents her/himself. Through art, s/he is able to reread, reinterpret, re-envision, and reconstruct her/his culture's present, as well as its past" (2015, 60). We are, all of us, informed by multiple lineages. Can the lineages of the past fuse with those of the present to craft solutions? Or will the imposed mergers miscarry? Oxfam partners with Bolivian climate change efforts to mobilize indigeneity. But what conception of indigeneity is carried forward in such attempts to gain autonomy and political purchase? Our common trope of indigeneity has various pitfalls. It too often frames a common theme of "unchanging indigenous peoples who live in harmony with natural surrounds." This assumes peoples and communities untouched by colonialism and capitalism. "Lo Andino" risks reification in a vision of native peoples as timeless, grounded in rural realities, and inherently connected to local ecologies. What is overlooked in this "return" to the past are the ways in which native peoples have been transformed by colonialization and capitalism, including the ways in which some indigenous peoples have contributed to the development of capitalism and benefited from such extractive industries as logging. Many communities see climate mitigation programs like REDD+ (Reduce Emissions from Deforestation and Forest Degradation) as beneficial not because they would return Bolivia to indigenous ways but because their market-based mechanisms promise to provide sufficient funds to address poverty.[11]

We have said that the multiple, infusing lineages can be resources for transformation. But our efforts to attend to the infusions of lineages can misfire if we look for fixed answers via a return to the past. Rather than harden the divide between the past and the present, border art's dance of fire disrupts such divides. As Anzaldúa explains, "each artist locates her/himself in this border *lugar*, tearing apart and then rebuilding the *place* itself. The border is the locus of resistance, of rupture, of implosion and explosion, and of putting together the fragments and creating a new assemblage" (2015, 49).

The framing of climate change issues through the lens of indigeneity in Bolivia is based on the recuperation of the indigenous Andean cosmovision of *suma qamaña* (Aymara) or *sumak kawsay* (Quechua), which translate into Spanish as *buen vivir* or *vivir bien* and into English as *good living* or *living well* (Huanacuni Mamani 2010, 15).[12] The ideal is offered as part of the *proceso de cambio*, the process of change led by President Morales, and is seen as presenting an alternative to colonialist and capitalist models. Rafael Quispe, the leader of the National Council of Ayllus and Markas of the Qullasuyu, explained that this goal will be met by a new model of development, one that returns to the "original" development model of the indigenous peoples: "We have to speak of a new model of development, an alternative to the system. Because both capitalism and socialism will go on changing the planet. And the development model of the indigenous peoples is the ayllu, the communitarian development model. We original peoples for thousands and thousands and thousands of years have been living in equilibrium and respect for our Pachamama (Mother Earth), from whom we emerged" (Weinberg 2010a, 21). The goal

---

11. To appreciate the complexity of this topic, see, for example, Cochrane 2014; Fabricant 2013; Fontana 2014; Perreault 2003; Perreault and Green 2013; Weinberg 2010b.

12. The World's People Conference on Climate Change and the Rights of Mother Earth, which was convened in Tiquipaya, Bolivia, in April 2009, presented as one of its imperatives the recuperation of the Andean cosmovision of *sumac kawsay*.

is to deploy the vision of ancient and unchanging indigenous lifeways as a model for changing the present and the future. Here we see the ayllu model of development wedded to "the universalizing of Buen Vivir as a broad-based indigenous construct for living differently, re-embedding the economic, social, and cultural into a system which lives in harmony with Mother Earth" (Fabricant 2013, 171). However, some have become concerned that the notion of *buen vivir* does not actually reflect indigenous lifeways but is rather "a discourse that was developed by intellectuals of the urban middle class in the 80s" (Chambi Mayta 2015, 30). Do these visions and discourses serve to address the millions of Bolivians living in urban areas whose lives are impacted by extreme poverty? Is this an instance of a modern, mastering mentality appropriating indigeneity? Can lineages be mastered without being lost?

Bolivia, like many South and Central American countries, has experienced large-scale migration from rural areas to urban areas. The city of El Alto, for example, expanded from approximately 11,000 in the 1950s to a city of 1,184,942 in 2010. The migration was often triggered by shifts in land ownership to more commercial farms and away from subsistence agriculture. How will the vision of *buen vivir* translate into the realities of cities like El Alto, with its lack of sanitation services, water scarcity issues, or its polluted waterways, like the Pallina River, which has become a foamy, pea-green soup that can no longer sustain fish or nourish crops, and other problems caused by poverty and inequality in urban settings? Should a concept like indigeneity be deployed as the other of capitalism? Can indigeneity be promoted without essentializing indigenous peoples or freezing them in time as unchanging peoples who live in harmony with nature? (See Macusaya 2015.) How do those who wish to deploy indigeneity avoid its commoditization by corporate agendas or even its misuse by the Bolivian government in ways that do not benefit indigenous people? Will such a vision obscure how environmental changes, many of which have negatively impacted human populations, have changed indigenous ways of life? Can such a vision work in a place like Bolivia that is deeply dependent upon resources like natural gas for economic development and social programming? Will it address the workings of power and politics associated with the fossil fuel industry?

And what of the negative tropes in such a worldview? The indigenous cosmovision as it is presented in *buen vivir* has many components: nature as a right-bearing entity, not a resource or an instrumental good; an emphasis on the harmony of human communities with nature, as part of nature, as dependent, rather than a view that would insist on the separation between the human domain and the natural domain. The view of earth as a nurturing mother is often woven with various gendered assumptions, many of which reinforce women's assigned role as caregiver by essentializing it and reinforcing heterosexist assumptions by naturalizing them. Consider the conception of Fernando Huanacuni Mamani, who is regarded as one of key intellectuals recovering and promoting the concept of *buen vivir* in Bolivia and who was appointed chancellor of Bolivia in 2017 by President Morales: "According to the original indigenous cosmovision, we are children of the Cosmos and Mother Earth; all that exists is generated by them. So too all that exists is paired. . . . Life emerges from this relation of complementary pairing . . . this implies going back to forming enduring relationships like our ancestors lived . . . it is necessary to re-establish the man–woman relationship but as an enduring relationship . . . one is a person only when one has been supplemented by forming a couple (man–woman or chacha-warmi), not before" (Translated by and cited in Cochrane 2014, 583).

There are also worries that the protection of indigenous lifeways overlooks the tremendous shifts in those very lifeways. Child labor laws have been a particular target of concern, as the Morales government has identified child labor in native indigenous, Afro-Bolivian, and intercultural communities as protected and designed to develop life skills and "strengthen community life within the framework of Vivir Bien" and thereby has exempted such children from child labor laws.[13] A 2009 study by the National Institute of Statistics of Bolivia identified more than eight hundred thousand children and adolescents aged five to seventeen engaged in economic activities, almost half of which are classified as dangerous activities (Chambi Mayta 2015, 35). As indigenous communities have been immersed in the market economy for decades and have been dealing with severe poverty due to limited job prospects for adults, many have argued that the treatment of indigenous child labor as exempt from child labor

---

13. Ley No. 548 Código de Niña, Niño y Adolescente. (Law N. 548 Boy, Girl and Adolescent Code), http://www.gacetaoficialdebolivia.gob.bo/, cited and translated in Chambi Mayta 2015, 32.

protection laws does a disservice to indigenous children while also ignoring underlying causes of extreme poverty in indigenous communities.

If we look to the past to reanimate the present, will we be able to overcome its oppressive power formations? A new synthesis will not be simple. Perhaps if we approach it with Anthropocenean sensibilities attuned to the formations of norms and borders, hierarchies and lifeways, the past can serve to reveal impediments as well as animate new possibilities.

FOLLOWING FIRE

Foucault was asked to take a position in the case of an individual who had previously been committed to a psychiatric institution and, during that time, had been declared mentally incompetent but who had, after his release from the institution, been held accountable for and convicted of two brutal murders. Foucault refused to take a position. He explains his decision in the following way: "What meaning would it have had to begin prophesying or to play the fault-finder? I have played my political role by bringing out the problem in all its complexity, prompting such doubts and uncertainties that now no reformer or president of a psychiatrists' union is capable of saying: 'This is what needs to be done.' The problem is now posed in such conditions that it will nag for years, creating a malaise. Changes will come out of it that are much more radical than if I were asked to work on the drafting of a law that would settle the question" (2000, 289–90).

Following Foucault into the field of climate ethics, we worry about the tendency of so many who work in this field to take a stand and dictate solutions. The desire is so pronounced. How can we act differently? Isn't the goal to draft laws or policies? Shouldn't they be governed by a set of principles? Given the multifaceted threats of climate change, isn't this what we *should* desire, namely, a response "that would settle the question"?

Perhaps before we take a stand or advocate for climate policies we need to more fully examine the ways in which the conceptual understandings and action choices pressed upon us often carry with them problematic histories and alignments. Following Foucault, we might rather work to create a malaise. Not to settle the question but to unsettle. To motivate further questioning and enliven the debate by cultivating uncertainty and attentiveness to what is ignored. Perhaps what we strive for are processes of engagement rather than solutions. To create an unease that emerges from and exposes the working of power relations. To display tensions. To expose complexities and, following the path of red and black ink, find the fissures and work to transform them. Anzaldúa reminds us of the importance of attunement to tensions and contradictions: "Like other new Raza narratives, mine are replete with contradictions, riddled with cracks. Though these holes allow light/insights to enter, they also cast shadows. Acknowledging and exploring estas sombras is more difficult when I myself have created them, and I risk reducing the complexities of race and culture. I'm always, already, a traitor por escribir y por mi lengua, and rewriting cultural narratives makes me even more of a malinchista" (2015, 74).

Foucault's malaise follows us into the field of climate ethics. The play of fire serves as a reminder that greenhouse gases are not inherently bad. Without them we would have no atmosphere, indeed we would not be. There is a hazy threshold. In taking a position we often forget to unsettle the questions. Polluting for whom? For which species? To which purposes and against which others? Adaptation for whom?[14] For which purposes? Perhaps what we need to set against the desire to settle the question are genealogies of greenhouse gas practices that enable, as Foucault phrased it, a "counter-network of power/knowledge, a history of the present capable of questioning the unquestionable" (2003, 8–9). Through such genealogies we might begin to see the complex exchanges between such practices as the use of synthetic fertilizers in farming and the military-industrial complex; between population growth and crop yields; between high-yield cropping practices and ice sheet melting; colonialism and environmental degradation; water toxicity and meat eating; farm workers and institutionalized patterns of oppression; rates of cancer and global business practices; species extinction and income inequalities. These genealogies could shed light, but the sombras will require ongoing attention to the complex permutation of capital, desire, hierarchy, and development.

As Foucault suggests, "Maybe the target nowadays is not to discover what we are, but to refuse what we are. We have to imagine and to build up what we could be to get rid of this kind of political 'double bind,' which is the simultaneous individualization and totalization of modern

---

14. For a discussion of the implications of what Bishop Tutu labeled *adaptation apartheid*, see Tuana 2019.

power structures" (1983, 216). We see this same attunement in Anzaldúa. Rather than an attempt to return to the past, she advocates "un proceso de crear puentes (bridges) to the next phase, next place, next culture, next reality... you don't build bridges to safe and familiar territories; you have to risk making mundo nuevo, have to risk the uncertainty of change. And nepantla is the only space where change happens. Change requires more than words on a page: it takes perseverance, creative ingenuity, and acts of love" (2015, 156).

This troubling of habits, this agitation of divides, this mistrust of settled questions is a movement in the threshold of new sensibilities in which we must become cartographers of the coming of the *terra incognita* of new desires and new attunements. Tracing lineages, becoming attuned to silences, setting the ground to stirring through enfleshed genealogical sensibilities opens us to the possibility of experiencing that which we could not previously experience, to see the flash of the fire of new conceptualizations, new comportments, new desires. Such troubling might kindle new sensibilities that rouse us from our stupor, that disrupt current sensibilities of denial. Rather than the pessimistic dystopian "welcome to the Anthropocene" that has been a repeated caution, perhaps we might rather welcome the genealogical creativity of Anthropocenean sensibilities.[15]

WALKING THROUGH FIRE

We begin with Anzaldúa's reminder that "las nepantleras, boundary crossers, thresholders who initiate others in rites of passage, activistas who, from a listening, receptive, spiritual stance, rise to their own visions and shift into acting them out, haciendo mundo nuevo (introducing change). Las nepantleras walk through fire on many bridges ... turning the flames into a radiance of awareness that orients, guides, and supports those who cannot cross over on their own" (2015, 152) and return to Anthropocenean sensibilities.

Anthropocenean sensibilities lead to terra incognita, unknown terrain. They involve movements into mundo nuevo. Welcoming them is

---

15. "Welcome to the Anthropocene" is the title of an editorial in *Nature* (2003) in response to the 2003 heat wave in Europe, which resulted in the deaths of tens of thousands of people (see Robine et al. 2008). The title has been often repeated; see, for example, the article by this title in *The Economist*, May 26, 2011.

becoming open to the emergence of new desires, ones in which our attentiveness becomes heightened to the mutual vulnerabilities that constitute the world, to flows of influences, and to economies of exchanges. Sensibilities unfold that incline us to learn to live in the midst of change, with an emerging acceptance of uncertainties that allows them to become animating rather than paralyzing. Uncertainties and unsolved problems are the cracks that can open us to the flash of fire, to the radiance of insights and transforming affections. Anthropocenean sensibilities can motivate us to be alert in our worldly vulnerabilities, to learn to be affected, to be provoked to feel and think anew, to attend to power exchanges and processes that are beyond the restricting boundaries of conceptual and moral formations.

In *Borderlands/La Frontera* Anzaldúa developed an analogous practice. She explained:

"The new *mestiza* copes by developing a tolerance for contradictions, a tolerance for ambiguity. She learns to be an Indian in Mexican culture, to be Mexican from an Anglo point of view . . . nothing is thrust out, the good the bad and the ugly, nothing rejected, nothing abandoned. Not only does she sustain contradictions, she turns the ambivalence into something else . . . a new consciousness—a mestiza consciousness—and though it is a source of intense pain, its energy comes from continual creative motion that keeps breaking down the unitary aspects of each new paradigm" (1987, 79–80).

To cultivate such a tolerance for contradictions, for ambiguities, we need tools to loosen the soil of conceptualizations and to set the ground to stirring. We might find resources for such tools in disparate locations. Jacques Derrida, for example, in his last interview with *Le Monde*, which appeared under the title "I Am at War with Myself," referred to his work and to the work of those to whom he was indebted as "an ethos of writing and thinking, an intransigent or indeed incorruptible *ethos* . . . without any concession even to philosophy," one that reflects a predilection for subtlety, "paradox, and aporia . . . an unrelenting war against *doxa*" (2007, 27–28).[16] In "Force of Law" we find this careful attention to the aporia concerning the unstable relation between law and justice through which

---

16. In the interview, Derrida lists those in his lineages as including Lacan, Althusser, Levinas, Foucault, Barthes, Deleuze, Blanchot, Lyotard, Kofman.

he teases out the contradictions, the undecidabilities, the impossible decisions, the unpresentables at the heart of justice. It is the injustice at the heart of justice that, Derrida explains, "deconstructs from within any assurance of presence, any certitude or any supposed criteriology that would assure us of the justice of the decision, in the truth of the very event of a decision" (1990, 965). For Derrida, justice remains an impossible event. Yet he insists that it is in its impossibility something that we must strive again and again to make possible. His war is a practice of attunement to events beyond established beliefs, confident rationalities, instituted values, and settled good sense . . . beyond possibility. As Hélène Cixous explains, for Derrida, "It is necessary that Democracy *remain to come*. It is necessary to think it and to think of it with a thought that will *always and still* remain beyond what is realizable. Beyond the possible, that is to say, beyond that for which I am prepared, beyond what I can claim, beyond what I, myself, a finite and delimited being, can do. Responsibility, in its secret splendor, consists in going further than one's own power. And this is to be lived, with difficulty, as he lived it, in the daily renewal of effort, fatigue, in a courageous insistence at the heart and core of discouragement" (2009, 43).

Derrida's attention to the unthought, indeed to the unthinkable, follows the same fault lines we advocate through Anthropocenean sensibilities. To think from the unsayables of current climate justice regimes, to think, dream, desire beyond what is now possible: these constitute our best hope for moving beyond the stranglehold of our current economies of thought and action.

What is not experienced as we experience Derrida is yet another aporia, that of the ever-shifting relation between affect and cognition, of ethos and episteme, of habits of thought and habits of action. For this experience, we return to Anzaldúa: "Back on the timber bridge, the wind shifts, whipping your hair away from your eyes. La Llorona's wail rises, urging you to pay heed. All seven ojos de luz blink 'on.' Your body trembles as a new knowing slithers up like a snake, stirring you out of your stupor. You raise your head and look around. Following the railroad tracks to the horizon, you note the stages of your life, the turning points, the rips in your life's fabric. Gradually the pain and the grief force you to face your situation, the daily issues of living laid bare. . . . As your perception shifts, your emotions shift—you gain a new understanding of your negative feelings.... By using these feelings as tools or grist for the mill, you move through fear, anxiety, and anger, and blast into another reality. But transforming habitual feelings is the hardest thing you've ever attempted" (2015, 131).

Bringing Anzaldúa to bear challenges us to remove the slash between cognition/affect and to cultivate the deep attunements in-between that can ignite shifts in sensibilities, moving us out of the stasis of denial to the movements of mutual worldly vulnerabilities. Through enfleshed genealogical sensibilities, we can begin to apprehend and learn to be affected anew by the complex imporings of affect-concept, cultural attunements-institutional inclinations, epistemes-norms. Transforming sensibilities requires crossing fiery bridges that begin with habituated ways of thinking and living, crossing over crevasses of uncertainty as we move toward possibilities for reorienting our perceptions, desires, and knowledge. We and not only other things reshape ... transform. Our affected thinking changes. Cuerpomentealma. Our reflections on ourselves change. Our desires change. As Anzaldúa puts it, we "blast into another reality." If we are fortunate.

Anzaldúa brings to bear the inaudible dimension of Derridean deconstruction. The importance of effecting an affective shift from an overemphasis on cognition to attunements beyond thought. These are indeed ways of "knowing" but ones that emerge through and give rise to affective responses and desires, habitual dispositions, bodily comportments. "I speak and write from what grounds me," Anzaldúa explains, "my physical body, the body of a female, a Chicana tejana, embedded in an indigenous Mexicana culture rich in symbols and metaphors, a body immersed in many cultures, a queer body" (2015, 182). Anzaldúa's emphasis is not reformation but transformation, and the falling apart that is part of it. "The who-we-are is currently undergoing disintegration and reconstruction, pulled apart, dismembered, then reconstructed" (2015, 74). Anzaldúa reminds us that we cannot simply think our way out of the economies of thought and practice that brought us to the Anthropocene.

The ethos of our work in this chapter, indeed in this book, echoes Foucault's desire for self-transformation. He reminds us: "Someone who is a writer is not simply doing his work in his books, in what he publishes, but that his major work is, in the end, himself in the process of writing his books ... the work includes the whole life as well as the text. The work is more than the work; the subject who is writing is part of the work" (1986b, 186). In a similar vein, Anzaldúa says, "Soy la que escribe ye se escribe/I am the one who writes and who is being written. Últimanente es el escribir que me escribe/It is the writing that 'writes' me. I 'read' and 'speak' myself into being ... I 'speak in tongues'—understand the languages, emotions, thoughts, fantasies of the various sub-personalities inhabiting me and the various grounds they speak from" (2015, 3). Practices of transformation thus emerge from unsettling the present actual.

So we who agree with Foucault and Anzaldúa attempt to create a malaise not only in ourselves but also in the communities around us. We attune ourselves to the unfathomable imporings of lifeways and landscapes and the convoluted infusions of injustice that shape them. We come to understand the deep histories of oppression infusing institutions, environments, and flesh. We animate thresholds, tensions, and contradictions on the way to allowing new lifeways to emerge. In the midst of the imporings of interrelationalities we can become open to being reanimated by new values. In this place we can embody new values, perhaps even new forms of normativity, but not ones that are fixed or universal. These would be mortal normativities, ones that emerge from and develop in response to modes of corporealization. Normativities that are themselves open, porous, vulnerable, changeable. But ones that afford an impulse for finding meanings and values that enhance our lives together. Norms that are deeply uncertain yet essential to action. In *Giving an Account of Oneself*, Judith Butler expresses the unknowability at the heart of ethical action. As she explains: "We must recognize that ethics requires us to risk ourselves precisely at moments of unknowingness, when what forms us diverges from what lies before us, when our willingness to become undone in relation to others constitutes our chance of becoming human. To be undone by another is a primary necessity, an anguish, to be sure, but also a chance—to be addressed, claimed, bound to what is not me, but also to be moved, to be prompted to act, to address myself elsewhere, and so to vacate the self-sufficient 'I' as a kind of possession" (2005, 136).

This is an impulse for an incalculable future, for terra incognita. Not a future limited by current ideologies undergirding conceptions of justice and freedom that reinforce humancentricness, garrison individualism, and harden assumptions of self-interest. We begin to find paths through uncharted territories. Paths that offer new possibilities for being together. Perhaps we can cultivate experiences from the in-between through the affective dispositions that arise in the space created by the unceasing reminder of the inevitable play of the world and the openness of bodies in that play—a play of influences and exchanges where we dwell in the midst of change, living in-relation. Through such an ethos of indwelling, we feel our way beyond. We live with uncertainty. Uncertainty and instability are unavoidable, for there will always be incalculable effects of action. But with Anthropocenean sensibilities, such an ethos has the potential to provide openings, thresholds through which new futures are imagined and perhaps lived. Here we agree with Butler: "If we speak and try to give an account from this place, we will not be irresponsible, or, if we are, we will surely be forgiven" (2005, 136).

We come to understand that to respond to climate change, to be affected, we must become undone in every way—conceptually, affectively, habitually—in order to give rise to new sensibilities. This means destabilizing outworn stories. Learning to live with change and uncertainty. Being subjected to the Anthropocene can be a provocation for transformation: of our ontological commitments, our sense of selves, our conceptions of agency, our ethos, our episteme, our affective lives, our sensibilities. This is the welcome of Anthropocenean sensibilities.

Anzaldúa was the first step on our journey in this chapter. She gives voice to our endingbeginning:

> Fuego, inspire and energize us to do the necessary work,
>
> and to honor it
>
> as we walk through the flames of transformation.
>
> May we seize the arrogance to create
>
> outrageously
>
> soñar wildly—for the world becomes as
>
> we dream it. (2015, 157)

An Infused Dialogue

BORDERS, FUSIONS, INFLUENCE

We begin our dialogue with borders, the demarcations between us, between my body and your body, human and nonhuman lives, habits of thought and institutional structures, nature and culture, reason and unreason, good and evil, self and other, subject and object. We find ourselves between the devil and the deep blue sea. Differences, distinctions, and borders are key to knowing and acting responsibly. Yet we are held captive by particular habits of understanding that police such borders and make them solid and rigid with unbecoming fervor. We desire to trouble borders when they are experienced in this way, to trouble these experiences with the aim of transforming habits of thought and embodied dispositions that find borders to be impenetrable and not dynamic. We want to engender new appreciations of shades of difference and porous, dynamic borders through the deep, ongoing play of fusions in-between.

We will provide an account of the ways in-between happens in differing circumstances. We intend to disrupt and displace legacies of substance ontologies with their instantiated borders and consequent bifurcations among things. We want to encourage attention to fusing, concrescent events as we come to understand the ways shades of differencing and porous borders happen. In-between comes about as continuous coalescing, a reminder of the deep interconnectivity of "things in the making" (James 1958, 263). We are attuned to the porosity of interrelationalities and interactions that compose differences, distinctions, and borders. In this attunement we deploy four concepts: viscous porosity, corporeal vulnerability, imporing, and anonymous agency in five meditations on the porous borders of nitrates; the discursive influence of fissured epistemic borders and the transformations that eventuate from those ruptures; the anonymous agency of paintings; agential fusions in the openness of wonder; and erotic love without objectivity. This chapter composes a rumination on fusions at the heart of reflections, physicality's extensive vulnerability, and astonishment in the appearing of things.

THE INTERRELATIONS OF NITROGEN

The current world population stands at over 7.5 billion. The United Nations predicts that by 2050 the population will have grown to almost 10 billion and that it will increase further to over 11 billion by the end of the century (United Nations 2017). To appreciate the nature of this transformation, consider that in 1900 the world population was about 1.6 billion. This fourfold increase in the span of about a century was supported in large part by significantly higher crop yields resulting from a variety of technological and chemical transformations in agricultural practices, including planting, irrigation, and harvesting technologies; fertilizers; pesticides; and new crop strains. Our focus here will be on the use of synthetic fertilizers.

The development of synthetic nitrogenous fertilizers in the early twentieth century paved the way for profound transformations in crop yields. Mass production of inexpensive nitrogenous fertilizers after World War II resulted in significantly higher crop yields per hectare of farmland by the end of the century, with, for example, wheat yields more than tripling and corn yields rising more than fivefold in the United States.[1] Synthetic nitrogenous fertilizers thus served to fuel the fourfold population

---

1. During the war, the United States built a number of plants to produce nitrogen, as it was one of the main ingredients in explosives. When the war ended, the capacity of these plants was turned from explosives to fertilizer, which in turn fueled the rise of high-yield crops like hybrid corn.

increase. Human well-being remains closely coupled with its infusions, for "modern cropping is highly dependent on constant inputs of nitrogen" (Smil 2011, 10). Without it, almost half of the world's food supply would fail, and roughly three billion people would face situations of food scarcity, leading to hunger, undernutrition, and, in some cases, starvation (Smil 2012).

The circulations of nitrogen offer insight into the viscous porosity of bodies, the intrinsic interrelationality of things in the making. Porosity calls attention to the in-between, the imporing and fusing of things, the emergent and complex constitution of what is. Nitrogen fertilizers are applied to croplands to increase yields. Nitrate is taken up by plant roots, providing amino acids, fueling chlorophyll as well as nucleic acids, supporting many of the biochemical reactions on which life is based. Attention to porosity serves to disrupt sedimented habits of making separations—between nature and culture, between subjects and objects. Not all of the nitrogen is taken up by crops. Some will leach into rivers and groundwater and influence algal blooms and expand dead zones. Nitrates in the water we drink are taken up through porous, fleshy interactions that sometimes result in cancer and neurological diseases. Appreciation of porosities interrupts inclinations to embrace the between, the persistence of the "addition"—biological *and* cultural—with its concomitant belief that the distinctions signify a natural and unchanging boundary. As we deploy the term *in-between*, the hyphen serves as a symbolic reminder to avoid the habit of shifting to the plus of additive accounts: nature + culture, material + semiotic. The infusions of synthetic fertilizers stimulate microbes in the soil to convert nitrogen to nitrous oxide at a faster rate than normal. The circulations of nitrous oxides in the atmosphere enhance the greenhouse effect, contributing to anthropogenic global warming (US Environmental Protection Agency 2015).

The viscosity of the porosity serves as a reminder that concrescences are not random. Only some concrescences are possible given the legacy of those that came before them. Only some things are in the making: "There is a viscous porosity of flesh—my flesh and the flesh of the world. This porosity is a hinge through which we are of and in the world ... there are membranes that effect the interactions. These membranes are of various types—skin and flesh, prejudgments and symbolic imaginaries, habits and embodiments" (Tuana 2008, 199–200). The in-between is a happening of influence, of imporing.

We wish to influence shifts of habits, affective dispositions, and attunements so as to catalyze transformations in ways of living—to learn to conceive and act anew, to break out of habits of thought and action that are grounded in sedimented images and concepts of essential substances and eternal realities. Attunements with occurrences of in-between can effect affective shifts to greater clarity and appreciation of the importance of corporeal vulnerability.

We will advance Judith Butler's conception of corporeal vulnerability in which she shifts the signification of vulnerability from weakness to an openness with the other, to the ability to affect and be affected (2005, 2009). We expand the significance of corporeal vulnerability as Butler presents it. Informed by the circulations of viscous porosity, we reach far beyond her restriction of corporeal vulnerability to the domain of the human. The viscous porosity of corporeal vulnerability is a reminder of the reciprocal vulnerability of things in the making. Each event, each concrescence, is what it is because of its capacity to be affected. Vulnerability is in the nature of things in the making, the openness of becoming; it is the possibility for imporing that is the wellspring of what is.

Corporeal vulnerability is a reminder of exchanges as well as of exposures: the influences and inflowings of nitrates and the flesh of plants and animals; the sites of exchanges between agricultural practices and atmospheric circulations; the coemergence of interrelations among social institutions and geophysical processes; the evolution of ecosystems and human well- and ill-being. Corporeal exchanges are not inherently positive or negative. They are the happenings of concrescences, whether beneficial or harmful, productive or destructive. Only through our viscous porosities, our interconnected openness in the world, can we be physically and psychically nourished as well as injured. Attunement to corporeal vulnerabilities and the influences that flow through them can open us to a new alertness, a new ethos as we live with the complex interrelations and elemental exchanges that constitute our world. This attunement can enhance our ability to be affected and encourage us to attend to the options presented by the now-expanded domains of interaction and mutual dependence.

POROUS BODIES OF KNOWLEDGE: FOUCAULT

We began at the site of borders. We will continue our attention to the various ways porous borders happen and to language appropriate for their happening as we turn to one of Michel Foucault's accounts of what we call *the imporing of epistemic borders*. With the neologism *imporing*, we have in mind the suffused movements that happen in the borders of things. The word elaborates *porosity* and in this section places emphasis on the mutational happenings of subtle but nonetheless unsettling influences and broken continuities in what Foucault called epistemes, that is, in the most profound and wide-ranging sensibilities in Western culture. In these mutational happenings, something passes without intention or design, not between but in-between the formations of orders of knowledge, meaning, and rational good sense. *Imporing* names the occurrence of that in-between. The part of Foucault's account in *The Order of Things* that will interest us describes imporings that were minute but whose effects over a long period of time were huge (1973c). The dynamic permutations and impacts in their particularity continued for more than a century without noticeable shifts in the defining formations. But infusions into them continued over a long enough time to effect increasingly significant mutational transformations. Those changes, as we will see, happened gradually until the infused episteme and its borders of difference were definitively altered. These constituted changes in fundamental senses of order and agency in knowledge of language, nature, and exchange; they—these changes—created a new episteme and the modern subject, the modern agent of representation. The subject of representation creates the dichotomy of subject/object. It—the subject of representation—inevitably re-presents, and what is re-presented is known as an object of consciousness.

A Short Excursus

Before we move further into an elaboration of the imporing of epistemic borders, we interrupt ourselves and return for a moment to the imporing of fleshy borders. We want to emphasize that imporings are not limited to conscious events. They do not define universal being or human nature. In their varieties they are their own kind of happenings *in* borders. Imporings constitute the inflowing and outflowing of influences that can fuse in the borders and compose a new event that is reducible to nothing other than itself.

Ammonium nitrogen (NH_4^+) is added to soil to fertilize plants. Under warm growing conditions, bacteria and NH_4^+ interfuse and occasion its transformation into nitrate nitrogen (NO_3^-) via nitrification. The stability of NH_4^+ is loosened through this imporing, and the porosity of NO_3^- is free to be leached from the soil. Nitrate accumulates in the groundwater, streams, and rivers and enters the water that we drink (Ward 2009). Nitrates bind to hemoglobin, and the happening in-between alters the hemoglobin, generating methemoglobin, which impairs oxygen delivery to tissues: "The health effect of most concern to the U.S. EPA for children is the 'blue baby syndrome' (methemoglobinemia) seen most often in infants exposed to nitrate from drinking water used to make formula" (US Environmental Protection Agency 1991). In this instance, not epistemes. Children.

We return to *The Order of Things* to consider anonymous agential fusions in the context of the transformation from what Foucault calls the episteme of Similitude to the episteme of Representation. In this book Foucault set himself the task of describing the transformations of rules of order and systems of regularity that function unconsciously and anonymously in the established knowledge and sensibilities of a given time. What are the tacit rules that allow things to come together—to concresce—in some ways and not others? "Concresce in some ways" in this context means the coming together of such various things as truths and orders that makes sense of the world. Foucault is giving an account of what he calls the rules of discursive space that function as a dynamic "positive unconscious of knowledge," in an effective, anonymous agency, when people make sense of the world (1973c, xii–xiii). *Similitude* is the name Foucault gives to the dominant episteme of the fifteenth and sixteenth centuries in western Europe. He describes it as a space of radiation in which all things in heaven and on earth share definitive similarities in their proportions and connections, a great chain of being that links all things in the universe by essential resemblances "in the vast syntax of the world" (1973c, 21, 25; see chap. 2.1 and also Lovejoy 1960). Within the jurisdiction of Similitude, orders enact the sense that everything enjoys a likeness to everything else. Orders enact the cosmic order. Sameness rules the spacing, gathering, and identity of all things. In the episteme of Similitude, the heavens, for example, are like the mountains in the principles that define their being. Being is One in the differences of what exists. Resemblance in all things, and not separated, interconnected, incompatible differences, constitutes the way all things concresce.

Within this epistemic domain, Foucault says, "to search for meaning is to bring to light a resemblance. To search for the law governing signs is to discover the things that are alike.... The nature of things, their coexistence, the way in which they are linked is nothing other than their resemblance" (1973c, 29). Knowledge of living things, for example, comprises what is essential in knowing the nature of signs and language. Sameness rules all differences, and knowledge of the universe is knowledge of the sympathetic draw of a seamless realm of complementary beings and processes: "The patterns from which [different kinds of things] are cut is the same" (1973c, 29).

Foucault finds one kind of porosity in this seemingly self-sufficient episteme. Similitude needs to confirm itself by the addition of new knowledge. In fact, it needs *to continuously* add to its self-confirmation by exploring yet unknown parts of nature and the rules that govern the discovered realities. In the rule of Similitude, dark spaces continued to appear that required classification (1973c, 30). Similitude's dark spaces, its porosity and its finitude, its vulnerability to what is unknown in it and its sense of incompleteness, constituted fractures in the tissue of its self-certainty. These fractures were located in its language, rationality, and knowledge, in the incompleteness of the sameness that Similitude required.

To take one example of its vulnerable porosity, knowledge of signifiers and signifieds showed that differences persisted in representation. The *what* that is represented—that is, the signified—is never the same as the signifier by which it is known. Representing perpetuates the differences between the reality of the *"what"* "that is known and the knowledge of it, not their samenesses. Representation as it came to be understood thus showed that to represent anything, by the very act of representing, engendered continuing differences that undercut Similitude's intuitive power of persuasion. Knowing and experiencing other things, whatever the things, did not follow the rules that established sameness.

Further, whereas scholars had found that syllables and words concresce because "there are virtues placed in the individual letters that draw them toward each other or keep them apart, exactly as the marks found in nature also repel and attract one another," linguists, in their newly developing discipline, found that language constitutes a break in that its order of attraction and repulsion differs from the order of attraction and repulsion of visible forms of nature (1973c, 35). Far from an order that establishes a seamless connection between language and nature, they—language and nature—are held apart in an absence of Similitude. A further complication emerged as linguists found that "language is a fragmented nature, divided against itself and deprived of its original transparency," transparency that, according to those in the know, it had prior to the Tower of Babel (1973c, 35). But now it is a fallen organism, defying the sameness that Similitude would bestow upon it.

An imporing happened in-between traditional, established knowledge and growing specializations. Scholars began to focus on the rules and histories of different grammars, for example. They studied such languages as Sanskrit, Chinese, and Greek as well as their own languages. Others studied the details of "natural lives," the flora and fauna around them in their particularities and classifiable differences. It is as though the new knowledge emerging from various kinds of specialization seeped in through the fissures, the dark spaces, of incompletion in the episteme Similitude. We can say that in the assurances of Similitude different kinds of knowledge, in their fusions, began, unbidden and unknown, to empower senses of difference and division. They opened regions of difference that constituted gaps (fissures) in the orders of things. They opened regions that lacked transparency with the very episteme that made possible sense and truth. Instead of surety about the universe, feelings of uncertainty, at first faint and probably unnoticed, emerged as though from nowhere. Fusions of different ways of knowing in-between these differences opened—let's call it an inclination to question—as learned people carried out their research in directions guided not by Similitude but by the research itself.

We return for a moment to the question of how signs present their signifieds. Within the episteme of Similitude, signs constituted a play of resemblances and differences that referred to a world of systematically ordered resemblances. But increasingly the knowledge of signs and of language could not verify the similarities that they should disclose (see Foucault 1973c, 35–36). How are signs, in their fallen dispersion and in the emerging specializations, to re-present a system of sympathetic resemblances? An influx of disturbing questions and problems concerning the Same and the Other arose with the multiplication of types of knowledge that were oriented by particular differences and not by Similitude. In time the problematic of re-presenting so infused issues of truth and sense that "at the beginning of the 17th century . . . thought ceases to move in the element of resemblance. Similitude is no longer the form of knowledge but rather the occasion of error. [Although] the chimeras of Similitude loom up on all sides . . . they are recognized as chimeras" (Foucault 1973c, 51).

According to Foucault's account, the episteme of Similitude was relatively stable (viscous) for more than two centuries but was nonetheless porous. Imporing happened, as we have seen, when specialized linguistic knowledge that had its sense by means of Similitude and that also undercut the pervasiveness of the resemblance that Similitude required influenced the culture's basic sensibility. That undercutting functioned as an anonymous agent in-between the dynamic formations of the rules and principles for orders of truth and sense in Similitude's dominion. Yet within that same episteme, scholarly knowledge began to show the multiple, intrinsic differences in language and semiotic rules. These in-between differences established relations of definitive dissimilarity that were beyond the reach of Similitude's sway. The result, in combination with other influences, was a slow formation of a new episteme that radically changed the prevailing space for truth and sense and in that change revolutionized Western culture.

One factor of the revolution was the emergence of the power of the subject/object axis in what is often called the modern era.

KANDINSKY: A PAINTING'S ANONYMOUS AGENCY

We have spoken of anonymous agency in the context of Foucault's account of the transformation of the episteme Similitude. We turn now to Wassily Kandinsky, an artist who developed a "totally new art," an art "'with forms that mean nothing and represent nothing and recall nothing,' yet which will excite the human spirit as only music had previously been able to do" (Weiss 1982, 34). His paintings compose remarkable instances of anonymous agency. The anonymous agencies of this totally new art, in their combinations of forms and colors, speak directly—immediately—to people's souls, their spirits, to their deepest feelings. They communicate directly in the sense that they are not mediated by rational reflection or specific meanings. As Kandinsky says: "Form alone, even though totally abstract and geometrical, has a power of inner suggestion. A triangle (without the accessory consideration of its being acute-or obtuse-angled or equilateral) has a spiritual value of its own. In connection with other forms, this value may be somewhat modified but remains in quality the same. The case is similar with a circle, a square, or any conceivable geometrical figure" (Kandinsky 2006, 32). His abstract paintings exist "solely for [themselves] in [their] own terms and [do] not call forth associations with anything outside [themselves]" (Whitford 1967, 15). What does that mean?

The formed colors of his abstract paintings impact attuned minds affectively and incite "spiritual" sensations for which he had no name.

Kandinsky frequently used transitive verbs when he spoke of the life of paintings. He said with respect to Monet's *Haystacks* that the paintings "grasped hold of you but moreover leave an indelible mark on the mind" (Kandinsky 1974, as cited in Lampe and Roberts 2014, 8). Paintings "feed the spirit . . . indeed the *Stimmung* [mood, disposition] of a picture can deepen and purify that of the spectator" (Kandinsky 2006, 2).[2] Paintings are, of course, marked by specific styles and traditions, but they also free themselves from the artist's control and intentions as they disclose

---

2. We understand *pure* to mean for him "unadulterated by rational reflection" as well as "spiritually lofty."

themselves to those who form a perceptive relation with them. Freed from its creator and to an important degree from its material limitations, the painting becomes anonymous and transcends the circumstances of its emergence (See Kandinsky 2006, 8, 11–12, 58). It constitutes what Kandinsky called a spirit of its own.

All manner of synthetic connections can develop from the force of a painting's "coursing energy of color and the wavy line" (Hiddleston-Galloni 2014, 4).[3] Paintings shimmer in their planes of color that are bordered by dynamic lines that do not form represented identities. The syntheses of lines and colors—their blending—form circles, triangles, squares, and rhombuses. The lines are blending borders of color with varied thicknesses and often interrupted directions. The colors in some instances appear to be directed by one spot of, say, bright red or intense black that gives vibrant tone—we are tempted to say, gives intonation—in the entire painting. In these paintings Kandinsky found spiritual vibrations emerging in these syntheses and rebounding in compound vibrations. These vibrations happen in the painting as colors and lines impore with a dimension of strange communicating—not unnatural communicating, we believe (in disagreement with Kandinsky), but with a different kind of communication in comparison with what people expect in an environment ruled by present-day common sense, rationality, and the dominance of the subject/object conception. Paintings happen as affective agencies and without objectification. This agency is where Kandinsky finds paintings' autonomous and independent lives.

In the shifting, shimmering planes of color the paintings communicate, Kandinsky said, "emotions beyond the reach of words" (2006, 12). A painting, then, engages the attuned viewer not primarily as an object but as an immediate region of vibrant affect, mind to mind, heart to heart, in ways whereby forms, colors, tones, and feelings interfuse in affective transmission. The viewer is *in* wordless feelings. They—the feelings—infuse one's nonreflective awareness. When we, for example, were quietly in the presence of Kandinsky's paintings, especially those after 1908, we found ourselves observers of feelings and senses that we underwent but

---

3. Hiddleston-Galloni used this felicitous phrase to refer to paintings in the Judendstil movement, what Kandinsky referred to as a "totally new art."

did not intend and for which we had no name. It is not that we were nonvoluntarily grasped and made objects of an agent's action. In a dimension of our minds, we were participant in a happening, a shimmering, intimating happening that we shared and did not own. It carried feelings without a determinate object. An anonymous agent seemed to transmit itself in its borders beyond its borders in a welcoming, pre-reflective dimension of our minds and shifted, if only for a short while, our sense of who and where we were. "Feeling," Kandinsky said, "is creative power, and ... it is the necessary guide by which [people] can enter into a work of art." Further, "if the spectator is deprived of the 'bridge' which gives him the possibility for entering this field of pure painting, and if he is deprived at the same time of the necessary feeling, he is disconnected. He thinks he has no longer any standards by which to appreciate art" (Kandinsky 1948, 820). No longer spectators in an immediacy without a bridge, we experienced the freedom of Kandinsky's art in its anonymous agency.

In our experience with Kandinsky's paintings, imporing happens in our exposure with them through our corporeal vulnerability in the vibrant affects of feelings and tones that arise by the synthetic connections of colors and lines. Those affects occurred in-between the borders that define us and the art's difference from us. The exposure is a happening that opens our awareness to a dimension of our lives that in its vitality is neither subject nor object, neither color nor line, neither idea nor image, but living affective immediacy. Vital oneness with the painting's communicated vitality takes place. We together experienced this immediacy at the Kandinsky retrospective exhibit at the Frist Center in Nashville, Tennessee: sitting quietly together with *Painting with Red Spot* we found ourselves in the vibrant affect of its shimmering colors and dynamic lines. In our quiet attunement with each other, forms and feelings and the warmth of our bodies where they touched infused in the painting's communication. We were attuned with the quiet that suffused the murmurings of those who with us engaged the painting; the sounds' vibrations often infused our attunement as shoes padded, heels clicked, and words whispered. We felt the vibrations of air and glimpsed movements as viewers shifted around us, their movements shifting our focus when we were no longer able to see this or that part of the painting and found ourselves immersed in a shimmering movement of the painting that was previously unheeded.

In the vibrations of the movements around us and, in a sense, through us, the lines and shimmering colors of the painting moved through us differently than before. Disturbances in the in-between, we might say. But in our experience the painting seemed to call us to ourselveswithit, call in the disturbance, bringing itself to our attention, infusing us as we felt the painting in this space happen—as we felt the happening happen in the vibrant silence of the moment.

Bodymind traces of those feelings wove themselves into this chapter, indeed into this book, as the anonymous agency of *Painting with Red Spot* became enfleshed and in that enfleshed border we found ourselves beyond, beyond subject/object, beyondourselveswithourselves in the vibrations of Kandinsky's paintings, beyond the words we use to speak of being in that border.

McCLINTOCK: FEELING WITH THE ORGANISM

We began at the site of borders. We then shifted to the organic, epistemic, affective in-between. Our aspiration is to inspire attunements to the ongoing play in the occurrences of in-between. In the previous section we called attention to the immediacy of concrescences of colors, lines, and affects through the play of the agency of a Kandinsky painting. Now we shift our perspective from art to the play of the world.

As John McDermott reminded us, we are habituated to "think of ourselves as 'in the world,' as a button is in a box, a marble in a hole, a coin in a pocket.... And yet, to the contrary, we are engaging in activities more descriptive of a permeable membrane than of a box. To feel is to be felt. To be in the world is to 'world' and to be 'worlded'" (1986, 129). We find ourselves in the midst of things. Physicality's extensive vulnerability is the site of becoming, the openness of living, reflection, and affect. It occasions in-between.

As we noted in chapter 6, attunements to imporing can open us to new habits of worldly indwelling. Our lives happen with our active, open intertwinings with things and events. As we have stressed, things in their physicality—human bodies, institutional practices, social organizations—impore. This imporing happens through the viscous porosity in which we world and are worlded. Perceiving a Kandinsky painting in the midst of the decline of the subject/object axis reminds us that heartmind emerges continuously in relations. We can see this relational in-between in Iris Marion Young's example of pregnant embodiment with its corporeal intertwining: "Pregnancy challenges the integration of my body experience by rendering fluid the boundary between what is within, myself, and what is outside, separate. I experience my insides as the space of another, yet my own body... the integrity of my body is undermined in pregnancy not only by this externality of the inside, but by the fact that the boundaries of my body are themselves in flux. In pregnancy I literally do not have a firm sense of where my body ends and the world begins" (1984, 49). Young shows that this bodily awareness happens without objectification, a bodying forth that dissipates the axis of subject/object.

Imporing happens not only through lines and colors or flesh with flesh but also in our relation to things. We find this attunement cultivated in the work of the cytogeneticist Barbara McClintock, who received a Nobel Prize in 1983 for her discovery of transposition—a DNA sequence that can "jump" or change its position within the genome. McClintock, who studied the mechanisms of the color patterns of maize seed and the unstable inheritance of these patterns, described herself as having developed a close relationship with the maize she cultivated and analyzed. She reported, "I start with the seedling [of maize], I don't want to leave it. I don't feel I really know the story if I don't watch the plant all the way along. So I know every plant in the field. I know them intimately, and I find it a great pleasure to know them" (Keller 1983, 198).

McClintock developed a relationship of empathy and cultivated attentiveness, what she called "listening to the organism." She called for a shift in sensibilities in scientific practice from imposition to attunement: *"Just let the material tell you"* (Keller 1983, 179). Her desire to listen carefully and her respect for complexity led her to cultivate a close relationship with the maize she studied. Eschewing the customary practice of having an assistant grow the maize, McClintock planted and tended the crops she studied. She viewed these interactions as a form of attention necessary for understanding. Indeed, in this attunement she came to know her plants so intimately that she could predict the structure of the cells' nuclei from external traits of the plants: "Before examining the chromosomes, I went through the field and made my guess for every plant as to what kind of rings it would have.... *I never made a mistake*" (Keller 1983, 102).

McClintock's feeling with the organism was a form of imporing, an undergoing of the maize's influence that resulted in a shift in her sensibilities: "I found that the more I worked with them the bigger and bigger [the chromosomes] got, and when I was really working with them I wasn't outside, I was down there. I was part of the system. I was right down there with them, and everything got big. ... I felt as if I were right down there and these were my friends" (Keller 1983, 117). Oneness with the chromosomes' felt vitality happened in the border of herself-with-chromosomes.

McClintock is so outside the subject/object axis! Hers was an imporing of an imporing. "The function of a gene," she explained, "can only be fully understood in terms of the cellular environment in which it operates. And the cellular environment, of course, is dynamic, changing constantly as a result of signals from other cells, including those that derive from events occurring in the external environment" (Meaney 2010, 48).

For McClintock, feeling with the organism was a source of marvel, of wonder: "Organisms can do all types of things; they do fantastic things. They do everything that we do, and they do it better, more efficiently, more marvelously" (Keller 1983, 179). Astonishment in the presencing of things is a happening of openness with the agential influence of things without objectification. Consider Merleau-Ponty's description of sensation: "The sensor and the sensible do not stand in relation to each other as two mutually external terms, and sensation is not an invasion of the sensor by the sensible.... in this transaction between the subject of sensation and the sensible it cannot be held that one acts while the other suffers the action, or that the one confers significance on the other.... As I contemplate the blue of the sky ... I abandon myself to it and plunge into this mystery, it 'thinks itself within me,' I am the sky itself as it is drawn together and unified, and as it begins to exist for myself, my consciousness is saturated with limitless blue.... I ought to say that *one* perceives in me, and not that I perceive" (1995, 214–15).

Here we see fusion at the heart of reflection, physicality's extensive vulnerability, and astonishment in being in-between.

THE POWER OF EROTIC LOVE WITHOUT OBJECTIFICATION

> A grammar lesson: "The lover died."
> "Lover" is subject and agent, but that can't be!
> The lover is defunct.
>
> Only grammatically is the dervish-lover a doer.
> In reality, with he or she so overcome,
>   so dissolved into love,
>   all qualities of doingness
>   disappear.
>
> —Rumi, "Rough Metaphors"

Human desire usually has an object of longing or hope. The more intense the desire, the more singularly prominent its object. *Sides* (the Latin stem for *-sire*), after all, means "heavenly body." When people desire, they want, crave, and even covet the desired, whether the desired is food, a professorship, or another's body. What is intensely desired, even if it is not heavenly, has the status of an object with exceptional and immediate meaning and draw. When simple desire finds satisfaction, the desired's attraction withers in its completeness, and the object fades into the ordinary environment, not unlike the disinterest we experience after we have overindulged in our favorite ice cream or the indifference to the other's presence we can experience on the morning after a casual sexual hookup.

We turn to the passion of desire for another. Can a kind of loving without objectification happen in the midst of intense erotic desire? How could an erotic exchange not objectify the desired one? Even if that kind of loving did happen, how could we speak of it? How could the experience of "I want you now, absolutely" not be cast in the forms my inflamed senses want for their satisfaction?

Much feminist ink has been spilled over sexual objectification and the myriad issues that arise from being female or male in a sociocultural context that sexually objectifies women as well as certain men. When we are made into the object of another's desire, whether willfully or without intent, with or without our consent, and whether or not we internalize that doing, we, so it is argued, become a means for another's satisfaction: "Sexual love makes of the loved person an Object of appetite; as soon as that appetite has been stilled, the person is cast aside as one casts away a lemon which has been sucked dry.... As soon as a person becomes an Object of appetite for another, all motives of moral relationship cease to function, because as an Object of appetite for another a person becomes a thing and can be treated and used as such by everyone" (Kant [1780] 1963, 163).

Ours is a quest for erotic love beyond objectification, where objectification ceases and becomes meaningless. Our concern is not that of Kant or even of the feminist ilk. We are *not* interested in judging erotic desire that objectifies. No doubt there are times when such objectification is detrimental to the one so objectified. We are well aware that the systematic objectification of certain groups of individuals can be an instrument of oppression. Through the various modes in which the subjectivity of certain groups is denied or seen as limited, objectification, often sexual objectification, and its various disciplinary practices serve as a means to police and minimize agency. Objectification can be in this way a vehicle for power. As Sally Haslanger has argued, "If one objectifies something, one views it as an object for the satisfaction of one's desire." She explains that it is through this process that sexist constructions emerge: "In objectifying something one views it as *having a nature* which makes it desirable in the ways one desires it, and which enables it to satisfy that desire. For example, if men desire submission, then in objectifying women men view women as having a nature which makes them (or, under normal circumstances, should make them) submissive, at the same time as they force women into submission" (2002, 229). Ours, however, is a quest for erotic love beyond objectification, where objectification ceases and becomes meaningless.

In the previous sections of this chapter we described how the porosity of borders happens in four contexts and used language that communicated without the imagery and conceptuality of a subject/object bifurcation. In this language we presented instances when anonymous agents function in immediate, nonreflective eventuations. These eventuations may be called "middle voice" events (a term we will discuss), in which the occurrence reverts to itself with neither transitivity nor passivity, where imporing in-betweens happen. These eventuations are without subject or object.

Before we turn to Rumi's poem and to erotic love without objectification, a few words about the middle voice and middle voice events. We are looking for ways of speaking and writing that emerge out of happenings that revert back to themselves and do not suggest subjective or objective functions. We saw, for example, that in Kandinsky's paintings vibrations of colors and lines present their own event in the event's occurrence. The event "voices" itself "without the intervention of regard for itself" (Scott 1990, 23). We also saw that nitrogen fuses through porous borders with plants as well as with humans, with a mix of positive and negative consequences, none of which is caused by a subject's acting on an object. When we really pay attention to the porosity of borders and the pervasiveness of fusions our reliance on subject/object formations will be disrupted. Instead of a subject's relating to something as an object, we found events of becoming, events that are in-between in the activity of becoming. We saw that there is no distance of one and then the other, neither an active subject nor a passive object. Rather, in their corporeal vulnerability, things are in the making. In these and other instances, when our grammar is not restricted by subject/object formations, we are able to speak of fusions and influences in borders of identity with middle-voiced enactments of anonymous nonsubjective agency.

A middle voice formation in early Sanskrit "may be reflexive, and on the other [hand], it may speak non-reflexively of an action in the action. For example, in a ritual the active voice for 'cleanse' or 'purify' may be used: 'Whatever of you the impure have polluted, that do I cleanse for you.' In the middle voice its sense might be rendered: 'whatsoever the impure has polluted, as to that for you through this let them become pure.' In the middle voice, the impure's becoming pure is expressed entirely in the verb form. Or, in the passive voice, we say, 'Let us be purified.' In the middle voice, we say, 'Let us become pure.' In the latter instance we are of the action that reverts to itself. It is a purifying action that makes pure. In the active voice the verb is for another. In the passive voice the verb acts on the subject. The middle voice is used when the subject is in some way specifically implicated in the result of the action but is neither the active subject nor the passive object of the action.... In the case of the intransitive verb, the active *drmhati*, for example, means 'to make (something) firm.' The intransitive middle *drmhate* means '(something) becomes firm' or, we might say, 'firming comes of its own action.' The middle voice of the verb, 'to die'—*mriyate*—we translate as 'dying occurs (of itself).'" Dying dies. "We translate *ayate* 'to be born' and 'birthing occurs (of itself).'" Birthing births. "This middle-voiced intransitivity is also found in the Greek middle perfect form, *phainesthai*, meaning 'to appear appearing or appearing appears,' and *gegonesthai*, 'to become becoming' or 'to come becoming.' In both instances the activity of the middle-voiced perfect expresses its temporal movement out of itself" (Scott 1990, 19).

Our thought is that imporing in viscous, porous borders can find linguistic expression best in intransitive middle voice phrasing. Later in the chapter as we talk of erotic love without objectification we will give accounts of events that find linguistic expression in middle voice phrasing. Now to a meditation based on Rumi's poem.[4]

An interplay emerges in an exchange of love, in loving interrelation, in all phases of the lovers' lives: when we, for example, are quietly close together at the end of the day, glancing at each other in the midst of a meal, holding hands while listening to a lecture, making love. Each happens, in these loving exchanges, not as a supplement but interconnected in a creative space of living. The exchanges pervade our daily lives and the ways we connect with all things. They carry us into the play of the world. They are neither active nor passive but shimmering in-between. They—these exchanges—pervade the lovers' memories and intentions, their values and judgments, their silence and suffering, their vulnerability and assertiveness. They give context for fulfillment and violation. When this kind of dynamic interplay fuels desire in erotic love, that desire for the other happens not within the one or the other but in the porous in-between.

The porosity of bodies when they interact erotically in love opens us in being together "dissolved into love." In this kind of experience, the erotic enactment of love is the happening of this in-between. A backing-and-forthing happens in it without apparent beginning or ending. Relating relates relating—together becoming a play of the senses, belonging together in a landscape of love's exchange, there already when "I want

---

4. We use this poem because of its descriptive power in presenting what we speak of by the phrase *erotic love without objectification*. However, Rumi's religious orientation and our orientation are considerably different.

you absolutely" begins its erotic dance, a happening that is not done while much else is done. In which:

> ... all qualities of doingness
> disappear.

As the relationship of love comes to bear sexually, beloveds are able to find themselves interfused in the porosity of the relationship. In the interfusing, loving loves. A word from the one to the other then is an exchange carrying them to and fro, an immediacy, not a separation, not a boundary, but a coming together in the midst of loving, a journey that carries lovers together, revealing a secret that bothtogether are and are not one. They are dynamically interconnected in loving, interfusing in such a way that they experience themselves in-between: sexually imporing, we might say, in a mutual flowing. Whose flesh? Whose breath? Whose touch? This experience describes an awareness that happens as erotic relating relates relating. This is an awareness that is absurd in a language that has sense only within the formations under the jurisdiction of subject/object. Our topic for this part of the chapter is found in the connected differencing of "doingness" as doingness continues the play of differencing and also disappears in erotic loving.

In the in-between of lovers, a kiss is neither the one's nor the other's. *Doingness disappears*. In-between, words are neither the one's nor the other's. Meaning occurs in exchanges of meaning. Listening happens in the midst of listening: "All saying is middle-voiced. This means that when I speak I undergo what I give expression to ... the *intimacy* of the two and the double requires that the spacing between these voices remains open precisely so that the two can remain in touch with each other ... [and] keep this circulation circulating" (Brogan 2012, 93).

Withdrawal of objectification happens in active relationships of love. The key thought is that the loving relationship enacts itself in erotic desire for another. "For another" suggests this one over there, the beloved object. But the lover's desire for the beloved is not an urge that relates to itself by seeking satisfaction with an agreeable object. Love in this instance transforms objectifying urge. Satisfaction is governed by mutual imporing delight. Delight suffuses, pours over, impores: *ex-stasis*, neither mine nor yours in the happening of desire. Loving desire returns and in returning is returned. When this dynamic interplay fuels desire in erotic love, that desire for the other happens ecstatically—in and beyond oneself. The dynamic interplay infuses. It is not done. Doingness disappears. Something else happens that we name in-between. It is a happening where passion opens in wonder and the beloveds, with all the doing, with all the differences, infuse. The in-between enacts itself.

In-between, of course, is not limited to erotic love. Indeed, we have used the term to elaborate the porosity of myriad borders. Consider yet one more example. Some therapists speak of moments in sessions, often called therapeutic moments, when the client and the therapist experience a kind of fusion, a blending that is not reducible to anything else, an event a therapist friend of Charles described as between the two and belonging to neither. In such occasions the moments between them form an in-between that neither person does (doingness disappears), an enacted communication beyond the borders of their singular personalities when new insights and psychological transformations can happen. The often life-changing anonymous agency of this in-between eventuates without initiative or reception, fully aware, without subjective control.

As we faced the inexpressible dimensions of such eventuations, E. E. Cummings's unreadable poem came to mind, a poem through the disarticulated words of which an image of a grasshopper comes to view both on the page and in our mind's eye:

```
                    r-p-o-p-h-e-s-s-a-g-r
              who
a)s w(e loo)k
upnowgath
         PPEGORHRASS
                        eringint(o-
aThe):l
     eA
       !p:
S                                    a
           (r
rIvInG              .gRrEaPsPhOs)
                                  to
rea(be)rran(com)gi(e)ngly
,grasshopper; (1994, 396)
```

The porosity of the letters ("r-p-o-p-h-e-s-s-a-g-r") mirrors the porosity of things in their becoming, disrupting the sedimenting of objects. The transliterative movements ("r-p-o-p-h-e-s-s-a-g-r," "PPEGORHRASS," "gRrEaPsPhOs") are a reflection of infusing movements in the happening of in-between. The porosity of the poem's words opens into the soaring, startling movement—leaping enacts itself.

The movements of the poem enact the inexpressible dimensions of a grasshopper's leap. Isn't it surprising to connect a grasshopper's leap to the happenings of erotic love? Isn't it remarkable that we find an inexpressible dimension in so many disparate happenings—from the ex-stasis of erotic love, to the therapeutic moment, to the movements of an insect? All three remind us that living actions are always in the midst of becoming, always in motion, always vulnerable in the infusing interrelations of their lives.

In this reflection on the power of love without objectification we have relied on poems that communicate their subject matter indirectly, as middle-voiced eventuations. In our effort to do justice to this art of communication, this border art, we use middle voice constructions and such neologisms as *bothtogether*, *heartmind*, and *imporing*. As philosophers we want to indicate the importance and value of including in our disciplined awareness attunement to occurrences that many of our most influential forebears have brushed aside or made unthinkable by the limits of their various rationalities. We note the often-subtle and pre-reflective predisposition toward various types of domination and control in thought, value judgments, and social practices that are formed when subjectivity, understood as the agency of an autonomous individuated subject, is the primary focal point. In this chapter our cynosures have been climate change and agricultural practices, anonymous agency in art, the porosity of epistemes, the infusion in-between a scientist and maize, and erotic love without objectification. Throughout our reflections in this chapter our project has been to maximize some of the opportunities provided by the decline of the authority of the subject/object axis.

One of our goals in this chapter is to increase attunements to happenings beyond the power of subject/object formations, to invoke happenings in-between. In the force of that attunement we do not want simply to hold an image in mind and describe that image to you so that you can also hold the image in mind. We, rather, want to catalyze a process, to write in ways that might incite happenings of in-between, processes of affecting, in which affect is neither ours nor yours but a toing and froing in-between.

We write this chapter, indeed this book, in our attunements to in-between. As we worked through the ideas that gave rise to this chapter, we found ourselves, in Teresa Brennan's words, attending to the transmission of affect, that is, in our words, to eventuations in-between (2004). There is nothing mystical about our dialogues. They are simply a type of communicating in which the affective aspects of our awareness and our thinking-together fuse and formations happen that neither of us could own. Some people might call that a kind of insight. Others, intuition. In any case, our differences, our borders between us, continued, yet something in-between happened, a happening beyond the between. As we became more and more attuned to the happening of fusions in-between, our thinking, indeed our very ways of relating, altered as we wrote in resonance with experiences *in* borders. Most of this chapter, which inaugurated several of the conceptions that define this book, emerged out of our dialogues, our infused dialogues, as we worked on it. We found too that we were thinking philosophically as we underwent occurrences that, while intimately connected with what we were thinking, were also beyond what we were thinking. They were liminal *and* apparent *and* beyond philosophy. The processes of our thinking throughout the chapter reverted back to themselves in what we were writing. Our primary task became one of remaining true to our experiences in the writing of this book.

If our attempt succeeds, we believe that the interfusing feelings and thoughts in our composition will provide an imporing occasion with the attentive reader, an occasion that considerably exceeds what we could intend and allows indirect disclosure of unsayable events as well as movements away from inevitable objectification by a representing subjective agency. If fortune smiles, the chapter's movements and contents will evoke an in-between, a fusion that "overcome[s] ... all qualities of doingness," as objectification disappears. Our intention is to compose an instance of border art philosophy that occasions an indirect disclosure of what exceeds considerably what we can say directly.

Instead of a grammar lesson with the sentence "The lover died," we might say that in the midst of thinking philosophically

> The single philosopher died
>
> With heshe in-between,
> > so dissolved into relation beyond thinking,
> > > all reflective qualities of active or passive presence
> > > > disappear in the midst of thinking.

We close now with a meditation on a poem by a master of expressing middle voice events, Wallace Stevens:

The House Was Quiet and The World Was Calm

The house was quiet and the world was calm.
The reader became the book; and summer night

Was like the conscious being of the book.
The house was quiet and the world was calm.

The words were spoken as if there was no book,
Except that the reader leaned above the page,

Wanted to lean, wanted much most to be
The scholar to whom his book is true, to whom

The summer night is like a perfection of thought.
The house was quiet because it had to be.

The quiet was part of the meaning, part of the mind:
The access of perfection to the page.

And the world was calm. The truth in a calm world,
In which there is no other meaning, itself

Is calm, itself is summer and night, itself
Is the reader leaning late and reading there. (1954, 358–59)

Stevens describes an event of fusion. But *describes* is an insufficient word for the poem's enactment. It is misleading as well. His language lets an event happen manifestly through the words. Metaphors compound and interplay with metaphors and with a subjunctive formation that seems to melt into the night: "summer night / Was like," "The summer night is like a perfection of thought," "The words were spoken as if there was no book." It is in the reader's absorption into the book, losing any sense of difference from the book, leaning into the book, wanting above all to be the site of the book's truth—wanting above all to be true with the book's truth—melding into the summer night as the night's quiet comes to be the meaning of the mind, the minding of the mind, the showing of the mind, the mind's undone intention—the night's quiet in the access of perfection to the page. The *truth* is a calm world; that is all. It, truth, is quiet, calm, is summer and night, itself is the reader of the late night as reading impores with house, quiet, world, calm, bookless words, anonymous agency, truth, fidelity, meaning, mind nothing missing summer night itself there, no other.

livingdying

PREFACE

In this book we have often turned to neologisms to write of inseparable differences that infuse with one another in their occurrences.[1] The words *living* and *dying* in their ordinary usage, for example, seem to name distinctly different kinds of realities. Often when people speak of a living person and a dying person, they think of two distinctly different ways of being, in effect two opposite kinds of existence. "Is she dying?" we might ask. "Oh no," we are told, "she's alive and well." With the neologism *livingdying*, however, we are able to blur the definitive borders that are often assumed in the expression *living and dying*. The conjunction *and* brings them together by holding them apart as opposites. In this chapter we want to show that the borders in livingdying are not well defined. They, the borders, are porous. They constitute thresholds—transformative powers of ambiguation and disorientation—that are inherent in mortal lives, *in* the structures that might appear thoroughly stable and by which we live together. Mortal identities are blended with dimensions of no identity, with no thing, with occurrences beyond the edges of our reasonable grasp, beyond the lives of our own events. We people *are* livingdying.

---

1. The neologisms in this book include *endingbeginning, imporing, cuerpomentealma, in-between, enfleshed, unreasonreason, spiritualimaginal,* and many others.

I turn now to a poem that blends human lives with the enormous repose of utter silence, with the "incredible depths" "of what is called life," where "nothing lives long": the inexhaustible treasure.[2]

INTRODUCTION

> Mountains, a moment's earth-waves rising and hollowing; the earth too's an ephemerid; the stars—
> Short-lived as grass the stars quicken in the nebula and dry in their summer, they spiral
> Blind up space, scattered black seeds of a future; nothing lives long, the whole sky's
> Recurrences tick the seconds of the hours of the ages of the gulf before birth, and the gulf
> After death is like dated: to labor eighty years in a notch of eternity is nothing too tiresome,
> Enormous repose after, enormous repose before, the flash of activity.
> Surely you never have dreamed the incredible depths were prologue and epilogue merely
> To the surface play in the sun, the instant of life, what is called life? I fancy
> *That* silence is the thing, this noise a found word for it; interjection, a jump of the breath at that silence;
> Stars burn, grass grows, men breathe: as a man finding treasure says "Ah!" but the treasure's the essence;
> Before the man spoke it was there, and after he has spoken he gathers it, inexhaustible treasure.
> —Robinson Jeffers (2001, "The Treasure," 100)

I will speak in attunement with livingdying. The attunement is poetic in its manner and connects inevitably with my own experiences. This attunement is guided by *how* livingdying happens in its immediacy. A different, valuable perspective on life and death focuses on *what* nurtures and kills, controlling powers, policies and procedures, skills, institutions, laboratories, objective commitments, and physical processes—on matters of concern within the broad horizon of healing and helping, oppressing and freeing, indifference and effective intervention in pathological practices.

---

2. This is the only chapter that is single authored. Charles will speak in his own name. Both authors worked through the chapter several times and made changes together.

Its language needs to be founded in careful methods, based on facts, and mediated by public discourse.

I, however, will speak only of livingdying, of how we people occur as I look for a manner of speaking of what cannot be said directly, look for a way to shape something intelligible and in consonance with the hollows of livingdying's turning. Stories and poetry will be important for what I say: I am saying now that *what* I say will not—cannot—say the event of livingdying directly, and that *impossibility* is intrinsic in the way of speaking of livingdying if we want—if we *desire*—to draw closer to livingdying and to our own eventuation in the sense we make as we speak. Desire to speak *in* awareness of livingdying permeates this writing.

This engagement will have no conclusion.

IMMEDIACY

Jeffers's poem "The Treasure" speaks of the immediacy of "*that*" silence, the "enormous repose" before, after, and in mountains, stars, time, birth, death, activity, language.... The immediacy of mere silence in all sounds, lives, and events, like shooting stars in silent darkness. Boundless repose enfolds—in-stills—movement. Silence, a soundless void, infuses the earth's life, stars' lives, our lives. Not *something* there before and after earth and stars. Nothing there in what is there. Nothing in the solidity of things. Nothing that as it were gives nothing: mere silence. Immediate silence in sounds and lives, silence that is ever silent, without time to qualify it. Silence in-dwells. It, without being an it, immediately infuses dying in living, gives, as it were, livingdying without conjoining two different things.

For Jeffers, *that* silence also inspires. He says in "Credo":

> ... The mind
> Passes, the eye closes, the spirit is a passage;
> The beauty of things was born before eyes and sufficient to itself; the heart-
>   breaking beauty
> Will remain when there is no heart to break for it. (2001, 147)

I believe that Jeffers understands his poetry to arise in attunement with silence that accompanies the noise of his voice—the "interjection of his breath"—silence that accompanies his written words—the interjection of his composition—silence that arises in an immediacy of the hush in the hollows of the inexhaustible treasure's turning, silence that he cannot say or write. His poetry arises in the silent traces of spirit's passage. "The Treasure," for example, is enmeshed in "the heart-breaking beauty" of "enormous repose": enormous repose that suffuses his own being. His poetry shadows this immediacy by indirection, by leaving unsaid the timeless silent beauty of things.

WEAVING A STORY

Weaving a story or a thought, by virtue of the weave, can provide nuance and shades of meaning that escape direct articulation. What appears at first to be a clear line of narration or thinking might disappear as that line blends with other story lines or with complex lineages embedded in the story or thought. The blending in the weave can permeate the narration, shade what seems initially transparent, and infuse what we expected to be clearly drawn conclusions with uncertainty and obscurity. The obscurity of seeming clarity, we might say. Consider Tim Ingold's description of a Navajo blanket: "What is most striking about the Navajo blanket . . . is that while the colored designs on its surface are strongly linear, these lines are not themselves threads. Nor are they really traces. Indeed when we look for the line in the blanket, however closely, we find only differences—namely, variations in the color of the threads, and row-by-row displacements in the locking position of the weft for each color. We could say that the line on the blanket exists not as a composite of the threads of which it is made, but as an ordered system of differences among them. Taken together, however, these differences add up to something positive, namely the perception of a continuous line on a coherent surface. And it is this perception that gives the line the appearance of a trace. Nevertheless the line formed on a woven surface as it is built up from threads is in reality unlike a line that is drawn on a surface that already exists" (2010, 28–29).

livingdying as well as the story of a life have their complexities, not entirely unlike a weave. The lives of people exceed the boundaries of meaning, exceed the sounds of lives. Silent earthliness plays its role. Perhaps better, silent earthliness is in the weave of a life. Jeffers's comment is a fit threshold for the story I will now tell.

> A little too abstract, a little too wise.
> It is time for us to kiss the earth again (Jeffers 2001, "Return," 499)

Funerals were family events in the small Oklahoma community where I grew up. In the semirural atmosphere, death was common. We butchered most of the meat we ate, killed criminals frequently, hunted and fished, and owned guns before we were teenagers. The earliest of the many funerals that I recall with specific vividness happened when I was probably four years old. Women on the front row of the small church were weeping and keening; sun-darkened men in old wool suits sat beside them with one arm on the back of the wooden pew. An open casket was in the front of the church. I could see the dead face just above the casket's side. Mother worried out loud that perhaps I shouldn't be there. I did not have bad dreams afterward, but I do have uncommonly clear memories of the event when death seemed like it belonged in the community and provided an occasion when the casket was lowered into the ground for something like kissing the earth again. I believe I grew up with a sense that life and death somehow blended, although I had no image of the way that intimacy happened.

The earth kissed back when ten-year-old Fraser Cartwright, my most admired friend, with his innocent, freckled face, was dead five days after he and I ran up and down a newly built dam. That was after the old one at the water-supply lake broke and drowned nearly a dozen or so people. No one thought of suing. It was just a damn shame. I never understood his gentle, naturally positive and sweet disposition, like when he, with my strong encouragement, bloodied the nose of a boy who bullied him and began to cry after he won. I certainly did not understand how he could die so quickly or why he would die at all after we came home, chilled by the late autumn air, drank hot chocolate and smiled over the cups at the fun we had. Seven days later I put on my freshly ironed Cub Scout uniform and with the rest of the Lion Cub Pack served as a pallbearer carrying the small casket out of the church to the hearse and from the hearse to the grave where we threw handfuls of dirt on it and returned Fraser to the earth while a dry prairie wind left us cold and moaned through the few trees in the cemetery.

FIGURE. 8.1

Charles and Fraser in September 1945 on their way to the first day of school.
Fraser died three months later. Photo courtesy of Mildred Scott.

His absence was strange. It is a bit strange to me now as I experience him and my friendship with him through the void of his absence. His death was up close, almost like something happened inside me. As I look back I cannot honestly say that on that day I experienced a space between living and dying. The lines between them, their borders, despite their difference, are porous and blurred as though there are only degrees and gradations, shades and intensities, not total or absolute difference. Earth to earth: does that mean first earth, then a space, and then a return to earth? Or that we are earthly, of the earth, never totally other—intimately earthly? On that day I believe I learned—properly mutely—that the earth somehow gave life and took it back at the same time, that none of it made sense, and that I, in some strange way, belonged to the earth like Fraser did. As I grew older, I learned that death scares some people who want to hold it separate from life and who like the image of life without death. That seemed odd to me, and I began to feel that what the preacher said didn't make any real difference to the earth.

"Nevertheless the line formed on a woven surface as it is built up from threads is in reality quite unlike a line that is drawn on a surface that already exists." Earthflesh. "It is time for us to kiss the earth again," to know that livingdying is dyingliving and it's all we are, our *exhaustible treasure*.

AH, THE EXHAUSTIBLE TREASURE: SEEING THE BRIGHTNESS OF THE WORLD

What might *exhaustible treasure* mean? Struggle to survive, not to exhaust our treasure? Killing to live? Does it mean blind urges to survive? Needing always in "divisions of desire and terror" (Jeffers 2001, 19)? Limited always? Needing nurturance of many kinds? Needing security? Needneeding? Finding earth in need? Our treasure is our mortal life? Earth-wed in time? Always, in her embrace, on the way to the earth's intimate kiss?

Perhaps *exhaustible* means killing in order not to die, killing to be secure, killing in concert with the mortality that delimits us.

Hear Jeffers again:

Salmon Fishing

The days shorten, the south blows wide for showers now,
The south wind shouts to the rivers,
The rivers open their mouths and the salt salmon
Race up into the freshet.
In Christmas month against the smolder and menace
Of a long angry sundown,
Red ash of the dark solstice, you see the anglers,

> Pitiful, cruel, primeval,
> Like the priests of the people that built Stonehenge,
> Dark silent forms, performing
> Remote solemnities in the red shallows
> Of the river's mouth at the year's turn,
> Drawing landward their live bullion, the bloody mouths
> And scales full of the sunset
> Twitch on the rocks, no more to wander at will
> The wild Pacific pasture nor wanton and spawning
> Race up into fresh water. (2001, 19)

Does this poem provide the metaphor for human life wherein the *treasure* is in empty silence, life in that repose that is nothing? Is the livingdying interim one of hopelessly securing, preying, killing, eating, attaching, and repelling in the forces of ancient passions, copulating, moving for a time and then falling into earth's depths? But we are of the *treasure*, of the repose. We are reposed—*en-treasured*, we might say—as we move and speak. With *only* empty silence, nothing. *Living* in/with empty silence, we *are* of the earth. We are always dyingliving. When we are attuned with our dyingliving we are in far more than the "red ash of the dark solstice." As a friend of mine, Sarah Russell, said in a conversation, "I'm not sure anyone can see the brightness of the world truly until they are dying."

There is brightness that lets us know the darkness, lets us know the darkness as Jeffers's "Salmon Fishing" lets us know it, brightness in the living perception, in the art, in livingdying by which the world shines beyond judgment. Perhaps the issue lies in the difference between blindness and brightness, between affirmation of *our* dyingliving and the ephemeral happening of events coming to pass.

Not long before he died, Jeffers wrote "Hand":

> Fallen in between the tendons and bones
> It looks like a dead hand. Poor hand a little longer
> Write, and see what comes forth from a dead hand. (2001, 701)

During his last ten years Jeffers wrote of many things—freedom from sexual passion, great poets, his granddaughter and daughter-in-law, fish and birds, stars, and always of life and death: "So we: death comes and plucks us: we become part of the living earth / And wind and water we so loved. We are they" (2001, 685).

He wrote of his dead wife and her great joy of her body in an untitled poem:

> It nearly cancels my fear of death, my dearest said,
> When I think of cremation. To rot in the earth
> Is a loathsome end, but to roar up in flame—besides, I am used to it,
> I have flamed with love or fury so often in my life,
> No wonder my body is tired, no wonder it is dying.
> We had great joy of my body. Scatter the ashes. (2001, 704)

That "dead hand" continued to write of love and loss, beauty and cruelty. I overhear in those late poems a brightness of spirit—a tired spirit, but bright nonetheless—who sees with pleasure "A great dawn-color rose widening the petals around her gold eye" (2001, "The Shears," 685). I find part of Jeffers's brightness in his unflinching presentation of human cruelty—of human beings as often "solitary, poor, nasty, brutish, and short" in Thomas Hobbes's phrase (1839–45, 13)—and his unflinching sense of livingdying—a sense without bitterness, defeat, or resistance, a sense of repose with love, astonishment, anger, pain, loss, and discovery, sensing and seeing with brightness that can cause people to glance away and wish for more darkness, wish for lives closer to the winter's solstice, and in that afternoon's dark, wish for a clear separation of life and death.

We, dyingliving, livingdying (whatever), are *always* living *in* our dying, always *in* the possibility of that brightness of mind that wants the world in its difference from our systems of grammar, meaning, and sense, *wants* the world in *its* livingdying, *wants* the edge where silence, utter silence, happens, where sound and movement begin always to pass.

Beyond Sensibilities

Epiphany

Like a single drop of rain,
  the wasp strikes
the windowpane; buzzes rapidly
away, disguising

error in urgent business:
  such is the
invisible, hard as glass,
unrenderable by the senses,

not known until stricken by:
  some talk that
there is safety in the visible,
the definite, the heard and felt,

pre-stressing the rational and
  calling out with
joy, like people far from death:
how puzzled they will be when

going headlong secure in "things"
  they strike the
intangible and break, lost,
unaccustomed to transparency, to

being without body, energy
  without image:
how they will be dealt
hard realizations, opaque as death.
   —A. R. Ammons

REVELATION

Epiphany: an intuitive grasp of reality through something, such as an event, usually simple and striking; an illuminating discovery, realization, or disclosure.

Ammons's poem begins with a double metaphor, a double distancing of the words from what the poem is talking about. Or is the poem talking about something ... like ... metaphorical distancing in which definitive completion is not possible? There are so many metaphors in the poem! The strike of the wasp against the transparent windowpane is like a single drop of rain striking a windowpane; and the wasp's striking and then buzzing away is like disguising an error, an error in not seeing the transparent. The windowpane is like the invisible and intangible (unrenderable by the senses) when people live primarily for the sake of what is sensible and definite around them, and what is definite and sensible around them appears as though it were not traversed by indefinite, invisible silence and lack of thinglyness. Such people live comfortably in the safety they find in the visible, "going headlong secure in 'things,'" live as though they were far from the unthinglike dimensions of their existence, far from what is opaque because it is transparent. They live far from their mortality, far from their bodies' ability to be no more, far from nothing, nothing beyond them and their busyness ... their busyness? Perhaps we might say, their insentience as they are face to face with transparency. These "far-froms" are in the closeness of what is opaque to them. Close upon them, we might say metaphorically, in their not seeing. The joy of such people arises without epiphany. Their epiphany will happen when they, as it were, strike the transparency of what has been invisible to them and break open in energy without image.

"Break open in energy without image." In part I of this book we worked with three extraordinarily creative thinkers. Nietzsche, Foucault, and Anzaldúa wrote in attunements with dimensions beyond rationalities and sharp bifurcations of values and truths. They wrote with prospects—visions—engendered in these attunements by questioning what is normally not subject to questioning, by perceiving oppressive silencing and outcasting, by growing alertness to the limits of their identified selves in the extended reach of their awareness and interconnectivity. They wrote with an energy and commitment in what we can call the epiphanies originating in their attunements beyond philosophy. We emphasized the happenings of lineages in the dimension of beyond. And yet *beyond*, as we used the word, has no essential nature, nothing to identify it other than being beyond sensible identification and reasonable grasp. In attunement with beyond, people can experience something like invisible lucidity—transparency—that loosens the hold of fixed identities and things whose importance to us can override most other aspects in our living. Attunement to beyond can have a liberating affect, an uncanny sort of disentangling that infuses people's attitudes and encourages disillusioned perceptiveness without imposing ordered meanings on the roiling, infinitely complex, and continuously shifting world in which they find themselves. Sometimes a new energy accompanies these kinds of experiences, energy that can happen with intensified clarity as things and people stand out in their differences—perhaps something like when colors intensify as a depression lifts. People see, as it were, the happening of the clarity, the happening of dimensions of occurrence that were previously invisible—perhaps like hearing the silence that happens in sounds. In this unexpected new experience and the imageless energy that can come with it, people's sensibilities might transform, and when people's sensibilities transform, their ways of living will shift. The world is no less complex and disordered, but a simultaneously normal and uncanny sense of flowing, unstable, and astonishing life might quietly infuse people's sense of being alive.

Metaphors both bear and shroud meanings ("opaque as death"). They elucidate and cloud as they bring the familiar to bear on the unfamiliar ("such is the / invisible, hard as glass"). The complex of lineages that informs a given situation deeply influences the meanings and intuitions sparked by metaphors; metaphors are themselves transient and shifty ("unrenderable by the senses"). Metaphorical transference provides something like a space for simultaneous obscuring and disclosing of the metaphorized subject, like silence where sounds happen. In these aspects metaphors are like myths: sometimes they are all about what they cannot say directly. They can constitute an art of letting something appear by indirection. Such is the myth of Metis, which, like "Epiphany," presents the elusiveness that also characterizes the medium of her presentation.

MÊTIS-INTELLIGENCE AND SHIFTING SENSIBILITIES

Metis was a Titan, a daughter of Tiethys and Oceanus, that watery coming together of the rivers and the sea. She was enfleshed fluidity, the embodiment of that kind of wise cunning that comes from immediate alertness to uncertainties, the limits of clear rationality, the instability of what seems reliable, firm, permanent. Metis is multiple and polymorphous, attuned to watery, unpredictable movements. She is beholden to no systems of value or comprehension. Metis is she "whose knowledge was greatest of gods and mortal men" (Hesiod 1983, 887). She "is applied to situations which are transient, shifting, disconcerting and ambiguous, situations which do not lend themselves to precise calculation or rigorous logic" (Vernant 1991, 4). Her name figures the skill to know when knowledge and judgment, normally recognized as wisdom in their combination, are ill advised; and thus mêtis-intelligence could offer wise counsel at odds with the day's wisdom as well as a tricky strategy that fools and misleads people. Metis represents the power of transformation—that shape-changing ability attuned to the uncertain movement of things. So, as Jean-Pierre Vernant says, "Metis must be tracked down ... in areas which the ... philosopher usually passes over in silence or mentions only with irony or with hostility so that, by contrast, he can display to its fullest advantage the way of reasoning and understanding that is required of his own profession" (1991, 5).

We can see why our Western philosophical traditions, preoccupied as they are with stabilities and transcendent standards for measuring virtues, often subordinated her kind of power and wisdom when we hold in mind that she in her artful, frequently devious, and crafty intelligence is attuned to the watery, winding, undermining becoming of things—of all things including truths, Gods, and goodness. Including too, we presume, her own image. Her wily ways must be appropriated and, to the extent possible, subjugated. Metis and mêtis-intelligence must be subjected to dominating, "higher" knowledge and virtue. And, of course, attempting to dominate Metis required cunning and devious strategies. Zeus set the standard. He, enamored of her cunning, of her ability to serve as his skillful adviser who provided sly, seductive tricks that ensured his reign, became her husband. When desire turned to fear, he sought to retain her within him, swallowing her. While she might be contained, she could not be codified, taught precision, or subjected and made to obey. For even in Zeus's stomach, we are told, she speaks from the belly. She speaks with that gut-wisdom that we too often ignore. A bodily cunning, that practical touch that opens to responsiveness and skillful, cagey improvisation.

The craftiness of mêtis-intelligence takes full advantage of the distance between what people find unquestionably virtuous and just, on the one hand, and the ambiguous imprecision of what happens, on the other. Such people's vulnerability, after all, lies in their trust of the security of the visible world and their normal ways of life. Mêtis-intelligence, in contrast, is transformative intelligence, an affective disposition, a responsiveness to the complex, shifting contours of situations. It stretches beyond the circumference of rational presentation and is often invisible to good sense. Mêtis-intelligence concerns happenings intangibly beyond the everyday busyness that occupies people and often determines the way they live their lives, just as this attunement concerns what is beyond the magnificent dreams of eternal forms and an abiding good toward which people can strive. It is not given to such prudent virtues as frugality, reasonable sanity, kindness, or honesty. Just a vague sense of her protean presence and the watery reality her intelligence makes evident can make many people scurry to sacred texts, rational systems, or other coves of comfort to find assurance that unifying meaning and purpose rule at the core of their lives. Mêtis-intelligence inhabits the indifferent borders of sensenonsense. In those borders there is no constancy of meaning, no grounds for stable identity. Being in those borders is invisibly far away from the feelings of profound rightness we experience when we securely go headlong into events that appear fitting and good through and through. We could wonder if Metis and Dionysus are infused in laughter as our constructions tremble in thresholds of becoming.

Mêtis-intelligence, as we understand it, inhabits those fluid, liminal spaces far beyond dreams of stabilities. It is an enfleshed wisdom that does not abide sharp categorizations but rather finds itself at home in cuerpomentealma; or should you prefer us to trace different lineages, we might say mêtis-intelligence finds itself at home in epistemepraxispoiesis, in wide-ranging generative and savvy, often wily and destabilizing perceptiveness. Mêtis-intelligence involves attunement to multiple lineages and the ways in which they can be woven together as well as undone (loosen the hold) and reentwined. It is a skill of attunement to what we have named *dimensions of beyond*, alert to fissures and tensions in those lineages, to their silences and unsayables. Mêtis-intelligence is enfleshed and open to transformations, responsive to change, ambiguity, and uncertainty. This intelligence is at the core of border art philosophy. It embodies the ability to twist free from categories, values, and practices that enfold us and to do so not in opposition but transversely—from the Latin *transvertere*, from *trans*, "across," and *vertere*, "to turn." It is this skill we need when we act, *not* from principles or values that we take to be certain, but rather in attunement with the protean lineages from which their value is derived.

Proceeding transversely is an artful skill. How else can we become open to the unthinkable? We have said that we cannot reason or argue or cajole or battle our way out of oppressive practices when the very concepts that structure our thought, the principles that guide our actions, and the institutions that subject us are shot through with the oppressive sensibilities out of which these oppressive practices emerge. What then? We have suggested practices of philosophy that enable us to conceive previously inconceivable thoughts, a practice we labeled border art philosophy, a practice of creative engagement. But how can we actually go beyond the sensibilities that function in our lives? How might transverse movements enable the generation of previously inconceivable feelings, thoughts, and intuitions? What relevance does mêtis-intelligence have when we attempt border art philosophy as we have described it? We will return to these questions.

In previous chapters one of our guiding thoughts is that meanings, axioms of behavior, and values are changeable, ambiguous, and localized. Rather than a preestablished human nature, a pre-formed and transcendental subjectivity, or a divine source of truth and goodness, we have given priority to multiple and simultaneously occurring sensibilities, which are often "transient, shifting, disconcerting and ambiguous ... which do not lend themselves to precise calculation or rigorous logic" (in the words of Vernant quoted above [1991]). The happenings of sensibilities are friendly to mêtis-intelligence in the sense that these occurrences are not compatible with clear-cut, precisely accurate theoretical comprehension. In their mutability and alterability, sensibilities compose in our unstable worlds the dynamic, viscous resources for various rationalities and moralities. People cannot live together without systems of accepted truths and principles, norms, values, moralities, and logics that make sense in particular cultures. These systems can also constitute a fabric of oppressive practices that call not only for obedience but possibly also for liberating critique and transformation.

"Call for liberating critique and transformation?" Where does that come from? This call comes in part from the instability of the sensibilities that generate our values, rationalities, convictions, and feelings of preference and aversion. Our sensibilities, we have seen, are fissured, cloven in the powers of differing and often contradictory lineages and established practices. We have noted that a person can have multiple and shifting feelings, feelings inclined, for example, to affirm the equality of all people combined with feelings of superiority in relation to some other groups of people or both attraction and fear when face-to-face with something beautiful and overpowering. The thought we want to underscore is that we are not limited by a unified sensibility that always repeats itself when we think about it. We can see with at least a degree of detachment, for example, what our prejudices are regarding some groups of people and how they function from the perspective of affirmation of the equality of all people. We can recognize anonymous powers that function in our lives by virtue of senses that are outside the jurisdiction of those powers—the ability to say no to them, to work to expose or weaken such powers or to look for avenues of escape from them. We can be aware of conflicting interests and evaluations in ourselves and make both judgments about the conflicts and plans for ways to deal with the conflicts that go on in our lives because of the differences that compose our sensibilities. We can hear the call to free ourselves and others, for example, from fabrics of oppressive practices because those fabrics do not constitute a whole cloth. There are parts of societies, parts of people's lives, that happen outside the oppression's jurisdiction. But the transformative processes can also proceed toward oppression as people, perhaps unwittingly, replicate oppressive practices in their liberatory efforts or as lineages of domination override the transformative practices. The lives of sensibilities are unpredictable. Metis is indeed cunning.

In this book we intend, by virtue of the affirmed sensibilities operative in our experience, to think transversely with the force of some of the elements in our lineages that are ignored, pushed aside, silenced, or forgotten in our dominant philosophical traditions. We intend to turn athwart of those traditions. We want to be answerable to the silences that infuse languages, conjunctions of events, and formations of identities, silences that haunt people's desire for unities and unbroken continuities. In our work we want to affirm the fissured and conflictual qualities of sensibilities, affirm the implications of those qualities, and affirm thinkers who have made the transversive turn. In our and their turning, we find prospects—exposures—to events beyond definitive schemas and structures, exposure to the aspects of the world figured by Metis and mêtis-intelligence. This is *where* the call takes us. In our understanding, as we respond to this call, we join Anzaldúa, Foucault, and Nietzsche as liberatory thinkers, not necessarily as "right" in what we and they think and not always free of the force of some of the practices and sensibilities for which we and they seek constructive options. But we are attempting nonetheless to liberate ourselves enough to generate transformative possibilities for acting decisively with liberatory goals as well as with uncertainty in the incongruous, shaded world in which we live.

How is it that sensibilities both constitute the originary base for our values and predispositions and happen in ways that are conflicting, even contradictory, in their tensions among diverse and mutating lineages? What might this kind of conflict look like in a person's life? Charles, in response to this question, will speak in his own voice for a moment: I grew up in the molding force of discordant, ambivalent convictions concerning Black people. During the 1940s I lived in a small town in Oklahoma in a family that was what I would call, given the social environment there, "moderately" racist. My mother and father believed that all humans are equal in the sight of God, recognized people of all races and nationalities as human, and affirmed separation of the races, especially in connection with marriage. They, in harmony with prevailing practices, affirmed segregation. In other words, I grew up in very fractured and self-contradictory sensibilities. I grew up knowing that God is love, that God loves Black people as well as White people, that Black people should be set apart from White people, and that White people had rightful power in setting the standards of how Black and White people should interact. These were not simply beliefs, but arose from pre-reflective "knowledge" that formed me. Of course, there were Black Christians. That the pastor of the Black Methodist church was the janitor of the White Methodist church that I attended seemed perfectly natural. Nothing is wrong with White folks going to the Black church to hear the singing, right? But Black folks did not come to White churches except as performing choirs. Without thinking about it, I also knew that there is something menial about Black people. Something subordinate. Something not designed for the standards of success among White people. By the time I was in high school, I had learned that blood transfusions between Black and White people are not a problem. I learned explicitly, by medical evidence, that human beings, regardless of color, have biological bodies that are much the same. That realization gave me something to think about at the same time that I (I planned to be a minister) was increasingly drawn by the implications in the sentiment expressed by the hymn "In Christ there is no East or West / in Him no South or North." I found myself at increasingly pronounced odds with neighbors and close relatives as I heard them speak using racist epithets about Black people being uppity and needing to be kept in their place. I became involved in a number of religious, statewide organizations and met people in them whom I respected and who were strongly opposed to segregation. Those contacts helped me to realize that I had been affirming segregation at the same time that I spoke out for equal rights. I became progressively aware that Black people in my southwestern society and in my own unconsidered "knowledge" of them were seen as both equal and not equal, both human and not quite human, both loved by God and best kept separate from White society.

In hindsight I can see that I was able to recognize my own racism because of the contradictions and ambiguities in my pre-reflective attitudes, the rifts in the very sensibilities that generated my values and identifications. Lineages of racism and equality without racism played active roles in my sensibility. I was able to see racist dispositions from the perspective of nonracist ones that happened in conflictual simultaneity. It was such a fractured sensibility! The values of equality, love, fairness, and empirically established truth were, when it came to Black people, combined with the values of inequality, separation, rejection, indifference, and domination. These incompatible values were fused into complex, divided, and ruptured sensibilities, sensibilities that defined me and many people in my society. It was the gaps and contradictions among those sensibilities—the ruptures—that allowed me to experience reflectively the tensions that led me to question myself and my White-dominated culture, to make judgments about aspects of sensibilities that were active in my awareness, values, and judgments even as I questioned them. I believe that I hit "the invisible hard as glass" transparency of contradictory attitudes and meanings, a transparency people can buzz away from in their busyness. The force of the ruptures and gaps, however, combined with my commitment at that time to the love of Christ, inclined me (in contrast to most of the churched people I knew in my hometown) not to turn away.

I was inclined—you do see, don't you, that this inclination shows the anonymous agency of my family and the lineages of Christian, Pauline love?—to learn how to listen to Black people, to hear them in their differences from me, to see with growing clarity how normal discriminatory attitudes were kin to acts of terrible violence and outspoken hatred toward them. In hindsight I can see how the ground was stirred, how I was unsettled enough that the civil rights movement could have a life-transforming influence on me, as I found myself at first both hesitant and strongly inclined to align myself, in spite of many important differences among them, with such leaders as Martin Luther King Jr., Fanny Lou Hamer, Diane Nash, James Farmer, Thurgood Marshal, Rosa Parks, Roy Williams, Angela Davis, Elaine Brown, and many others. This process took place over a period of many years and continues up to this day, exposing layer after layer of racism in my life.

Was I in a process that approached a kind of intelligence—mêtis-intelligence—that would please Metis? Perhaps give her to smile as I struggled with myself, my society, and my broad culture at a threshold of vibrant change in the midst of confused disorder the future of which I could not see. This is the kind of intelligence that thrives on ambiguity and cunning. A kind of cunning intelligence that inclines activists to use wily strategies of opposition—to make transversive moves—such strategies as nonviolence to resist and overcome violent dominations, grassroots organizing in local communities for voter registration and solidarity in the face of violence, skillful use of guilt to weaken opposition, civil disobedience, the creation of organized outlets for publishing their views and beliefs, the formation of organizations of solidarity that are able, in addition to resisting head-on opposition, to advance different ways of perceiving and knowing, the use of undercover infiltrators, and so forth. These are diverting, sometimes sly and shrewd tactics that arise from feelings and knowledge born not only of experiences of oppression but also of the rips and fissures in powerful, ambiguous sensibilities that allow people to say *"No!"* when they have been taught to say "Yes, sir, yes ma'am." Is Metis, as it were, present in happenings of those rips and fissures, those tensions and ambiguities? Metis, who is not present in the myths that present her. Who speaks in the silent gaps and is disclosed by indirection. Metis, who might be enacted as mêtis-intelligence in the ambiguities of sensibilities, whose "knowledge" can turn out not to be knowledge at all. Cunning, devious Metis, silently active as mêtis-intelligence in the warp and woof of values and meanings for living.

BEYOND NORMS

What do you hear when you hear the word *norm*? How do normativities circulate in your life? Have you been told that you deviate from the norm? Or that you are not normal? Or that you engage in unnatural acts? How did such proclamations affect you? Did you experience them with shame or celebration? Confirmation or rebellion?

We speak of norms as codes or principles that prescribe actions, that is, make certain actions right and others wrong. Norms may be understood to be situated and flexible, like, for example, cultural codes regarding when it is acceptable to hug another person. Or the norms may be viewed as universal and rigid, like prescriptions for moral action—the thou-shalt-nots. Norms inform so many of the ways we experience ourselves and others. Am I trustworthy? Too fat? Too loud? Sufficiently courageous? Above or below the norm?

Norms subject us. They craft us into the types of subjects that we are. Where would we be without norms? They help us get through life in so many different ways. They get under our skin and provide the stuff out of which we fashion our lives, adjust our goals, determine what we will eat and what we will avoid. They even inform whom we love and whom we ignore. The productive power of norms arises from both what they permit and what they forbid. We might ask, "What can we do about norms?" Or *should* it be "What should we do about norms?" Perhaps we need to ask as well, "What can norms do with us?"

The problem with norms is that they carry with them their contraries, their deviations. Abnormalities are not always aberrant, but the line between different and deviant is a slippery one. Take sexual norms. Although we allow for some flexibility in sexual tastes, for many there is a boundary that goes well beyond mere taste and into the realm of the abnormal, the deviant, the immoral. Where do you find that boundary? How does it color your dispositions? Are there certain types of sexual relations that you see as always acceptable, as good, as right? And if you allow flexibility in what is permitted, are there, nonetheless, domains that are not permitted—immoral, criminal, pathological no matter where or why? What are the boundaries between mere difference and immoral behavior?

Liberatory theorists often critique norms—norms that normalize particular sexual practices, gender role expectations, habits of comportment, and lifestyle expectations, to name a few. Many norms are woven out of lineages of oppressive practices and reinforce the racism, sexism, ableism, and complex et ceteras so many liberatory thinkers wish to address. So we ask again: What can we do about norms? When we see that a norm is oppressive, how should we respond? How can we make a difference? Debates rage within this domain. Do we identify the right norms, the ones that do not oppress? Do we, as Butler says, "distinguish among the norms and conventions that permit people to breathe, to desire, to love and to live, and those norms and conventions that restrict or eviscerate the conditions of life itself" (2004, 8)? Is this a form of "getting it right"? This desire for an unoppressive normativity, a pro-normativity, we might say, reinscribes the debate, does it not? The moment we deem something right, or normal, or natural, we plow the ground for designating its opposite, that which is immoral, abnormal, or deviant. And here we find the wellspring of oppression. So perhaps we might set ourselves against norms, the stance some have referred to as antinormativity.[1] But

---

1. Queer theorists such as Leo Bersani, Lee Edelman, Eve Kosofsky Sedgwick, and Michael Warner have been labeled antinormative theorists. Indeed the editors of the

here don't we find a similar logic of opposition, if only from a different direction? Such oppositions risk animating the very thing that is opposed by keeping it in play through their contestations.

We find ourselves at an impasse, a paradox, trapped once again, choices returning us to the very thing we desire to trouble, to resist. As Butler phrases it: "The paradox of subjectivation (*assujetissement*) is precisely that the subject who would resist norms is itself enabled, if not produced, by such norms" (1993, xxiii). The aporia of liberatory theory reappears and seems to encircle us in inextricable bonds.[2] When we are without passage (*a-poros*) we might turn to Metis to provide a path, a *poros*, a transverse movement, a position *in* the border.[3]

To help us with this movement we consider this passage from Sarah Kofman's essay "Beyond Aporia?" Kofman reminds us that "*poros* refers only to a sea-route or a route down a river, to a passage opened up across a chaotic expanse which it transforms into an ordered, qualified space by introducing differentiated routes, making visible the various directions of space, by giving direction to an expanse which was initially devoid of all contours, of all landmarks. To say that a *poros* is a way to be found across an expanse of liquid is to stress that a *poros* is never traced in advance, that it can always be obliterated, that it must be traced anew, in unprecedented fashion. One speaks of a *poros* when it is a matter of blazing a trail where no trail exists, of crossing an impassable expanse of territory, an unknown, hostile and boundless world, an *apeiron* which it is impossible to cross from end to end; the watery depths, the *pontos*, is the ultimate *apeiron* (*paron* because *aperion*), the sea is the endless realm of pure movement, the most mobile, changeable, and polymorphous of all spaces, a space where any way that has been traced is immediately

---

special issue of the journal *differences* titled "Queer Theory without Antinormativity" claim that antinormativity is "a guiding tenet of queer inquiry" and is "central to its self-definition" (Wiegman and Wilson 2015, 3). Their interpretation of queer theory has been the subject of critique. See, for example, Jack Halberstam's review of the issue (2015).

2. We recall here the paradox of liberatory theory we introduced in chapter 5.

3. Poros, Plato tells us in the *Symposium*, is the son of Metis (203b). *Poros* means way or resource.

obliterated, which transforms any journey into a voyage of exploration which is always unprecedented, dangerous and uncertain" (1988, 10).

Rather than offering a normative response to the normativity debates—do it this way, not that way—we might follow Metis and proceed *transversely*, with a side movement, with cunning. We might understand *beyond normativity* in this way. A way to signal a difficulty with accord as much as with opposition, for both keep the very divisions we wish to interrupt circulating. So we move, neither in opposition nor accord, but in a crosswise motion attentive to lineages, to the fluidity of their entwinings, to the gaps and the fissures, the contradictions and tensions. To what is gathered and what is passed over in silence. We move transversely to expose the aporias, the happenings beyond normativities that might open us to new possibilities, take us beyond the logic of the either/or, for or against. Mêtis-intelligence provides cunning possibilities, passages that bring orders to the fluid movements of norms, not *the* order, but paths, possible ways of weaving and reweaving lineages. "Where any way that has been traced is immediately obliterated." Each path creates in its wake both openings and closures. Moving transversely, we give ourselves over to "a path that must be engaged and traversed each time for the first time" (Naas 2008, 68). Such transverse movements provide not a method but ways to maneuver, attunements, winding, flowing paths, but ones that must be recovered, reinvented with each movement rather than providing a principle that remains constant, a replication of the same. Each response to norms will enable and, in enabling, exclude. There is no Right path. There is no way in which silences and unsayables can be uttered and made stable. Norms there are, but they are mortal norms, fleshy, lineage-born, "mobile, changeable, and polymorphous." We come to understand that the paths of norms are like the transfiguring ruses of Metis, in which she is not authentic at one moment and inauthentic at another but is always both at once, multiple, shifting. The either/or of opposition/accord arises from a desire for stability, certainty (or at least less uncertainty), and purity. But the *poros*, the path charted with mêtis-intelligence, the willingness to question the value of values themselves, will be a "voyage of exploration which is always unprecedented, dangerous and uncertain." With cunning, perhaps we can become attentive to unsayable dimensions of experience that, in their indirection, provide entryways to transformed lifeways. Attunements beyond norms.

Where does this leave us, and where does it lead us? This *poros* might lead in watery ways to an understanding of Foucault's statement: "So my position leads not to apathy but to a hyper- and pessimistic activism" (1984, 343).[4] And perhaps, in this way, our lives might become a work of art (cf. 1984, 350).

DECISIVENESS

Is pessimism necessarily the sign of decline, decay, failure, exhausted and enfeebled instincts, as it was with people of India, as it is to all appearances now with us, we "modern" people and Europeans? Is there a pessimism of strength, an intellectual predisposition toward what is hard, gruesome, evil, toward what is problematic for life, pessimism that arises out of well-being, out of overflowing good health, out of the fullness of life?

—Nietzsche, "Attempt at a Self-Criticism" (1886; our translation)

"Attunements beyond norms," we said. In this chapter we seem to be left in watery ways with Metis and her son, Poros, functioning as metaphors for the lives of norms and with attunements to nothing specific "where" shifting, mutating, and often contradictory lineages constitute our pre-reflective inclinations, values, and meanings. Drowning might seem more likely than hyper-, pessimistic, and presumably decisive activism! And what's with pessimistic hyper-activism? Is it—pessimistic hyper-activism—the best lifesaver we can have in the flowing river of becoming? Living not just without stable norms but with pervasive instability might not sound like much of a life. And while we are seeing the specter

---

4. The full quote is as follows: "I am not looking for an alternative: you can't find the solution of a problem in the solution of another problem raised at another moment by other people. You see, what I want to do is not the history of solutions, and that's the reason why I don't accept the word alternative. I would like to do the genealogy of problems, of problématiques. My point is not that everything is bad, but that everything is dangerous, which is not exactly the same as bad. If everything is dangerous, then we always have something to do. So my position leads not to apathy but to a hyper- and pessimistic activism."

of not much of a life, we recall that in the first section of this chapter we described a burst of imageless energy that can happen when people are liberated from a type of blindness in their busy, crowded, everyday lives by attunement to a dimension that we call beyond, an energy exemplified in the works of Nietzsche, Foucault, and Anzaldúa, and an energy that we too experience. Energy that inclines people to experimentation, creativity, and transformation. Energy that leaves them wondering how they might act and how they might position themselves to remain attuned with it.

So what's the point of the previous section? In affirming the instability of norms and the priority of sensibilities and attunements beyond norms, we might appear to have undercut the possibility for hope. Are there no definitive boundaries that can keep us on course for justice and moral goodness? No borders for right knowledge and genuine truth? No stabilities? Even with energy without images, doesn't living in an unguided, indifferent, continuously shifting world sound like a fine basis for unending contention, for the ceaseless and "turbid ebb and flow / Of human misery" (Arnold 1910, 226)? Aren't we in dark harmony with Matthew Arnold's poem "Dover Beach"?

> for the world, which seems
> To lie before us like a land of dreams,
> So various, so beautiful, so new,
> Hath really neither joy, nor love, nor light,
> Nor certitude, nor peace, nor help for pain;
> And we are here as on a darkling plain
> Swept with confused alarms of struggle and flight,
> Where ignorant armies clash by night. (1910)

Isn't there a deep pessimism embedded in our thoughts and words?

The word and concept of pessimism are oppositionally paired with the word and concept of optimism, and that pair is often joined with the opposites good and bad: pessimists expect bad things to happen, and optimists expect good things to happen. *Good* and *bad* can refer to moral goodness and immoral badness, such good happenings as times of peace, the fall of an unjust ruler, or progress in overcoming poverty; or such bad ones as unending human misery, repeatedly bad results for actions intended as good, or unavoided anthropogenic climate disaster. People can feel a basic optimism when they "know" that life has deep and permanent meaning that gives purpose even to tragic events, or they might be inclined to pessimism if they "know" that life is meaninglessness at its core. We, however, do not think within the sway of such oppositional pairings or assumptions of such stabilities.

We have affirmed throughout this book that meanings and values are mortal, that simultaneous endings and beginnings constitute thresholds beyond which the path is unclear, uncharted. Lineages, institutions, all manner of power-networks, social interrelations, class hierarchies, and economies extend our environments and our awareness; we could continue the list of flowing anonymous agencies—of in-fluences, of emanations, that play constitutive roles in us as subjects. Stable, fixed transcendental subjectivity is a fiction. The point is that humans in the influences of anonymous agencies are continuously changing, multidimensional, self-reflexive events. That is neither good nor bad. "The world" does not offer a fundamental purpose or direction for life. No single, unifying order gives order to the multiple orders of worldly lives. That is neither good nor bad. All living things die. That is neither good nor bad. So, you ask, how do we live in such a world? A world that is neither good nor bad?

Perhaps the question is rather: How do we *desire* to live in the world? Apathetically? Without passion even though passion intensifies people's living experiences? Even though it generates energy to be? Are we able to be passionately in the world without a felt need to make the world conform to our—we people's—formations of reflective awareness, our rationalities, our values? Isn't being able to form, reform, and transform our lives in the eventuation of influences that reach far beyond our grasp a remarkable ability? Is the word *wondrous*—a wondrous ability to form, reform, and transform our lives—too much here? To live in such passion is no small thing.

We have been speaking in the force of Foucault's word *hyper*. Hyperactivism, he said. Passionate, intense, excited activism. Activism that can happen in politics, in education, in the ways we live our lives in relation to other lives, in writing and in art. You very likely can think of other ways. He added *pessimistic*, a word that we hear in Nietzsche's sense of a pessimism of strength that means for Nietzsche, yes, life as it happens offers no basis for hope, no escape from the turbid ebb and flow of human misery and death. But the strong ones, he says, affirm life nonetheless in its beauty, in its—far from mere being—its intensities and passions, its adventures. They recognize possibilities for continuous creativity in spite of suffering, setbacks, and pain. They find possibilities for self-affirmation and self-creation.

We have chosen, however, not to describe this activism and attitude as pessimistic because of the term's current use in bifurcations with optimism and with good and evil. We find ourselves nonetheless with a predilection for seeing the world as it appears, the world as indifferent to whatever happens in it, as indifferent to gruesome, horrifying, intolerable events, to boring, apathetic, insipid, and vapid ones, as well as indifferent to beautiful, wonder-filled, courageous, and life-enhancing events. We agree with Foucault, Nietzsche, and Anzaldúa that with passion, with energy that comes in attunement with beyond as we have spoken of it, people can feel overfull, incited to give themselves to making differences, to speaking out against intolerable conditions they find themselves or others subjected to, to learning how to ask questions that dislodge the confidence attached to many axiomatic values and meanings, to creating new values, developing new ways of knowing, exposing what they find wrong and hidden from view, staying in tune with the feelings of being alive and wanting yet more of being alive. We are speaking of passionate, committed engagements, of hyper-activism.

We have in mind decisiveness in the midst of countless options for action or inaction. We are not speaking of specific, commanding values or imposed options. Rather, we have in mind the resoluteness that can come with the energy and decisiveness that arise from people's affirmative sense of being alive when they are released from oppressive busyness or rigid, dogmatically affirmed categorical values. A desire, a strong inclination that seems to emerge beyond thought (thought comes later), beyond reason. An urge, we might say. An urge that becomes a felt need: I need to act; I cannot let this go; I want to make this situation different. The situation might be a person's own life, an intolerable complex of oppressing powers, a person or people who need help, an opportunity to build an institution or to save a life, a book that needs to be written, a painting that is waiting, a project that needs to be thought through and planned. Built into the decisiveness we have in mind is a sense of life and living that affirms itself in the action it takes.

The sense we have in mind escapes tight grasp. The sense in its nascence is like being on the edge of something like a space where time seems to shudder and a possibility appears, perhaps at first like the arrival of a dream, but a real possibility nonetheless, one with a direction calling for decisiveness. People with this sense are in a threshold that composes endingbeginning, where beginning happens in the immediacy of ceasing happening. The threshold is almost transparent as individuals feel the immanence of passion, possibility, loss of what was happening, and uncertainty before the indefinite future. In that transparency the threshold opens into a darkly shaded—is it watery?—uncharted region of experiences. People could well experience a shock of being in-between, the experience of endingbeginning, a shock of definite liminality, definite indefiniteness, decisiveness suspended in interfusing indecisiondecision—decisiveness put to the test. It's not too late for individuals to buzz away from the threshold's hit, buzz busily away from the liminality, preoccupied with relief that one's life is to be guided by stable moral commands and all that stuff that needs to be done.

Imagine that some people make it through the strange currents of misty indefiniteness and face the challenge of turning liminal possibilities into realities. Imagine that the passion and sense of being alive—*really alive*—are infused with decisive determination that inclines individuals to pay attention to the movements of things: to endingsbeginnings, to what are taken to be defining moments or limits, attention to those dynamic borders, to the lives of defining limits of people and things, to identities and differences and their mutating interconnections. How do those porous borders and limits happen? Borders and limits that define locales, things... *all* identifiable things?

HYPER-ACTIVISM

Borders happen as ever-shifting ways of defining differences and identities? They are like inconstant and porous demarcations? Our, Nancy's and Charles's, sense of life emphasizes change, becoming, an interfusing porosity among events, lineages, and identities. That sense also strongly inclines us to pay attention to what persists in streams of becoming, to what endures for a time, to durations, to what is much the same from moment to moment. The word *viscous* helps us to understand the consistency of what lasts, the often-tenacious durability of things. When we put *viscous* and *porous* together and speak of viscous porosity we have a term to describe enduring things that are not like rigid fixtures in the world but are like borders through which influences can flow, like the porosity of cultural borders, personal borders, geographical borders, moral borders. The liveliness of passionate decisiveness engages the liveliness of borders with a wily cunning that takes its cues from the ways events, people, things are alive in the specific situations in which their lives take place, from what nurtures them or suppresses and stifles them. Genealogical sensibilities help us to put in question what seems stable, inevitable, unchangeable, inflexible and to reveal the shifts and fissures, the endingsbeginnings, the often subtle and shaded movements that are occluded by finding safety in the definite, comfort in the stable.

A Short Excursus

Often when people think of borders, they think with words using the Proto-Indo-European root *sta-*, which means to stand, make firm, something standing and secure. A stable, for example, provides a securing enclosure for animals. It is built to stand firm in all kinds of weather, to safely store provisions and equipment. But, we note, it is always subject to change. Indeed, a stable needs repair, usually consistent repair, to keep it as it was, and, in time, it will need replacing. An under*sta*nding stabilizes a mutual agreement and has the sense of holding firm or grasping. But it is not necessarily long lasting. The question of borders is not their existence but their constitution. Are they constituted by agreements? By constructions—the wall in *la frontera*, the attitudes that recognize all southern asylum seekers as criminals? By terrain—bordered by mountains, a river, a shore? By emotions—you are at the limits of her tolerance? In any case, we have been careful in our use of *sta-* words, especially those suggesting stasis and static. We are wary, for example, of using statistics to establish *stable* facts whereby we can understand the way enduring things stand. The stance of statistics tends to occlude the dynamic, mutating lives of things.

We are speaking of decisiveness in an indifferent world filled with shifting, identifiable things that in their viscous porosity become different from the way they are. When we speak of decisiveness we are speaking of a passion that fuels hyper-activism. This passion drives us toward making a difference in a world of fissures, complexity, uncertainty, and change. The fissures, complexity, uncertainty, and change provide sources in and beyond our sensibilities that inform our responsiveness. The hyper-activists with whom we join labor in the seams of oppressive practices, paying particular attention to the ways those practices are held in place by assumptions of stabilities (that's just how those people are; women were made to do such work; there has always been poverty). Thinking otherwise is a passionate commitment to the otherwise of orders, beliefs, values, and institutions.

Genealogical sensibilities orient and inform hyper-activism. They, with their fissures and contradictions, can provide the unstable ground for the ways people engage the durability of things. In our engagement with our three thinkers in part I and in our engagements in part II, we have followed such seams as those in the lineages of moral orders and authoritative knowledge; the establishment of a new moral order through the construction, suppression, and exclusion of unreason; the fissures in formations of identities; the lineages of the transatlantic slave trade as they continued to circulate in energy extraction; the preoccupying certainties and practices in ways of living without a sense of "what" we call beyond.

Beyond. *Decisive* does not mean *incisive*. Unutterable, inconceivable, shaded, and vague dimensions of events do not disappear with decisiveness. As people carry out their passionate commitments, an art of indirect disclosure is nonetheless required for thoughtful awareness *if* the unsayables are to appear, to present themselves, not as re-presentations but as occurrences beyond the borders of objectification and literal speech.

This art of indirect disclosure, as we have seen, happens in many ways. Kandinsky's art. Our experience of "Waldinneres" that we describe in the preface of this book. Nietzsche's discursive movements beyond good and evil. Foucault's engagements with unreason. Anzaldúa's *arte* in writing and speaking of nepantla. Indirect disclosure: the happening of what is meant and cannot be viewed, read, or heard directly. It—the happening—considerably exceeds what the viewer, reader, or listener directly perceives. We are speaking of a kind of attunement, an art of alertness, and an art of thinking that allows what is not representable to present itself, an art that diminishes the importance of clarity and increases the value of nuance, shades of meanings, metaphors, attitudes, complex depths, movements of more or less fading lucidity. It is an art of perceiving beyond the ordinary borders of cognizance.

We are putting to work Foucault's use of *hyper-activism* in the context of passionate decisiveness. The word *hyper* has an ancient Greek overtone of "over," "beyond," "above." In that context of meaning, *hyper-activism* does not mean "hyperactive" in the sense of impulsiveness or inattention and distraction. The word, to the contrary, suggests exceptional—we could say abnormal—attention, alertness, and action without specifying what the center of attention should be.

Foucault modifies hyper-activism with the word *pessimism*. Although we are not using *pessimism* constructively for reasons we stated above, we interpret that modification to mean that hyper-activism is never finished. As we have seen, he and we do not expect lasting solutions to the problems we encounter. Rather, decisive hyper-activism is oriented toward a continuing future of, not problems that need solutions, but uncountable, altering thresholds where truths, expectations, and certainties die and unexpected and uncertain conditions begin to emerge. The transformative potential of hyper-activism emerges from the potential for moving hyper-activists beyond truths and certainties, moving them to desire difficult engagements in living, mutating borders. This is a practice that, Foucault explains, "is precisely to bring it about that [people] 'no longer know what to do,' so that the acts, gestures, discourses that up until then had seemed to go without saying become problematic, difficult, dangerous" (2000, 235). And this means, as Anzaldúa so clearly illustrates in her writing and her living, that we must continually question, affect, and change "the paradigms that govern prevailing notions of reality, identity, creativity, activism, spirituality, race, gender, class, and sexuality" (2015, 2).

When hyper-activists confront oppressions and what they identify as injustices they, in their decisiveness, might be tempted to look for normative principles to guide their transforming, interrupting, and exposing actions. That, of course, would turn activism into yet another reform. Rather, in the language Hélène Cixous uses to speak of Jacques Derrida's practices of activism, we find ourselves "on the side of those who are current victims, in a precise *historical* moment, of violence and the denial of justice, but without ever letting [ourselves] be *appropriated* by a cause or a party.... Without illusion, without ever giving the opposition good/evil a chance to seduce, knowing full well that there is always more contamination in store" (2009, 44.) The expectation of living without illusion might itself be an illusion, but we accept the importance of disillusionment and as far as possible pay primary attention to undeceived appearances. We want to focus on specific situations, on "current victims," as Cixous says. We want enfleshed engagements that might loosen the power of the identities that have been imposed on us. We want to begin with particular events and relations of power, to find the effects of past occurrences and present habituations that cause abuse, brutality, subjection, and unnecessary suffering for people and other living things along with the destruction of the living spaces—the environments—of the world.

Although uncertainties and instabilities confront us from all directions, misery and what we find to be injustices certainly happen. These are the kinds of enfleshed events we want to begin with decisively when we act politically. And with our goal of transformation rather than reform, we begin with the knowledge that moral orders and standards of normalcy are often among the most problematic and dangerous power formations that we encounter. We begin, not by following principles, but by placing them in question. We begin with dynamic legacies that function in sensibilities and with the forces, incompatibilities, and conflicts that are in play in them and that disclose their finiteness and porous quality. We begin with the fissures, gaps, and unspeakable silences that are both in sensibilities and beyond them. We find in these beginnings the guides for hyper-activism as well as for the definitive conceptions in this book.

Epilogue

Our chapters emerged from in-between. Two very different authors, the polyphony of two voices speaking as one. Writing in-between Nietzsche, Foucault, Anzaldúa. We write to hear what is not quite in the texts but which can be glimpsed through attunements with their provocations. We offer no methods, sets of rules, or procedures. Not even a guidebook. But a desire for attunements with beyond.

You have noticed, we are sure, that our goal for this book has not been to persuade you of the normative rightness or goodness of any of the thoughts and positions we have engaged. Engagement—preferably deep engagement—with those thoughts and positions, on the other hand, has been one of our goals. Attunements with beyond have their ways of pushing us beyond the arguments, descriptions, values, mastering concepts, favorite issues, and even truths that characterize our thought and the thought of our considered authors. That push, we have said both directly and indirectly, comes in the experiences that accompany the words and concepts. A phrase, thought, feeling, orientation, or new prospect gets under our skin and excites a movement. These are experiences that happen when the engagements are intense and many types of transformations become possible. "Nietzsche was a revelation to me," Foucault wrote. "I felt that there was someone quite different from what I had been taught. I read him with a great passion and broke with my life, left my job in the asylum, left France: I had the feeling I had been trapped. Through Nietzsche, I had become a stranger to all that" (1988, 13). Such experiences, we have said, take people out of the sense that they are each autonomous subjects as distinct to extended ones. They show us that in being subjects we are living connections *in our eventuations* with images, cultures, peoples, places, a vast range of often-conflicting values, and liminal thresholds into which we cannot see clearly. These experienced elements in our extensiveness happen in and through lineages and their continuous mutations. They, the experiences, can rattle the cages of our certainties, not by substituting those certainties with new certainties, but by holding certainty in question—not eliminating certainty, but experiencing it in question. Each of our considered philosophers thinks with transformations of feelings in mind, with, we believe, desire for particular kinds transformations.

With desire for particular kinds of transformations? Doesn't that just revert us back to repetition of frames, sensibilities, concepts that animate desire for the good, for the right, for the true? Or can we, have we, perhaps identified a threshold to the enfleshment of a new ethos, one in which we desire not fixed, universal, ahistorical normativities, but rather mortal normativities. Norms that are fleshed, open, fluid, porous, vulnerable— deeply uncertain, yet essential to action. Norms that we are committed to and which commit us. A desire for mundo neuvo, new possibilities in our living together. What we suggest is not a simple task. As Butler cautions, "the desire to foreclose an open future can be a strong one, threatening one with loss, loss of a sense of certainty about how things are (and must be) . . . it may be that what is right and what is good consist in staying open to the tensions that beset the most fundamental categories we require, in knowing unknowingness at the core of what we know, and what we need" (2004, 180, 39).

Do we want to persuade you that our claims are true? Agreement is usually nice. But "want" in the sense of strongly desire? Yes and no. We believe that the stakes for our interconnected lives are high in the issues that we have raised. We think that the imagery and pre-reflective power of prioritizing subjectivity are profoundly and mischievously misleading. Our values incline us toward transformative thinking like that found in liberatory thought, genealogical thought, thought that begins with deep social dissatisfactions and suspicions of many traditions that are received as axiomatic for our lives—as well as astonishment in being alive. We wish to be like Anzaldúa's nepantleras: "Nepantleras function disruptively. Like tender green shoots growing out of the cracks, they eventually overturn foundations, making conventional definitions of otherness hard to sustain" (2015, 84). We valorize the importance of alertness to structural oppressions and the oppressing consequences of many values. But at times that we think of as our better times we see ourselves as in processes that we neither define nor could control if we wanted to. Yet in our decisiveness we intend to contribute to the lives of the processes of philosophical engagements, to the intensification of people's caring about genealogical sensibilities and happenings that are beyond our schemas of sense, for example. We want to contribute to the lives of the processes of philosophical engagements rather more than we want to be right, to be certain, to be possessors of the truth. Is that the truth, what we just said? Well, yes. Sort of. At least it's correct. But saying it is rather more dull, don't you think, than experiencing the wonder of actually engaging transformatively and feeling the emergence of new options, new prospects, new angles of alertness, and the living reality that seems to come only from experiences of devotion, decisiveness, and affection that allow "the" truth to blow with the winds of time? And isn't it true that you must have chaos in yourself to give birth to a dancing star (Nietzsche 1966c, section 5)?

Beyond Philosophy. There are many ways to interpret this phrase. Questions that are raised and reverberate throughout our chapters. Our intention was to cultivate attunement to its many senses, listening as Metis whispers in our ears, and in so doing, provoke a response. If this book has been successful, if our work opens out beyond to the possibilities of doing otherwise in the practices of thought and response, feeling and habits, then we conclude our reflections not at the end of philosophy but with openings beyond philosophy.

What did you expect?

BIBLIOGRAPHY

Aamons, A. R. 2017. "Epiphany." In *The Complete Poems of A. R. Ammons*, edited by Robert M. West, 128. New York: W.W. Norton.
Anzaldúa, Gloria. 1987. *Borderlands/La Frontera: The New Mestiza*. San Francisco: Aunt Lute Books.
———. 1996. "To Live in the Borderlands Means You." *Frontiers: A Journal of Women Studies* 17 (3): 4–5.
———. 2000. *Interviews/Entrevistas*. Edited by AnaLouise Keating. New York: Routledge.
———. 2012. "Interview with Gloria Anzaldúa." In *Borderlands: La Frontera*, 4th ed. San Francisco: Aunt Lute Books.
———. 2015. *Light in the Dark/Luz en lo Oscuro: Rewriting Identity, Spirituality, Reality*. Edited by AnaLouise Keating. Durham, NC: Duke University Press.
Anzaldúa, Gloria, and AnaLouise Keating. 2002. "Introduction." *This Bridge We Call Home: Radical Visions for Transformation*. New York: Routledge.
———. 2009. *The Gloria Anzaldúa Reader*. Durham, NC: Duke University Press.
Arnold, Matthew. 1910. *The Poetical Works of Matthew Arnold*. London: Macmillan.
Baptist, Edward E. 2014. *The Half Has Never Been Told: Slavery and the Making of American Capitalism*. New York: Basic Books.
Beckert, Sven. 2014. *Empire of Cotton: A Global History*. New York: Alfred A. Knopf.
Berlin, Ira. 1992. *Slaves without Masters: The Free Negro in the Antebellum South*. New York: New Press.
Bersani, Leo. 2010. *Is the Rectum a Grave? and Other Essays*. Chicago: University of Chicago Press.
Blackmon, Douglas A. 2008. *Slavery by Another Name: The Re-Enslavement of Black Americans from the Civil War to World War II*. New York: Doubleday Books.
Bollaín, Icíar, director. 2010. *También la Lluvia* [Even the rain]. Produced by Juan Gordon, Pilar Benito, Eric Altmayer, Monica Lozano Serrano, and Emma Lustres. Written by Paul Laverty. Distributed by Vitagraph Films.
Bradley, Raymond S., Mathias Vuille, Henry F. Diaz, and Walter Vergara. 2006. "Threats to Water Supplies in the Tropical Andes." *Science* 312: 1755–56.

Brennan, Teresa. 2004. *The Transmission of Affect*. Ithaca: Cornell University Press.
Brogan, Walter. 2012. "The Middle Voice of Charles Scott: The Intimacy of Attentiveness and the Life of Wonder." *Epoché* 17 (1): 89–97.
Buber, Martin. 1970. *I and Thou*. Translated by Walter Kaufmann. New York: Charles Scribner's Sons.
Butler, Judith. 1993. *Bodies That Matter: On the Discursive Limits of "Sex."* New York: Routledge.
——. 2004. *Undoing Gender*. New York: Routledge.
——. 2005. *Giving an Account of Oneself*. New York: Fordham University Press.
——. 2009. *Frames of War: When Is Life Grievable?* London: Verso.
Chambi, Mayta, Rúben Darío. 2015. "'Vivir Bien': A Discourse and Its Risks for Public Policies. The Case of Child Labour and Exploitation in Indigenous Communities of Bolivia." *Alternautas* 2 (2): 28–38.
Cixous, Hèléne. 1976. "The Laugh of the Medusa." Translated by Keith Cohen and Paula Cohen. *Signs* 1 (4): 875–93.
——. 2009. "Jacques Derrida: Co-Responding Voix You." In *Derrida and the Time of the Political*, edited by Pheng Cheah and Suzanne Guerlac, translated by Peggy Kamuf, 41–56. Durham: Duke University Press.
Cochrane, Regina. 2014. "Climate Change, Buen Vivir, and the Dialectic of Enlightenment: Toward a Feminist Critical Philosophy of Climate Justice." *Hypatia* 29 (1): 576–98.
Cook, Simon J., Ioannis Kougkoulos, Laura A. Edwards, Jason Dortch, and Dirk Hoffmann. 2016. "Glacier Change and Glacial Lake Outburst Flood Risk in the Bolivian Andes." *Cryosphere* 10: 2399–413. doi:10.5194/tc-10-2399-2016.
Cummings, E. E. 1994. *E. E. Cummings: Complete Poems, 1904–1962*. Edited by George James Firmage. New York: Liveright.
Derrida, Jacques. 1988. *Limited Inc*. Evanston, IL: Northwestern University Press.
——. 1990. "Force of Law: The 'Mystical Foundation of Authority.'" Translated by Mary Quaintance. *Cardozo Law Review* 11 (5–6): 920–1045.
——. 2007. *Learning to Live Finally: The Last Interview*. Translated by Pascale-Anne Brault and Michael Naas. Houndmills, Basingstoke, UK: Palgrave Macmillan.
Deyle, Steven. 2005. *Carry Me Back: The Domestic Slave Trade in American Life*. New York: Oxford University Press.
Edelman, Lee. 2004. *No Future: Queer Theory and the Death Drive*. Durham: Duke University Press.
Eribon, Dedier. 1991. *Michel Foucault*. Translated by Betsy Wing. Cambridge, MA: Harvard University Press.
Fabricant, Nicole. 2013. "Good Living for Whom? Bolivia's Climate Justice Movement and the Limitations of Indigenous Cosmovisions." *Latin American and Caribbean Ethnic Studies* 8 (2): 159–78. doi:10.1080/17442222.2013.805618.
Ferrer, Ada. 2014. *Freedom's Mirror: Cuba and Haiti in the Age of Revolution*. New York: Cambridge University Press.
Finkelman, Robert B., and Glenn. B. Stracher. 2011. "Environmental and Health Impacts of Coal Fires." In *Coal and Peat Fires: A Global Perspective*, edited by Glenn B. Stracher, Anupma Prakash, and Ellina V. Sokol, vol. 1, *Coal—Geology and Combustion*, 115–25.

Fontana, Lorenza. 2014. "The 'Indigenous Native Peasant' Trinity: Imagining a Plurinational Community in Evo Morales's Bolivia." *Environment and Planning D: Society and Space* 32 (3): 518–34.
Foucault, Michel. 1972. *The Archaeology of Knowledge*. Translated by A. M. Sheridan Smith. New York: Pantheon Books.
———. 1973a. *The Birth of the Clinic: An Archaeology of Medical Perception*. Translated by A. M. Sheridan Smith. New York: Vintage Books.
———. 1973b. *Madness and Civilization: A History of Madness in the Age of Reason*. Translated by Richard Howard. New York: Vintage Books.
———. 1973c. *The Order of Things: An Archaeology of the Human Sciences*. New York: Vintage Books.
———. 1977. *Language, Counter-Memory, Practice*. Edited by Donald F. Bouchard. Translated by Donald F. Bouchard and Sherry Simon. Ithaca, NY: Cornell University Press.
———. 1980. *Power/Knowledge*. Edited by Colin Gordon. Translated by Colin Gordon, Leo Marshall, John Mepham, and Kate Soper. New York: Pantheon Books.
———. 1982. "The Subject and Power." *Critical Inquiry* 8 (4): 777–95.
———. 1983. *Michel Foucault: Beyond Structuralism and Hermeneutics*. Edited by Hubert Dreyfus and Paul Rabinow. Chicago: University of Chicago Press.
———. 1984. "On the Genealogy of Ethics: An Overview of Work in Progress." In *The Foucault Reader*, edited by Paul Rabinow, 340–72. New York: Pantheon Books.
———. 1985. *The Use of Pleasure*. Translated by Robert Hurley. New York: Pantheon Books.
———. 1986a. *The Care of Self*. Translated by Robert Hurley. New York: Pantheon Books.
———. 1986b. *Death and the Labyrinth: The World of Raymond Roussel*. Translated by Charles Ruas. London: Continuum.
———. 1988. "Truth, Power, Self: An Interview with Michel Foucault." In *Technologies of the Self: A Seminar with Michel Foucault*, edited by Luther H Martin, Huck Gutman, and Patrick H. Hutton, 9–15. Amherst: University of Massachusetts Press.
———. 1997. *Michel Foucault: Ethics, Subjectivity, and Truth*. Edited by Paul Rabinow. Translated by Robert Hurley et al. New York: New Press.
———. 1998. *Michel Foucault: Aesthetics, Method, Epistemology*. Edited by James D. Faubion. Translated by Robert Hurley et al. New York: New Press.
———. 2000. *Power*. Vol. 3 of *The Essential Works of Foucault, 1954–1984*. Edited by James D. Faubion. Translated by Robert Hurley. New York: New Press.
———. 2003. *Society Must Be Defended: Lectures at the Collège de France 1975–1976*. New York: Picador.
———. 2006. *The History of Madness*. Edited by Jean Khalfa. Translated by Jonathan Murphy and Jean Khalfa. London: Routledge.
Fox-Genovese, Elizabeth, and Eugene D. Genovese. 2008. *Slavery in White and Black: Class and Race in the Southern Slaveholders' New World Order*. New York: Cambridge University Press.
Genovese, Eugene D. 1998. *A Consuming Fire: The Fall of the Confederacy in the Mind of the White Christian South*. Vol. 41. Athens: University of Georgia Press.
Genovese, Eugene D., and Elizabeth Fox-Genovese. 2011. *Fatal Self-Deception: Slaveholding Paternalism in the Old South*. Cambridge: Cambridge University Press.

Glikson, Andrew Y. 2014. *Evolution of the Atmosphere, Fire and the Anthropocene Climate Event Horizon*. Dordrecht: Springer.

Global Carbon Project. 2017. *Carbon Budget and Trends 2017*. Last modified November 13, 2017. http://www.globalcarbonproject.org/carbonbudget.

Grandin, Greg. 2014. *The Empire of Necessity: Slavery, Freedom, and Deception in the New World*. New York: Metropolitan Books/Henry Holt.

Gyasi, Yaa. 2016. *Homegoing: A Novel*. New York: Knopf.

Halberstam, Jack. 2015. "Straight Eye for the Queer Theorist: A Review of 'Queer Theory Without Antinormativity.'" Bully Bloggers. Last modified September 12, 2015. https://bullybloggers.wordpress.com/2015/09/12/straight-eye-for-the-queer-theorist-a-review-of-queer-theory-without-antinormativity-by-jack-halberstam/.

Haraway, Donna. 2007. *When Species Meet*. Minneapolis: University of Minnesota Press.

Hartman, Saidiya V., and Frank B. Wilderson III. 2003. "The Position of the Unthought." *Qui Parle* 13 (2): 183–201.

Haslanger, Sally. 2002. "On Being Objective and Being Objectified." In *A Mind of One's Own: Feminist Essays on Reason and Objectivity*, edited by Louise M. Antony and Charlotte E. Witt, 209–53. Boulder, CO: Westview.

Henry, Patrick. 1775. Speech to the Virginia Convention, March 23, 1775. http://www.history.org/almanack/life/politics/giveme.cfm.

Hesiod. 1983. *Theogony*. Translated by Apostolos N. Athanassakis. Baltimore, MD: Johns Hopkins University Press.

Hiddleston-Galloni, Anna. 2014. "The Beginnings in Munich: 1896–1908." In *Kandinsky: A Retrospective*, by Angela Lampe and Brady Roberts. New Haven, CT: Yale University Press.

Hobbes, Thomas. 1839–45. *Leviathan*. In *The English Works of Thomas Hobbs*, edited by W. Molesworth. London: John Bohn.

Hoffmann, Dirk, and Daniel Weggenmann. 2013. "Climate Change Induced Glacier Retreat and Risk Management: Glacial Lake Outburst Floods (GLOFs) in the Apolobamba Mountain Range, Bolivia." In *Climate Change and Disaster Risk Management*, edited by Walter Leal Filho, 71–87. Berlin: Springer. doi:10.1007/978-3-642-31110-9_5.

Huanacuni Mamani, Fernando. 2010. *Vivir Bien/Buen Vivir Filosofía, Políticas, Estrategias y Experiencias Regionales*. Lima, Peru: Jr. Carlos Arrieta.

Ingold, Tim. 2010. "The Transformation of the Line: Traces, Threads, and Surfaces." *Textile: The Journal of Cloth and Culture* 8 (1): 10–35.

———. 2015. *The Life of Lines*. Abingdon, UK: Routledge.

Irons, Charles F. 2008. *The Origins of Proslavery Christianity: White and Black Evangelicals in Colonial and Antebellum Virginia*. Chapel Hill: University of North Carolina Press.

James, William. 1958. *Essays in Radical Empiricism: A Plural Universe*. New York: Longmans, Green.

Jeffers, Robinson. 2001. *The Selected Poetry of Robinson Jeffers*. Edited by Tim Hunt. Stanford, CA: Stanford University Press.

Johnson, Walter. 2017. *River of Dark Dreams: Slavery and Empire in the Cotton Kingdom*. Cambridge, MA: Harvard University Press.

Kandinsky, Wassily. 1948. *Kandinsky: Complete Writings on Art*. Vol. 1. Edited by Kenneth C. Lindsey and Peter Vergo. Philadelphia: De Capa.

———. 1974. *Regards sur le passé et autres textes, 1912–22*. Edited with an introduction by Jean-Paul Bouillon. Paris: Hermann.

———. 2006. *Concerning the Spiritual in Art*. Translated by M. T. H. Sadler. Boston: MFA Publications.

Kant, Immanuel. (1780) 1963. *Lectures on Ethics*. Translated by Louis Infield. New York: Harper and Row.

Keller, Evelyn Fox. 1983. *A Feeling for the Organism: The Life and Work of Barbara McClintock*. New York: W. H. Freeman.

Kinouchi, Tsuyoshi, Tong Liu, Javier Mendoza Rodríguez, and Yoshihiro Asaoka. 2013. "Modeling Glacier Melt and Runoff in a High-Altitude Headwater Catchment in the Cordillera Real, Andes." *Hydrology and Earth System Sciences Discussion* 10: 13093–144. doi:10.5194/hessd-10-13093-2013.

Kofman, Sarah. 1988. "Beyond Aporia?" In *Post-Structuralist Classics*, edited by Andrew Benjamin and translated by David Macey, 7–44. London: Routledge.

Kuenzer, Claudia, and Glenn B. Stracher. 2012. "Geomorphology of Coal Seam Fires." *Geomorphology* 138: 209–22.

Lampe, Angela, and Brady Roberts. 2014. *Kandinsky: A Retrospective*. New Haven, CT: Yale University Press.

Lorde, Audre. 1984. "The Master's Tools Will Never Dismantle the Master's House." In *Sister Outsider: Essays and Speeches*. Berkeley, CA: Crossing, 110-113.

Lovejoy, Arthur. 1960. *The Great Chain of Being*. New York: Harper Torchbook.

Lugo, Alejandro. 2008. *Fragmented Lives, Assembled Parts: Culture, Capitalism, and Conquest at the U.S.-Mexico Border*. Austin: University of Texas Press.

Macusaya, Carlos. 2015. "El Vivir Bien." MINKA Digital. http://www.minka.tk.

Maffie, James. 2013. *Aztec Philosophy: Understanding a World in Motion*. Boulder: University Press of Colorado.

Marcin, Tim. 2017. "What Has Trump Said about Global Warming: Eight Quotes on Climate Change as He Announces Paris Agreement Decision." *Newsweek*, June 1. http://www.newsweek.com/what-has-trump-said-about-global-warming-quotes-climate-change-paris-agreement-618898.

McDermott, John. 1986. "The Aesthetic Drama of the Ordinary." In *Streams of Experience*, 129–40. Amherst: University of Massachusetts Press.

Meaney, Michael. 2010. "Epigenetics and the Biological Definition of Gene × Environment Interactions." *Child Development* 81 (1): 41–79.

Merleau-Ponty, Maurice. 1995. *Phenomenology of Perception*. Translated by Colin Smith. New York: Routledge.

"Metal, Mineral, Coal and Stock Markets: Current Prices, Market Conditions and Commercial Statistics of the Metals, Minerals and Mining Stocks: Quotations from Important Sources." 1909. *Engineering and Mining Journal*, January 16.

Miller, James. 1993. *The Passion of Michel Foucault*. New York City: Simon & Schuster.

Mississippi. 1866. *Laws of the State of Mississippi, Passed at a Regular Session of the Mississippi Legislature, Held in Jackson, October, November and December, 1865*. Jackson: Mississippi State, 82–93, 165–167.

Moore, Jason W. 2015. *Capitalism in the Web of Life: Ecology and the Accumulation of Capital*. New York: Verso.

NAACP et al. 2012. "Coal Blooded: Putting Profits before People." http://www.naacp.org/climate-justice-resources/coal-blooded/.

Naas, Michael. 2008. "Fire Walls: Sarah Kofman's Pyrotechnics." In *Sarah Kofman's Corpus*, edited by Pleshette DeArmitte and Tina Chanter, 49–74. Albany: State University of New York Press.

NASA. 2018. Accessed April 2018. https://climate.nasa.gov/.
Nietzsche, Friedrich. (1886) 2005. *Die Geburt der Tragödie: Versuch einer Selbstkritik.* Urbana, IL: Project Gutenberg. Accessed June 1, 2019. https://www.gutenberg.org/ebooks/7206.
———. 1966a. *Beyond Good and Evil.* Translated by Walter Kaufmann. New York: Vintage Books.
———. 1966b. *The Birth of Tragedy.* Translated by Walter Kaufmann. New York: Vintage Books.
———. 1966c. *Thus Spoke Zarathustra.* Translated by Walter Kaufmann. New York: Viking.
———. 1967. *On the Genealogy of Morals.* Translated by Walter Kaufmann and R. J. Hollingdale. New York: Vintage Books.
———. 1997. *Untimely Meditations.* Edited by Daniel Breazeale. Translated by R. J. Hollingdale. Cambridge: Cambridge University Press.
Oliver, Mary. 2016. *Upstream: Selected Essays.* New York: Penguin Press.
Parks, Rosa, and Gregory J. Reed. 1994. *Quiet Strength: The Faith, the Hope, and the Heart of a Woman Who Changed a Nation.* Grand Rapids, MI: Zondervan.
Perreault, Thomas. 2003. "'A People with Our Own Identity': Toward a Cultural Politics of Development in Ecuadorian Amazonia." *Environment and Planning D: Society and Space* 21: 583–606.
Perreault, Tom, and Barbara Green. 2013. "Reworking the Spaces of Indigeneity: The Bolivian Ayllu and Lowland Autonomy Movements Compared." *Environment and Planning D: Society and Space* 31 (1): 43–60. doi:10.1068/d0112.
Pew Research Center. 2013. *King's Dream Remains an Elusive Goal: Many Americans See Racial Disparities.* Washington, DC: Pew Research Center. http://www.pewsocialtrends.org/2013/08/22/.
Pyne, Stephen J. 2001. *Fire: A Brief History.* Seattle: University of Washington Press.
Ramirez, Edson, Bernard Francou, Pierre Ribstein, Marc Descloitres, Roger Guerin, Javier Mendoza, Robert Gallaire, Bernard Pouyaud, and Ekkehard Jordan. 2001. "Small Glaciers Disappearing in the Tropical Andes: A Case-Study in Bolivia: Glaciar Chacaltaya (16° S)." *Journal of Glaciology* 47 (157): 187–94.
Rilke, Rainer Maria. 1984. *Letters to a Young Poet.* Translated by Stephen Mitchell. New York: Random House.
Robine, Jean-Marie, Siu Lan K. Cheung, Sophie Le Roy, Herman Van Oyen, Clare Griffiths, Jean-Pierre Michel, François Richard Herrmann. 2008. "Death Toll Exceeded 70,000 in Europe during the Summer of 2003." *Comptes Rendus Biologies* 331 (2): 171–178. doi:10.1016/j.crvi.2007.12.001.
Robins, Nicholas A. 2011. *Mercury, Mining, and Empire: The Human and Ecological Cost of Colonial Silver Mining in the Andes.* Bloomington: Indiana University Press.
Robinson, Michael D. 2017. *A Union Indivisible: Secession and the Politics of Slavery in the Border South.* Chapel Hill: University of North Carolina Press.
Rothman, Adam. 2007. *Slave Country: American Expansion and the Origins of the Deep South.* Cambridge, MA: Harvard University Press.
Rumi, Jalal ad-Din Muhammad. 2004. *The Essential Rumi.* Translated by Coleman Barks, with John Moyne. San Francisco: Harper One.
Scheman, Naomi. 1993. *Engenderings: Constructions of Knowledge, Authority, and Privilege.* New York: Routledge.

Schermerhorn, Calvin. 2015. *The Business of Slavery and the Rise of American Capitalism, 1815–1860*. New Haven: Yale University Press.

Schneiderman, Jill S. 2017. "The Anthropocene Controversy." In *Anthropocene Feminism*, edited by Richard A. Grusin, 169–95. Minneapolis: University of Minnesota Press.

Scott, Charles E. 1990. *The Question of Ethics*. Bloomington: Indiana University Press.

Sedgwick, Eve Kosofsky. 1990. *The Epistemology of the Closet*. Berkeley: University of California Press.

Sharma, Bhavna. 2006. *Contemporary Forms of Slavery in Bolivia*. Anti-Slavery International. http://www.antislavery.org.

Smil, Vaclav. 2011. "Nitrogen Cycle and World Food Production." *World Agriculture* 2: 9–13.

———. 2012. *Harvesting the Biosphere: How Much We Have Taken from Nature*. Cambridge: MIT Press.

Stevens, Wallace. 1954. *The Collected Poems of Wallace Stevens*. New York: Vintage.

Sublette, Ned, and Constance Sublette. 2015. *The American Slave Coast: A History of the Slave-Breeding Industry*. Chicago: Chicago Review Press.

Toomey, Diane. 2013. *Coal Pollution and the fight for Environmental Justice*. Yale Environment 360. Last modified June 19, 2013. http://e360.yale.edu/features/naacp_jacqueline_patterson_coal_pollution_and_fight_for_environmental_justice.

Trump, Donald. 2018. Interview with Piers Morgan, January 28, 2018. Transcript available at https://blogs.spectator.co.uk/2018/01/donald-trumps-interview-with-piers-morgan-full-transcript/.

Tuana, Nancy. 2008. "Viscous Porosity: Witnessing Katrina." In *Material Feminisms*, edited by Stacy Alaimo and Susan Hekman, 188–213. Bloomington: Indiana University Press.

———. 2019. "Climate Apartheid: The Forgetting of Race in the Anthropocene." *Critical Philosophy of Race* 7 (1): 1–31.

Turetsky, Merritt R., Brian Benscoter, Susan Page, Guillermo Rein, Guido R. Van Der Werf, and Adam Watts. 2014. "Global Vulnerability of Peatlands to Fire and Carbon Loss." *Nature Geoscience* 8 (1): 11–14.

United Nations Department of Economic and Social Affairs, Population Division. 2017. *World Population Prospects: The 2017 Revision, Key Findings and Advance Tables*. New York: United Nations. https://esa.un.org/unpd/wpp/Publications/Files/WPP2017_KeyFindings.pdf.

US Environmental Protection Agency. 1991. *Integrated Risk Information System: Nitrate*. http://archive.epa.gov/teach/web/pdf/nitrates_summary.pdf.

———. 2015. *Overview of Greenhouse Gases*. http://epa.gov/climatechange/ghgemissions/gases/n2o.html.

Vernant, Jean-Pierre. 1991. *Cunning Intelligence in Greek Society and Culture*. Translated by Janet Lloyd. Chicago: University of Chicago Press.

Ward, M. H. 2009. "Too Much of a Good Thing? Nitrate from Nitrogen Fertilizers and Cancer: President's Cancer Panel—October 21, 2008." *Reviews on Environmental Health* 24 (4): 357–63.

Warner, Michael. 1999. *The Trouble with Normal: Sex, Politics, and the Ethics of Queer Life*. Cambridge, MA: Harvard University Press.

Weinberg, Bill. 2010a. "Beyond Extraction: An Interview with Rafael Quispe." *NACLA Report on the Americas* 3 (5): 21.

———. 2010b. "New Water Wars in Bolivia: Climate Change and Indigenous Struggle." *NACLA Report on the Americas* 43 (5): 19–24.
Weiss, Peg. 1982. "Kandinsky in Munich: Encounters and Transformations." In *Kandinsky in Munich, 1896–1914*, by Wassily Kandinsky, Solomon R. Guggenheim Foundation, Solomon R. Guggenheim Museum, San Francisco Museum of Modern Art, and Städtische Galerie im Lenbachhaus München, 18–83. New York: Solomon R. Guggenheim Museum.
"Welcome to the Anthropocene." 2003. *Nature*, August 14, 424, 709. doi:10.1038/424709b.
"Welcome to the Anthropocene." 2011. *Economist*, May 26, 13.
Whitford, Frank. 1967. *Kandinsky*. London: Hamlyn.
Wiegman, Robyn, and Elizabeth A. Wilson. 2015. "Introduction: Antinormativity's Queer Conventions." *differences* 26 (1): 1–25.
Winterson, Jeanette. 1996. *Art Objects: Essays on Ecstasy and Effrontery*. New York: Alfred A. Knopf.
Wrangham, Richard. 2009. *Catching Fire: How Cooking Made Us Human*. New York: Basic Books.
Young, Iris Marion. 1984. "Pregnant Embodiment." *Journal of Medicine and Philosophy* 9: 45–62.

INDEX

abnormality, 106; difference and deviance in, 237; and madness, 82–83
absolute understanding, 103, 103n18
acceptance and legitimacy, 15
activism: Anzaldúa on, 191; and cultivation of malaise and in-betweenness, 190–91; and métis-intelligence, 235. *See also* hyper-activism
Aeschylus, tragic dramas of, 28
affect and feelings: affectional vulnerabilities, 19; in Anzaldúa's enfleshed genealogical sensibilities, 120–21, 133, 134, 169; attunement to, 156, 191; in Nietzsche's new knowledge, 50, 56; process of affecting, 6; and sensibilities, 15, 16, 17, 53–54, 69, 164; transformation in, 165, 187, 189, 191, 195; transmission of, 202, 214. *See also* art; Brueghel the Elder, Jan; imporings; Kandinsky, Wassily
agency, pre-reflective, 17, 164
Alabama, coal and convict leasing in, 175–76
alternative knowledge, 14
Ammons, A. R., "Epiphany," 226–27, 228
anonymous agency: concept of, 18–19; of imporings, 121, 157, 171; of lineages, 119, 235; in paintings, 193 (*see also* Kandinsky, Wassily); in reading Anzaldúa, 136. *See also* sensibility and sensibilities
Anthropocenean sensibilities, 164–65, 164–65n1, 169–71, 186–87, 191

Anzaldúa, Gloria: and attunement to tensions, 135–36, 185; and attunement with beyond, 112; autohistoria of, 110–16; border arte of, 131, 134–38, 140, 141, 155, 160; and borderlands, 17n14, 18; corporeal spirituality of, 121, 141; and the Coyolxauhqui imperative, 126–29; on critiques, 148; cuerpoespíritu of, 130–31, 132, 133, 138; and denial of dichotomies, 120; enfleshed genealogical sensibilities of, 19, 109, 116–22, 133, 160–61; function and practice of writing for, 136, 138, 170, 177, 190; genealogies in, 13, 13n13; multiple lineages of, 113, 189; multivocality of, 111–12; poetic and aesthetic awareness of, 142; resonance and attunement with beyond in, 8–9, 24; response to oppression, 127, 128; and self-transformation, 146, 166, 186, 188–89; sexuality of, 113, 116, 134, 189; spiritual *mestizaje* of, 114, 123, 187; on transcendence of duality, 119, 169–70; and transformation-with-others, 138–40; translational practices of, 110n2. *See also* conocimiento; falling apart; nepantla; nepantleras
Anzaldúa, Gloria, writings of: *Borderlands/La Frontera*, 115, 119, 129, 136–37, 187; *Light in the Dark/Luz en lo Oscuro*, 115, 123–24, 125, 128, 165–66; "To Live in the Borderlands Means You," 157

Apollo, 28
aporia: in Derrida, 187–88; in liberatory theory, 238; transverse movement to expose, 239
Arnold, Matthew, "Dover Beach," 241
art: and affirmation of tragic life through, 49n15; anonymous agency of, 18, 201, 203; and the extraordinary, 75n6; as foreign territory, 153; importance to thinking and morality, 27–28; inspiration and implementation into, 31–33; relationship with beyond, 135, 137. *See also* Kandinsky, Wassily
ascesis, 22, 99, 160
asceticism: games of truth in, 100; and human living, 50n16; Nietzsche's war with, 41, 42, 43, 50–54
attunement: animation of others' experience of, 9, 23, 24, 158–59, 213–14, 251; as art of alertness, 247; authors' experience of, 4–5, 7, 147; and being in borders, 21–22; beyond norms, 240, 241; genealogies and shifts in, 15; to the unthinkable, 126, 165; in the writing process, 4–5, 9, 141–42, 147. *See also* anonymous agency; Anzaldúa, Gloria; beyond; *Beyond Good and Evil*; border art philosophy; conocimiento; corporeal vulnerabilities; Derrida, Jacques; enfleshed happenings; Foucault, Michel; happenings; hyper-activism; imporings; in-betweenness; Kandinsky, Wassily; liberatory philosophy; livingdying; McClintock, Barbara; mêtis-intelligence; Nietzsche, Friedrich; *On the Genealogy of Morals*; sensibilities of denial; sensibility and sensibilities; silence; thresholds; unreason; unsayables; viscous porosity
authoritative knowledge: "games of truth" in use of, 99–100; and silencing of venereal disease patients, 87; silencing power of, 81
authors: "An Infused Dialogue," 6; dialogues as instance of border art philosophy, 214; goals for this book, 249–51; hopes for readers, 11, 23–24, 26, 29, 53–54, 109, 153, 162

Bachelard, Gaston, 161
Beauvoir, Simone de, 161

Bechtel Corporation, 179
becomings, 118, 125, 155, 209
beginnings, new: attunement to, 14; and genuine change, 148; requirements for, 186, 251; in self-overcoming, 33–34; shiftings as a result of, 131
beyond: attunement with, 118, 141, 249; comprehensibility of, 3; concept of, 8, 8n9, 9, 24, 108; and creativity, 130, 150; dimensions of, 121, 129–30; epiphanies in attunement with, 227–28; Foucault's attunement with, 106–7; nepantla as, 125. *See also* Anzaldúa, Gloria; border art philosophy; creative energy and conception; Foucault, Michel; happenings; human life and living; liberation; Nietzsche, Friedrich; silence; transformation; unsayables
Beyond Good and Evil (Nietzsche): dangers to the human soul, 35–38; free spiritedness and truth, 30–35; relationship with *Thus Spoke Zarathustra*, 42; temporality in, 39–40; ways of living in beyond, 38–39, 40–41
Black Americans and criminalization of, 174–75
black lung disease, 176–77
Blackmon, Douglas, 176
Blanchot, Maurice, 161
bodies: porosity of, 118–19; reading and writing through, 118–19; relationality of, 119; and shaping of identity and mind, 118. *See also* corporeality
Bolivia: Amazonian climate change in, 178–79; child labor laws in, 183–84; Platform for Climate Change, 180; poverty in, 178, 178n9, 181, 182; rural-to-urban migration in, 182; use of indigenous structures and practices in, 180; water security in, 178–79
border art, concept of, 21, 27, 29, 69–70. *See also* Anzaldúa, Gloria
border artists, 49, 134–38, 140, 180, 181
border art philosophy: and alertness to the risks of uncertainty, 160–61; attunement with lineages and borders in, 156, 157; attunement with nonrational and

nondiscursive dimensions in, 29; book as instance of, 214; concept of, 142, 155–56; creative experience of, 158; cultivation of, 70; description of, 20–22, 27; ever-becomingness of, 156; experiential excitement in, 159; methodology of, 161–62; métis-intelligence at core of, 231; multilineal sensitivities in, 157; *poiesis* of, 158, 161; relations to feelings and affect, 69–70, 135, 154, 159, 161, 214; in socioenvironmental issues, 24–25; transverse movement in, 231

borderlands: in Anzaldúa's life and thought, 134; sensibilities as, 17, 17n14

borders: being *in* borders, 11, 21, 69, 104, 157–58, 238; as ever-shifting, 244–45; and moments, 11; porosity of, 7, 109, 127; pushing boundaries as impulse for writing, 129–30; and sensibilities, 76, 165; thinking experimentally in, 71–72, 72n1; and transformations, 18; unsettling to transform habits of thought, 192. *See also* Anzaldúa, Gloria; border art philosophy; imporings; in-betweenness; thresholds

Brennan, Teresa, 214

bridges, 114, 123, 124, 128, 139, 140, 186

Brueghel the Elder, Jan, *Forest View*, xi–xii, 11, xiin1

buen vivir (good living): as alternative model of development, 181–83; and climate change, 181n12; negative tropes in, 182–84

Burning Mountain (Australia), 171

Butler, Judith: and concept of corporeal vulnerability, 195; *Giving an Account of Oneself*, 190, 191; and grids of intelligibility, 152–53, 156; on norms, 237; on openness to tension and uncertainty, 250; on the paradox of subjectivation, 238; and risk of ethics, 166, 190

capitalism, 173, 177, 180–81

Cartwright, Fraser, 221–22, 222*f*

chiasm and interconnectedness of differences, 10

Christianity: and banishment of lepers, 85–86; craziness and normality in rituals of, 86–87n14; and morality, 60n25; new love of, 61; and self-authorization in division of lepers from sanctified, 86

Cixous, Hélène, 161, 188, 248

climate change: and circulation of nitrogen, 194; coal seam fires' effect on, 171; denial of, 163–64; and fissures in current sensibilities, 169; and genealogies of greenhouse gas practices, 185; human responsibility for, 170; and need for transformation of our sensibilities, 164–65; questions related to overcoming, 178; solutions to, 184–85; thinking from the unsayables, 188

coal and coal industry: and coal seam fires, 171; and convict leasing, 175–76; incendiary lineages of, 171; mortality and illness of convict miners, 176–77; racism and environmental exploitation in, 173; as seen through enfleshed genealogical sensibilities, 171–77

Coal Blooded: Putting Profits before People, 172

Cochabamba Water War, 179, 179n10

Codex Tezcatlipoca, née Codex Fejérváry-Mayer, 109–10, 109–10n1

cognition, limits of, 120–21

Collegium Phaenomenologicum, 4, 4n1–2

colonialism, 117, 117n7, 173, 178n9

communities-beyond-communities, 139

concrescences: corporeal exchanges in, 168, 195; Foucault's use of term, 197; occurrences of, 194, 195; Similitude and, 198

conflict: genealogies and, 14; productive capacities of, 139–40; sensibilities and, 17, 233

conocimiento: and border arte, 133–38; concept of, 124, 124n8, 132–33, 160; as key to Anzaldúa's enfleshed genealogical sensibilities, 133–34; in liberatory work, 148; as tool, 166, 169–70

convict leasing, 175

corporeality: and anonymous agency of paintings, 203–4; asceticism's denial of goodness in, 51, 52; attunement to, 35; as basis for Anzaldúa's work, 115–22, 133, 141; and enfleshed sensibilities, 35, 167; in engagement with truth and beyond, 34; of the human soul, 37; knowledge and, 120; priority of, 50

corporeal vulnerabilities, 193; in becomings, 209; concept of, 195; and corporeal exchanges, 195; and imporings when experiencing art, 203–4; as site of becoming, 204
correctional institutions, 93–94
Coyolxauhqui and Coyolxauhqui imperative, 116, 116n5, 126–29, 166
Coyote, the trickster, 168
creative energy and conception: in attunement with beyond, 135; birth and death in, 31–33; the child as metaphor for ecstasis of, 34; engendered in beyond, 130; power of imagination in, 133–34, 135; sparks and wonder in, 32, 33
creative experiences, Foucault's instigation of possibilities for, 72–73
cruelty: in Jeffers's poetry, 225; lineages in, 13, 108; and purity, 68; self-inflicted, 60, 100
cuerpomentealma: concept of neologism, 116; in conocimiento, 124, 133, 169; experience of, 140, 141; in nepantla, 122; rebirth of, 127; in transformation, 120, 189
cultural sensitivity, 139–40
Cummings, E. E., "r-p-o-p-h-e-s-s-a-g-r," 212–13

death, Foucault and boundary of, 79, 79n9. See also livingdying
decent reforms, 91, 148, 149, 161–62
decisiveness, 162, 243–45, 246, 247
depth, dimensions of: in art, xii; in human soul, 37; through philosophical thinking, xii–xiii
Derrida, Jacques: activism of, 248; as border art philosopher, 161; on creativity, 152; deconstruction of, 166, 187–88, 189; ethos of writing, 187; writing lineages of, 187n16
dichotomy and dualism: creation of, 196; refusal of, 8, 10, 35, 38, 53, 61, 77, 141–42
Dionysian dimensions in Nietzsche's work, 39–40, 53, 54
Dionysus, 28, 46, 150
disorder, lineages in, 13. See also madness; unreason
distance, dimensions of: in human soul, 37; painter's skill in creating, xi–xii; and silence, 78; through philosophical thinking, xii–xiii. See also in-betweenness
doingness, 211, 212
domain of unreason, 96

edges, and formlessness beyond the edges, 22, 24
eleutheria, concept of, 150–51
endingbeginning, 162, 191, 244
enfleshed happenings: in border art philosophy, 156 (see also viscous porosity); and enfleshed freedom, 140; and enfleshed genealogical sensibilities, 35, 167, 171–77, 186, 189 (see also Anzaldúa, Gloria); and enfleshed wisdom, 230; and experiencing art, 204; transformations as, 145. See also corporeality; hyper-activism; Metis, myth of; mêtis-intelligence; phusis
enslaved people. See slavery
environmental exploitation and racism, 172, 173, 177
epistemology, imporings in, 196
Eribon, Didier, 78
erotic love: enactment in the in-between, 210–11; and sexual objectification, 193, 207–8
eternal life, through life-denying values, 51–52
eternal recurrence, temporality of, 46–50, 48n13, 49n15
ethics, split in unity of, 95
everyday life: with the instability of the intangible, 25; nonrational dimensions in, 76; occurrences of in-between in, 11, 23; unreason and normalcy in, 77
extended authorship, 5–6, 131–32

falling apart, 126–29, 155, 189
feminism and sexual objectification, 207, 208
fire in human life: cooking and transformation of the body, 167; as corporeal exchange, 168; as the differentiator with other species, 166–67; humans' transformation of the earth, 168–70; migrations enabled by, 167; in mythology, 168
fleshiness. See corporeality; enfleshed happenings

form and formlessness, in beyond, 22, 24
Foucault, Michel: attunement with beyond in, 8–9, 24, 106, 227–28; curiosity of, 99, 101, 102, 103–4; *division* in thought of, 86; essence of his work, 71–72n1, 72; and "games of truth," 99–101; genealogies in, 13, 14, 72, 73–74, 166; and the imporing of epistemic borders, 196; and a language of unending exchange with change, 83; liberation from philosophical canon, 148; motivation for work of, 99; on Nietzsche, 55n18, 159, 249; on origins, 12; philosophical task of, 157; and "positive unconscious of knowledge," 121; reading Foucault, 71–72; response to dangers, 240, 240n4; on role in fault-finding, 184; self-transformation of, 100–104, 106, 189–90; sexuality of, 79n9, 81, 102; on silence, 78–79, 80; on silencing, 78–81; and truth, 8, 106, 152; uncertainty in thought of, 160; ways of living, 105, 145–46, 185–86; on writing and thinking, 9, 99, 100–101, 189–90. *See also* hyper-activism; madness; silence; silencing; unreason

Foucault, Michel, writings of: *The Archaeology of Knowledge*, 73; *The Birth of the Clinic*, 73, 74; *History of Sexuality*, 104; *Madness and Civilization*, 73, 74; *The Order of Things*, 73, 74, 196, 197–200; *The Use of Pleasure*, 99. See also *History of Madness*

freedom: language of, 150; practices of, 102–4

free spiritedness: enabled by curiosity, 99; and finding joy and laughter, 35; and the human soul, 37; and life-denying subjugation to Western morality, 38; reliability and irresponsibility in, 65–66; and self-direction, 66, 67; and self-transformation, 100–101; wonder and creativity in, 32–35

fusion and interfusion: as assemblages of processes, 77; experience of, 6, 10–11; genealogies and, 14; in painting, xii; poem as enactment of event of, 215; of voices and conceptualizations, 4–5. *See also* concrescences; imporings

gender. *See* Anzaldúa, Gloria; borders; *buen vivir* (good living); oppression

"Genealogical and Corporeal Temporalities" (course), 4, 4n2, 7, 7n6

genealogical responsibility: in interrupting moralities and religion, 54; and making promises, 64–65, 64–65n28; and normative ethics, 64; sovereign individuals and, 66–68, 67n31

genealogical sensibility and sensibilities: in Anzaldúa, 13n13; concept of, 19–20; corporeality and transformation in, 40–41; as enfleshed in Anzaldúa, 117–18; forms of, 109; and hyper-activism, 246; Nietzsche's desire for alternatives to European morality, 52–54; as practices of border art philosophy, 158; and questioning, 245; and re-creation of oppression, 162; and undoing life-denying values, 151. *See also* Anzaldúa, Gloria; climate change

genealogy and genealogies: concept of, 13–14; developing genealogical knowledge, 54; emergence of, 14–15; as practices of border art philosophy, 158; and sensibilities, 15; and striking change, 15–16. *See also* Anzaldúa, Gloria; Foucault, Michel; genealogical sensibility and sensibilities; lineages; Nietzsche, Friedrich; *On the Genealogy of Morals*; transformation

German National Socialist Party, 60n25

God, deteriorating social power of, 46–47, 161

Goethe, Johann Wolfgang von, 26, 26n1

good and bad: conjunctive space between, 57–59, 58n23; etymological evidence for, 55–56n19; lineages of, 55–56, 55n18; Nietzsche's move away from dualism of, 62; as opposites, 56–57; power, good, and truth of the noble, 57nn21–22; and power in ranking values of, 58; and priestly power, 60n25

good and evil: conjunctive space between, 60; lineages of conjunction of, 61; Nietzsche's move away from dualism, 61–62; and priestly power, 59–60

Greek culture: affirmation of tragic life in, 49n15; art of tragedy and mythmaking in, 28–29; genealogies in mythology, 13; tragedy of life and beautiful art in, 30n7

Gyasi, Yaa, *Homegoing: A Novel*, 176

happenings: body, life, spirit, and beyond in, 115; in concept of beyond, 7n7, 8, 21, 142; in everyday living, 23; invoking in-betweenness, 213–14; and mêtis-intelligence, 230, 231, 236; nepantla as, 122–23; openness to, 11, 119, 206, 250–51; thinkers attuned to, 22–23, 69. *See also* aporia; border art philosophy; borders; corporeal vulnerabilities; imporings; in-betweenness; limit-experiences; lineages; objectification; transformation; uncertainty; unreason; viscous porosity

Hartman, Saidiya, 150

Haslanger, Sally, 208

Hebrew/Jewish people and traditions, 60n25

Hebrew Scriptures, genealogies in, 13

herd cultures: concept of, 35; moral and theoretical formations of, 39; in oppressive systems, 57, 162

History of Madness (Foucault): experiential basis for, 80–81; formation of unreason in, 72, 98; quasi-mad authorship of, 83–84; on silencing in separation, 82–83; versions of, 73n4. *See also* madness; networks of obscure complicities; social excommunication; unreason

Hobbes, Thomas, 225

Hölderlin, Friedrich, 77

Hollingdale, R. J., 41

holograms, similarity of unreason to, 98

Hôpital Sainte-Anne (Paris), 80–81, 82

Huanacuni Mamani, Fernando, 183

human life and living: actions as becomings in, 212–13; affirmation in the face of tragedy and indifference, 29–31, 33–35, 48n14, 62–63, 109; Andean *buen vivir* (good living), 181–83; 181n12; and asceticism, 50, 50n16; in attunement with beyond, 45–46; autonomy of individuality in, 104–5, 250; decisiveness in, 243–44; in the definite and sensible, 227; energy from attunement with beyond, 228, 243–44; eternal recurrence in affirmation of life, 48–49; in experience with uncertainty, 73, 159–60, 250; falsifications and ignorance in, 30–31; Foucault's ethics of, 107; in Greek culture, 30n7; interconnectivity with the environment, 165; madness as nonrational dimension of, 75; Nietzsche's conception of ways of living, 38–41; purity in, 37, 59, 68, 118, 239; roots of, 133; self-care and self-transformation, 102–4; simplicity of falsifications and ignorance in, 34–35. *See also* free spiritedness; identity; lineages; madness; morality; norms and normativities; self-transformation; sensibility and sensibilities; sovereign individuals

human soul: lineages as agencies in formation of, 108; and Nietzsche's self-transformation, 37–38, 42; site of its own transformations, 64; Western lineages and conceptions of, 33, 36–37

human subjectivity, 18, 250

hyper-activism: and the art of indirect disclosure, 246–47; in confronting oppression, 248; and continual change, 244–45; decisiveness and, 246; engagements of, 243; Foucault's concept of, 162, 240, 240n4, 242, 247; informed by genealogical sensibility, 246; practice of, 247; where to begin, 248

identity: in constant state of flux, 125, 128, 136; dimensions of mortal identities, 217; dual identities, 112; experience of transparency, 228; genealogies and senses of, 16; melding of divergent nonnormative identities, 94, 95–96, 97; multiple lineages in, 132; new happenings from infusion of lineages, 131; process of formation, 132; reconceptualization of, 6; relationality of, 119–20; resistance to categorizations of, 137; sensibilities' function in, 17; transformation in, 126–29, 166. *See also* falling apart; nepantla

ignorance, educated, 31

immorality: disease and, 87; sanctioned by objectification and confinement, 89–90; unreason as region of, 95

imporings: of epistemic borders, 196; in erotic love, 211; in experience with art, 203–4; of fleshy borders, 196–97; as happenings of influence, 195; in McClintock's feeling for the plant, 206; and middle voice phrasing, 210; in openness of wonder, 193; and specializations of knowledge, 199; through viscous porosity, 196. *See also* fusion

in-betweenness: concept of, 10–11; in erotic love, 212; experience of, 6; and fire myths, 168; and interconnectivity of becomings, 192; and intimacy, 22; and polyvocality, 4–5; and possibilities for new ways of thinking and knowing, 158; of reason and unreason, 83; sensation as experience of, 206; sensibility's location of, 17; and the way it happens, 192. *See also* border art; imporings; Kandinsky, Wassily; McClintock, Barbara; viscous porosity

indigeneity: and the ayllu, 180, 181–82; conceptions of, 180; political appropriation of, 182; and rights activists, 179; shifts in indigenous lifeways, 183; traditions in, 128

indirect disclosure, art of, 7–9, 21, 214, 246–47

individuality, autonomy of, 104–5

indwelling, ethos of, 191, 204

Ingold, Tim, 220

intimacy, enriched meaning in, 22

Irigaray, Luce, 161

Jansen, Maarten, 109–10n1

Jeffers, Robinson: "Credo," 219; "Hand," 224; "Return," 221; "Salmon Fishing," 223–24; "The Shears," 225; "The Treasure," 218, 219; untitled poem, 225

Judenstil movement, 202n3

justice, modern systems of, 108

Kandinsky, Wassily: and anonymous agency of paintings, 201; on Judenstil movement, 202n3; middle voice of paintings of, 209; on paintings' communication of vibrant affect, 202–3; *Painting with Red Spot*, 203–4; on spirit of paintings, 202

Kant, Immanuel, 208

Kaufmann, Walter, 41

Kofman, Sarah, "Beyond Aporia?," 238–39

Kunsthaus (Zürich), xi

leadership, 55–56

leprosy and banishment: as sanctioned by God, 85–86; and self-authorization of divide with the sanctified, 86

LGBTQ population, genealogies as catalysts for, 16. *See also* queerness

liberation: aporia of liberatory theory, 238; code-switching and, 111–12; contradictions in efforts of, 111; and critique of norms, 237; effect of attunement with beyond, 228; and new shackles from old beliefs, 148; Nietzsche's and Foucault's understanding of, 108; paradoxes in work of, 147; in philosophical thinking, 233; and practices of power, 147–48; reasoning with ties to Western sensibilities, 154; of the self, 101–4; work of, 139. *See also* oppression

liberatory, roots of term, 148, 150

liberatory philosophy: challenges to values and goals in, 151; dealing with the paradoxes of, 147–53; divergent streams in, 149; engaging in, 148–49; need for creativity in, 151–52; and openness to uncertainty and the unthinkable, 152; and paradox of liberatory theory, 238; and reorientation to transformation of sensibilities, 155; transformation of thinkers in, 152; and writing to open us to transformation, 155. *See also* decent reforms

life-energy, release of, 59, 60

limit-experiences, 79n9, 80, 105, 107, 147
lineages: anonymous enactment of, 18; awareness in border art philosophy of, 158–59; complexity of, 13, 124, 125; definitions and connotations of, 11–12; moving beyond, 141–42; multiplicity of in each person, 132, 133; as mutational and permeable, 109; and the nature of lines, 12–13; sensibilities' conflicting lineages, 17; tensions and contradictions in, 123. *See also* anonymous agency; Anzaldúa, Gloria; coal and coal industry; cruelty; good and bad; good and evil; identity; morality; oppression; social excommunication; truth
livingdying: attunement with, 218–19, 224; author's early experiences with death, 221–22; belonging to the earth, 223; brightness in, 225; exhaustible treasure in, 223–25; immediacy of silences in, 219–20; porous borders as thresholds in, 217; as a weaving, 220–21
Lorde, Audre, 148
love: dynamic interconnection in, 210; essay on, 3–4; withdrawal of objectification in, 211. *See also* erotic love

madness: and abnormality, 82; fuzziness of term, 74–75, 74n5; medical senses of, 76, 78; psychiatry and silencing of unreason, 82–83; and psychology's illusion of mastery of, 83; and reforms toward healing of, 91–92; during the Renaissance, 88; and social exclusion through containment in asylums, 87. *See also* Foucault, Michel; *History of Madness*; norms and normativities; social excommunication; unreason
Maffie, James, 115n4
marginalized people, genealogies' transformative power for, 15
Mbembe, Achille, 161
McClintock, Barbara, 205–6
McDermott, John, 204
meaning and meaninglessness: in borders, 230; and dimensions beyond, 23, 29, 69, 109; dimensions in philosophical thinking of, xii–xiii; generation of, 16, 25; in in-between, 211; instability of, 106; in life itself, 241–42; and Similitude, 198. *See also* asceticism; *Beyond Good and Evil*; border art philosophy; conocimiento; genealogical responsibility; good and bad; good and evil; liberatory philosophy; livingdying; nepantla; *On the Genealogy of Morals*; Stevens, Wallace; unreason
mental health: appropriateness of treatment for, 75; healing the disordered with compassion, 91–92; and mental institutions, 16, 87–88, 105
Merleau-Ponty, Maurice, 206
metaphor of the child, 33–35
metaphors and unsayables, 228. *See also* Metis, myth of; *poros*, concept of
Metis, myth of, 229–30, 236, 239
métis-intelligence: attunement to weave of lineages, 230–31; author's experience with, 235; as enfleshed wisdom, 230; as transformative intelligence, 230; and transverse thinking, 233; in Western philosophical traditions, 229
Mexican culture, importance to Anzaldúa' life and work, 114
middle voice and middle voice events, 11n10, 208–10, 211, 212–13, 215
Miller, James: on Foucault's obsession with death, 79n9; on Foucault's psychiatric hospital experience, 81n11; and Foucault's silences, 78
Mississippi, vagrancy laws in, 174
moments, occurrences of, 11
Monet, Claude, *Haystacks*, 201
Morales, Evo, 179, 181
morality: dangers of, 43–44, 248; lineages of, 45; noble and slavish, 56–57nn20–21, 66n29; self-transformation from critiques of, 43–44; slave revolt in, 60n25, 61; soul sickness and fear as basis for, 52; as universe of dualisms, 38. *See also* immorality
moral rationality and moral judgments: in exclusion of people with venereal disease, 87; and institutionalization of people judged to lack reason, 88, 89–90
mythology, 168. *See also* Metis, myth of

NASA Global Climate Change site, 163
Navajo blankets, 220
Nazi purification mania, 96–97
neologisms, to denote inseparable differences, 217, 217n1
nepantla: centrality in Anzaldúa's transformative experience, 114–15, 149, 169, 186; concept of, 8, 115, 115n4, 116, 151; as constant state of displacement, 123; as dimension where things fall apart, 126–27, 146
nepantleras, 125, 129, 135, 138, 139–40, 186, 251
networks of obscure complicities, 93–97
Nietzsche, Friedrich: on actions and judgments, 58n24; and affirmation of life, 29–31, 33–35, 48n14, 62–63, 109; alertness to occurrences beyond good and evil, 29; and art of asking questions, 43–44, 62, 146, 161; attunement with beyond in, 8–9, 24, 93n26, 146; on augmenting activity, 26; contradictions in thought of, 48n13; development of genealogies by, 27, 36, 40, 57, 60n25, 62, 69; on history, 26n1; and the human soul, 36–38; importance of art to thinking and morality, 27–28; on Jewish people, 60n25; on laughter and living, 28, 28n5, 45–47; and life forces of stabilization and deformation, 28–29; and pessimism, 240, 242–43; ranking values in good *and* evil, 54–64; self-overcoming concepts in thought of, 47, 68; self-transformation of, 145; and split in ethics, 95; and truth, 30–35; and unreason, 77; use of term *beyond*, 27, 38–41; on ways of living, 38–41; writing and thought of, 227–28. *See also* eternal recurrence, temporality of; good and bad; good and evil; nobility; *On the Genealogy of Morals*
Nietzsche, Friedrich, writings of: "Attempt at a Self-Criticism," 240; *Beyond Good and Evil*, 27n3; *The Birth of Tragedy*, 27–28, 30n7; *Free Spirit*, 30; *Joyful Wisdom*, 42; *Thus Spoke Zarathustra*, 33, 42, 47–48n13, 48; *Twilight of the Idols*, 42; *Untimely Meditations*, 26n1. See also *Beyond Good and Evil*; *On the Genealogy of Morals*

nitrogen and nitrates: and blue baby syndrome, 197; corporeal vulnerabilities and, 195; population and crop yields, 193–94; wartime lineages of, 193n1
nobility: goodness in, 55–56; power, good, and truth of, 57–58
nonsense, speaking coherently of, 98–99
norms and normativities: and antinormativity, 237–38, 237–38n1; crafting of lifeways with, 236–37; dangers of, 248; genealogical sensibilities and, 236; and intimacy with madness, 75; mortal normativities, 190, 239, 250; new forms of, 190; using mêtis-intelligence to maneuver, 239

objectification: of Black Americans, 175; erotic love without, 193, 207–8, 210–11; as homeland of unreason, 89; movement away from, 214; by Nazis, 96–97; and oppression, 208; and silencing, 96; society's lust for, 92
Oliver, Mary, 22, 75n6
On the Genealogy of Morals (Nietzsche): and cheerfulness in transformation, 45–46; confrontation with the ascetic priest in, 50–54; and the danger of European moralities, 43; eternal recurrence, temporality of, 46–50; formation of lineages in, 49–50; genealogical responsibility, 64–68, 69; genealogical temporalities in, 44–45; new knowledge and transformation from, 50; as polemic, 41–43, 50n17; positive spirit in, 42–43
oppression: alertness to, 251; Anzaldúa's response to, 127, 128; in games of truth, 100; genealogical sensibility in, 19; genealogies and, 14; going beyond the sensibilities of, 154–55; infusion into the body, 120; lineages of, 13, 237; power of unreason to break, 93; reasoning out of, 135; re-formations of, 154; from systematic objectification, 208; as written on the body, 117. *See also* liberation
ordinariness, reconceptualizing, 7

Pascal, Blaise, 82n12
Patterson, Jacqueline, 172

Pérez Jiménez, Gabina Aurora, 109–10n1
pessimism, 240–43, 247
philosophy: compelling intensity of, xii; continuous change in, 142; contribution to, 251; cultivation of border alertness in, 69–70; Foucault's view of, 99, 100–101; liberatory philosophy, 147; limits in professional philosophy, 141; transverse thinking in, 233; Western traditions in, 229, 233. *See also* border art philosophy; texts
phusis, 116, 116n6
physicality. *See* corporeality
Pinel, Philippe, 91–92, 100
Plato, *Symposium*, 238n3
poiesis, 22, 131–32, 155, 158
polemic, term of, 41
Pólemos, 41, 42
polyphony: of philosophical thinkers, 8, 249; responsiveness to, 5; in understanding beyond, 109–10
polyvocality: in authorship, 4–5; of Nietzsche and Foucault, 109
poros, concept of, 238, 238n3, 239
power in social structures: attunement to, 19; and configurations of truth, 100; dynamic relations of, 74. *See also* authoritative knowledge; morality; norms and normativities; objectification; oppression; silencing
pregnancy and borders, 205
priestly caste, menacing spirituality of, 59–60
promises: memory and keeping, 64–65, 64–65nn28–29; and sovereign individuals, 66
psychology and psychiatry: Foucault's questioning of, 105–6; as "games of truth," 99–100; illusion of, 83

queerness, 16, 237–38n1. *See also* Anzaldúa, Gloria
Quispe, Rafael, 181

racism: author's experience of conflicts in sensibilities regarding, 233–35; changing sensibilities around, 154; in the flesh, 177; and forced labor, 174–75, 178n9; incorporation into social practices, 173–74, 173n6, 177; and "people of color," 172n5; relationship with coal, 172; the South's internalization of, 173–74; and transversive behavior to overcome, 235–36
reason: dimensions of occurrence beyond schemas and, 77; irreconcilable conflict with unreason, 95; as social and moral normalcy, 91. *See also* unreason
REDD+ (Reduce Emissions from Deforestation and Forest Degradation), 181
redemption, Nietzsche's dream of, 63, 63n26
reform efforts: and absence of transformation, 149n1, 150, 150n2; decent reforms, 91, 148, 149, 161–62; as games, 100; by hyper-activists, 248; as reformulations, 149–50
religious creatures: and the hunt for souls, 36–37; physical transformation of, 38–39
religious passion, 46
representation: and the nature of language, 199; subject of, 196; transformation of Similitude to, 197–200
resistance: to authority, 91; borders as locus of, 181; to classification, 137, 138; to ecclesiastical power, 88; through code-switching, 111. *See also* activism; oppression; silencing
resonance: experience of, 5–6; with happenings, 21; with texts, 20–21
ressentiment, 56n20
Riggins, Stephen, 78
Rilke, Rainer Maria: *Letters to a Young Poet*, 3; and unsayables, 6
Rio Grande valley, 117n7
Roman Catholic Church, 88
rules, and measurement, 12, 12n12
Rumi, "Rough Metaphors," 207, 210, 210n4, 211
Russell, Sarah, 224

Sade, Marques de, 95
Sanskrit, middle voice formation in, 209
Scheman, Naomi, 12n12
self-sacrificial love, lineages in, 108

self-transformation: in attunement with unsayables, 130; as crisis, 126–27; entering into art of, 126; openness to and process of, 141; from tensions and conflicts in sensibilities, 235. *See also* Anzaldúa, Gloria; Foucault, Michel; Nietzsche, Friedrich

sensibilities of denial: archetypal examples of, 164; and forced labor after Civil War, 174–75; moving out of, 189; transformation of, 165, 168

sensibility and sensibilities: arising from asceticism, 51–52; as assemblies of anonymous agencies, 18; concept of, 16–18, 164; crafting of, 139; genealogies and transformation of, 16; instability and unpredictability of, 232; and mêtis-intelligence, 231–32; Nietzsche's attunement with life, 35; Nietzsche's shift in, 43–44, 53–54; and "positive unconscious of knowledge," 121; tensions and conflicts in, 233–34, 236; and unresolved conflict in nepantla, 122; where and when they happen, 69. *See also* affect and feelings; genealogical sensibility and sensibilities; genealogy and genealogies; lineages

sexuality: and Anzaldúa, 134; norms and abnormality in, 237; and objectification into unreason, 94, 95. *See also* erotic love; queerness

signifiers and signified, 198–99, 200

silence: about, 21n15; and activism, 248; and alertness, 29; attunement to, 5, 21, 22, 106, 220; being answerable to, 233; and beyond, 70; in *Beyond Good and Evil*, 29; and border art philosophy, 159; and death, 79–80, 79n9; in human life, 218, 219, 224, 227; in livingdying, 225; in North American Indian culture, 78; in sounds, 228; stability of, 239; in temporality, 53; and unreason, 98; and writing, 145, 155

silencing: as attractive and repellent, 78–79; in medical practice, 80–81, 82–83. *See also* social excommunication

Similitude, 197–200

slavery: and coal industry, 173–74, 175–76; Nietzsche's understanding of slave morality, 66n30; population increase in, 174n7; as social death, 79–80

social death, 79–80

social excommunication: of lepers for their salvation, 85–86, 88; and lineages of expulsion and banishment, 83–84; of people with venereal disease, 87–88; self-authorization in division of sanctified and unholy, 86; of those "fit for confinement," 94–95; of unreason, 88–91. *See also* networks of obscure complicities

Sophocles, tragic dramas of, 28

sovereign individuals, 66–68

Spillers, Hortense, 161

spirituality: evil and, 59; and spiritual sickness, 60n25

stability and change, 245–46

stabilizing normalcy, 74–76, 77–78

Stevens, Wallace, "The House Was Quiet and The World Was Calm," 215–16

structuralism, Foucault and, 73–74

subject/object bifurcation, disruption of, 208, 209, 213

suffering, meaning of, 50

synthetic fertilizers, 193–94

temporality: in context of beyond, 39–40; of decline and growth of human *geists* and souls, 49–50; and ordered time, 40. *See also Beyond Good and Evil*; eternal recurrence, temporality of; *On the Genealogy of Morals*

Tennessee Coal, Iron, and Railroad Company, 175, 177

texts: attunement to meaningnonmeaning in, 23; as a blending in a weave, 220; engagement with, 249; in-between experiences of, 11; with openness to ideas, 19–20; and reading practices, 109–10, 147; sensibilities in, 32

therapeutic moments, 212

thresholds: being in, 104, 142; endings and beginnings as, 242; and fissures in lineages, 124, 125, 156; liminality of, 21, 25, 62, 160; to transformations, 27, 124–25, 126, 191. *See also* border artists; borders; transformation

transformation: and attunements to occurrences beyond value and good sense, 27; concepts and beliefs as continual process of becoming, 28, 250; corporeal dimensions in, 121; genealogical sensibility in, 19, 20; genealogies in, 13, 15, 16; of habitual feelings, 120; Metis as representative of power of, 229; multiple lineages as resources for, 181; nepantla as site of, 124; practices of, 189–90; in reading Anzaldúa, 111, 112; from sensibility defined by linear time, 48–49; and spirit's self-overcoming, 34, 68; through attunement to unsayables, 9; through writing, 146; transformation-with-others, 138–40; and a willingness to be undone, 153. *See also* Anzaldúa, Gloria; border artists; Foucault, Michel; Nietzsche, Friedrich; *On the Genealogy of Morals*; self-transformation

transversive thinking and behavior, 231, 233, 235, 239

Trump, Donald, on climate change, 163–64

truth: exposure of lineages in, 158; games of, 99–100; instability of, 106; Nietzsche on, 26; Nietzsche's formulation of, 30–35; in relation to nobility, 57, 57n22

Tuke, Samuel, 91–92, 100

uncertainty: animating potential of, 187; cultivation of, 29, 158, 160; Foucault and, 105; living with, 25, 191, 233, 250; Nietzsche on, 62; responsiveness to, 152, 213, 246; and self-transformation, 101, 102

unemployed poor, 95

unreason: as dimension of living, 76; domestication through silencing, 90; eventuation of, 106; Foucault's use of term, 76–77, 78; instability of concept, 98–99; lineages of, 93; perceived dangers of, 92–93; power to incite creativity, 93; readers' engagement with, 71–72; reforms to normalize, 91–92; silencing of, 96–97; social reality of, 84–90, 93; as threat in the seventeenth and eighteenth centuries, 89. *See also* madness; networks of obscure complicities; objectification; silence; silencing; social excommunication

unsayables: Anzaldúa's speaking to, 110; attention to, 130, 239–40; attunement to, 5–6, 9, 21, 135–36; concept of, 8; indirect disclosure and, 214, 246; indirect disclosure of, 214; and metaphors, 228; openness to, 126, 140; questions surrounding, 7; thinkers attuned to, 22–23

value, problem of: ranking in, 62; value of morality, 54–55

Vernant, Jean-Pierre, 229

violence: and human cruelty, 68, 68n32; and keeping promises, 65n29; and need for evil, 61

viscous porosity: of bodies in erotic love, 210–11; and circulation of nitrogen, 194; concept of, 167–68; and concrescences, 194–95; Cummings's poem, 212–13; and enduring things in borders, 245; of nitrates, 192–93; and Similitude, 198, 199–200

vital signs of the planet, 163

Waldinneras. *See* Brueghel the Elder, Jan

warriors, 55–56, 65–66n30. *See also* nobility

Winterson, Jeanette, *Art Objects*, 153

wonder and astonishment: and affirmation of life, 62, 243; and erotic love, 212; in experience, 32–34, 250–51; and feeling with organisms, 206; in human transformability, 242; in Jeffers's poetry, 225; openness to, 119, 193; and soul-sickness, 51–52

Wrangham, Richard, 167

Wynter, Sylvia, 161

Young, Iris Marion, 196

NANCY TUANA

is DuPont/Class of 1949 Professor of Philosophy and Women's, Gender, and Sexuality Studies at Penn State University and the founding director of the Rock Ethics Institute (https://rockethics.psu.edu/). She is author of *The Less Noble Sex: Scientific, Religious, and Philosophical Conceptions of Woman's Nature* and *Woman and the History of Philosophy*.

CHARLES E. SCOTT

is Professor of Philosophy at Pennsylvania State University and Distinguished Professor of Philosophy Emeritus and Research Professor of Philosophy at Vanderbilt University. He is author of *The Lives of Things* and *Living With Indifference*.

www.ingramcontent.com/pod-product-compliance
Lightning Source LLC
Chambersburg PA
CBHW030529230426
43665CB00010B/816